P9-EDI-280

# DIGITAL
# COMPUTER PROGRAMMING

# General Electric Series

## WRITTEN FOR THE ADVANCEMENT OF
## ENGINEERING PRACTICE

DIGITAL COMPUTER PROGRAMMING
   by D. D. McCracken

THE ART AND SCIENCE OF PROTECTIVE RELAYING
   by C. Russell Mason

APPLIED ELECTRICAL MEASUREMENT
   by Isaac F. Kinnard

AIRCRAFT GAS TURBINES
   by C. W. Smith

AN INTRODUCTION TO POWER SYSTEM ANALYSIS
   by Frederick S. Rothe

D-C POWER SYSTEMS FOR AIRCRAFT
   by R. H. Kaufmann and H. J. Finison

TRANSIENTS IN POWER SYSTEMS
   by Harold A. Peterson

SERVOMECHANISMS AND REGULATING SYSTEM DESIGN, TWO VOLUMES
   by Harold Chestnut and Robert W. Mayer

TRANSFORMER ENGINEERING
   by the late L. F. Blume, A. Boyajian, G. Camilli, T. C. Lennox, S. Minneci, and
   V. M. Montsinger, Second Edition

CIRCUIT ANALYSIS OF A-C POWER SYSTEMS, TWO VOLUMES
   by Edith Clarke

CAPACITORS FOR INDUSTRY
   by W. C. Bloomquist, C. R. Craig, R. M. Partington, and R. C. Wilson

PROTECTION OF TRANSMISSION SYSTEMS AGAINST LIGHTNING
   by W. W. Lewis

MAGNETIC CONTROL OF INDUSTRIAL MOTORS
   by Gerhart W. Heumann, Second Edition

POWER SYSTEM STABILITY
   Volume I—Steady State Stability; Volume II—Transient Stability;
   by Selden B. Crary

MATERIALS AND PROCESSES
   by J. F. Young, Second Edition

MODERN TURBINES
   by L. E. Newman, A. Keller, J. M. Lyons, and L. B. Wales;
   edited by L. E. Newman

ELECTRIC MOTORS IN INDUSTRY
   by D. R. Shoults and C. J. Rife; edited by T. C. Johnson

# DIGITAL

# COMPUTER PROGRAMMING

### D. D. McCRACKEN

*Manager-Training, Computer Department*
*General Electric Company*
*Phoenix, Arizona*

*✳5 10.78*
*M13d*

One of a series written by General Electric authors
for the advancement of engineering practice

JOHN WILEY & SONS, INC., NEW YORK
CHAPMAN & HALL, LTD., LONDON · 1957

SECOND PRINTING, SEPTEMBER, 1957

Library of Congress Catalog Card Number: 57–8891

Printed in the United States of America

# PREFACE

This book is written for the person who needs to know how problems are solved on a modern stored program computer. The person seeking such information in the past has had to rely on printed materials which are directed either toward those who only want to know the end product of computing—what computers can do, how much money they can save, etc.—or toward those who want the details of operation of a particular machine. *Digital Computer Programming* provides a general introduction to the entire field, with emphasis on the basic principles. It is written for people with no previous knowledge of computing who want to know how to prepare the detailed "instructions" for the computer, as well as for people whose work is so closely related to computer applications that they need to know what is involved in programming.

The book begins with a rudimentary discussion of the elements of a computer and their relationships. It presents the fundamental ideas of programming with detailed examples and explanations. These examples are written for a mythical computer called TYDAC, which stands for TYpical Digital Automatic Computer. This "paper" computer is intended primarily as an aid to learning rather than as a compilation of all the features of available equipment. It is generally representative of the major trends in present computer building. The examples are written in a form which makes it possible, if desired, to study them without detailed knowledge of the characteristics of the illustrative computer. The book presents many of the programming techniques which must be known to make efficient use of the equipment, and thus helps to answer the question, "Now that I know how the machine works, how do I solve my problem?"

It is anticipated that the book will be useful, in different ways, to two main groups of readers. Those who read it without having an actual machine to practice with will find that what they learn can easily be applied to a real situation later. This is because the primary concern is not with details and peculiarities of a particular machine, which must be the concern of a machine manual, but with the *principles* of programming. In fact, much of the textual matter is a general discussion of ideas which apply equally to any computer, without direct reference to TYDAC.

Those who have a computer at hand while they read the book will find several desirable features. Possibly the most important is that the chapters which do not apply to a particular situation can be omitted without loss of continuity: at least half of the chapters may be omitted or included at will. This group of readers will find little difficulty in applying the illustrations to their particular machine, partly because of the format of the programs and partly because TYDAC is an uncomplicated machine. In a classroom situation, the instructor can fairly easily rewrite the illustrations. The many exercises are in no way dependent on the features of TYDAC.

Both groups of readers will find that the text is self-contained. If necessary, it may be read without an instructor or reference material, either to provide a general background knowledge of computer programming or as a supplement to a manual.

Practically none of the technical material of the book is original with me. I am indebted to all those who have developed and made available the material presented here. All the computer manufacturers were most helpful in supplying material on their equipment.

I wish to acknowedge my appreciation to P. M. Thompson, W. C. McGee, and Dr. H. R. J. Grosch of General Electric Company, for encouragement in the very early stages of this effort; to F. G. Gruenberger of General Electric, who read the manuscript and made many valuable suggestions; to R. C. McGee of General Electric, who supplied most of the material for Chapter 7; to members of my staff who assisted in the clerical work; and to my wife, for her patience during the writing.

D. D. McCRACKEN

*Phoenix, Arizona*
*March 1957*

# CONTENTS

CHAPTER

1 Computing Fundamentals 1
2 Coding Fundamentals 13
3 Binary and Octal Number Systems 30
4 Decimal Point Location Methods 52
5 Address Computation 66
6 Loops in Computing 74
7 Flow Charting 87
8 Index Registers 98
9 Subroutines 111
10 Floating Decimal Methods 121
11 Input-Output Methods 132
12 Magnetic Tape Programming 150
13 Program Checkout 159
14 Relative Programming Methods 170
15 Interpretive Programming Methods 178
16 Double Precision Arithmetic 191
17 Miscellaneous Programming Techniques 198
18 Automatic Coding 211
Numerical Operation Codes for TYDAC 218

APPENDIX

1 Summary of TYDAC Instructions 219
2 Minimum Access Programming 227
3 Externally Programmed Computers 231
4 Octal-Decimal Integer Conversion Table 236
5 Octal-Decimal Fraction Conversion Table 244
6 Bibliography 247
Index 249

# 1 COMPUTING FUNDAMENTALS

## 1.0 Introduction

Programming a problem for solution on a digital computer is basically a process of translating from the language convenient to human beings to the language convenient to the computer. The language of the problems to be solved is mathematics or English statements of decisions to be made; the language of the computer is simple arithmetic and elementary choices, expressed in coded numerical form. By and large, we are at present required to present problems to the computer in *its* language.

In order to put the problem in the required form, we must learn in some detail the functions of the various parts of a computer, and the precise manner in which orders are given to the machine. This chapter presents the framework of the subject; later chapters will provide the details. Section 1.1 discusses the over-all picture and defines some of the basic terms. Section 1.2 gives an initial description of the mythical computer used for illustration in the text. The succeeding sections trace the development of present equipment, sketch the steps in computer solution of a problem, and list some typical computer applications.

## 1.1 Computer Organization

A modern digital computer usually consists of several boxes or racks of mechanical and electronic equipment, connected together by electric cables. In this array we find five distinct functions being performed: *input, memory, arithmetic, control,* and *output*. Figure 1 is a block diagram of these functions, showing the relationships among them.

The input section of a computer ordinarily consists of devices which take information from punched cards, paper tape, or magnetic tape, and place it in memory. In technical language, this is called *reading*. The function of the input device(s) is essentially to translate from the external form in which the information is represented, such as a punched card, to the form in which the same information is stored in memory.  The *information* in question may be anything which can be stored in memory: numbers to be used in the calculation, *instructions* which tell the machine what to do, numbers or letters to be used later as column headings on the output, etc.  The single arrow from the input box to the memory box in Figure 1 implies that the information goes only *to* memory—further operations must take the information from memory to other sections of the machine.

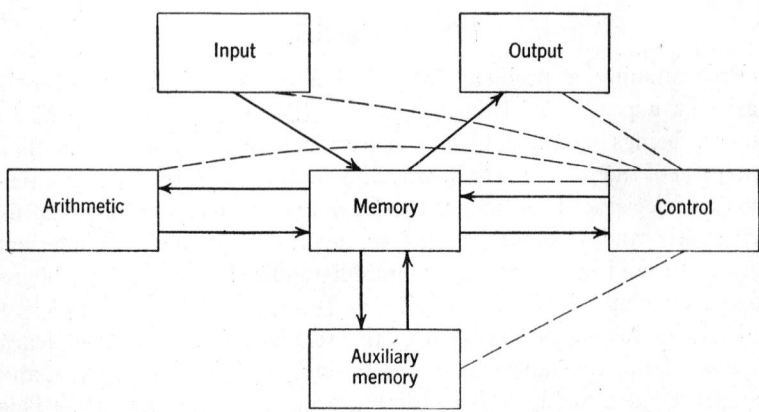

Figure 1.  Functional parts of a digital computer and their relationships.  The solid lines represent information flow, the dashed lines control signals.

It is difficult to find good analogies between large computers and things more familiar, and the analogies are apt to be misleading. Nevertheless, it may be helpful to characterize the input function as equivalent to the keyboard of a desk calculator.  Of course, the difficulty with this analogy is that a desk calculator has no real internal memory.

The memory or storage of a computer is the nerve center of the machine.  All information must travel through it.  All numbers must be in it before any arithmetic manipulations can be carried out.  All the instructions which tell the machine what to do must be in memory before they can go over to the control section.  The memory needs to be large and fast, i.e., it should be able to hold many numbers or instructions—from 1000 to 30,000 in present equipment—and be able to send these to the arithmetic or control sections with a minimum delay—as short as about 10 microseconds in the fastest machines at the time of writing.  If it is not technically or economically feasible to build a high-speed memory large enough to hold all the information required, a solution is to store the part not currently needed in a larger, but slower, auxiliary device. As indicated in Figure 1, the auxiliary memory "communicates" only with the main memory.

The present trend is for the main memory to be built around magnetic cores in large machines, and magnetic drums in the smaller. Auxiliary memory is almost always magnetic tape, with magnetic drums also being used in the large computers. Electrostatic and mercury-delay storage are still employed in some machines, but are being superseded in the newer ones. Descriptions of the operation of these devices will be found in works listed in the bibliography.

The arithmetic section of the computer does what its name implies. It is here that the actual work of problem solution is done. In addition to the four arithmetic operations, this section can *shift* numbers right and left, and assist in certain operations which make it possible for the computer to make *decisions*. It corresponds in a desk calculator to the wheels and gears and shafts that actually do the calculation.

*Register* is a term commonly used in connection with several of these basic functions; this is simply a device for temporarily storing a piece of information while or until it is used. A register corresponds quite closely to the dials on a desk calculator, which are wheels that temporarily store the numbers on which arithmetic is done. In our case, it is not only numbers which may be stored in a register but also instructions.

The control section of a calculator has the function of *interpreting* or *decoding* the instructions stored in memory, and then sending signals to the rest of the parts telling them what to do. In the diagram we see two solid lines, implying that instructions are sent to and from (usually *from*) memory to control; the dashed lines imply electric signals sent to the rest of the machine, based on these instructions.

The control section is equivalent to the buttons which are pushed to start the various arithmetic operations on a desk calculator, but the analogy is quite incomplete. The arithmetic and control sections are the hardest functions to point to in looking at a machine. The input and output devices are usually separate frames, as are memory and the magnetic drums and tapes if any. The arithmetic and control sections, on the other hand, are made up of ordinary-looking electronic components, and the equipment constituting the two functions is usually in the same cabinet. Incidentally, there are usually one or more boxes to which no reference has been made here: the power supply. This omission simply points up that we are looking at a computer from the standpoint of what it does and how the information flows, not from the standpoint of electrical engineering.

The output section has the obvious purpose of recording in convenient form the answers to the problem or anything else in memory. The media may be punched cards, printed pages, or paper or magnetic tapes. The chart shows that information may be recorded (or *written,* in the jargon) only from memory. For our purposes this is true, although *electronically* the arithmetic unit may be involved.

The word *instruction,* which has been used repeatedly, should be amplified. Anyone who has used a desk calculator realizes that it is necessary to have some sort of pattern to the operations so that the operator can get into a routine. This pattern consists of a sequence of specified arithmetic operations on specified quantities. Analyzing or breaking down the process further, we see that doing a desk calculation consists of doing a series of distinct steps, each step involving one arithmetic operation and one new piece of information.

The situation in the electronic computer is not so different. For a problem to be solved on a computer, it must be broken down into a series of precise steps, each involving one arithmetic operation and one piece of information (two or three in some machines) in addition to the result of the previous step. The difference between this situation and the desk calculator is that with the desk calculator the sequence of operations is in the operator's head, whereas to satisfy the computer the sequence must be written down in a rigidly defined form. The appearance of these instructions will be elaborated in the next chapter; we may say here that they are usually stored in memory as ordinary numbers.

After defining several more terms, we shall look at the flow of information as a typical instruction is executed. The first term is *program.* A program is simply a collection of instructions which carries out some purpose such as solving a particular problem. We speak of modern computers as being *stored program* machines. As a verb, to program means to write the instructions necessary to tell a computer how to solve a problem, along with the planning necessary before the detailed instructions can be written. The word *code* is sometimes used almost as a synonym for program, but often it implies a lower level of activity which involves a smaller amount of planning. *Word* is used in computing as a generic term to cover either a number or an instruction or a group of characters to be used for some other purpose. It is roughly equivalent to *piece of information* as used previously.

Suppose now as a very simple example that two numbers are to be added. The two numbers, and, in the type of machine to be considered in this book, three instructions, have to be loaded into memory by the input device(s). Actually, many other instructions have to be in memory to instruct the machine to bring these in, but we can without great inconvenience ignore this fact.

The first instruction moves from memory to the control unit, which analyzes the coded instruction to determine what operation is called for and where in memory to locate the first number. After this analysis or interpretation, the control unit sends out signals to the appropriate units, calling for the specified number to move to one of the arithmetic registers in preparation for the next operation. The second instruction is similarly interpreted and the control unit calls for the second of the two numbers to move from memory to the arithmetic unit and be added to the first number. The third instruction sends the sum back to memory. Finally, the sum is written on an output device; this also requires many more instructions, which fact can be temporarily ignored.

In Chapter 2 we shall discuss the same example in terms of the *details* of machine characteristics.

## 1.2 TYDAC

Much of the material of later chapters will be illustrated by writing codes for TYDAC, which, in the tradition of naming computers by acronyms, stands for TYpical Digital Automatic Computer. This machine is a compilation of representative characteristics of present computers, and of course exists only in this book. This section is a description of the major features of TYDAC, showing the relationship to the material of the previous section.

The input of TYDAC is assumed to include punched cards, a special typewriter, and a paper-tape reading device on the typewriter. The memory is taken to be 2000 words, each holding ten decimal digits and sign. Each word may be either a number to be used in the calculation or a (coded) instruction. No assumptions or statements are made about the physical type (whether magnetic cores, drums, etc.) or the speed of the memory. Four magnetic tapes are assumed as auxiliary memory.

The arithmetic unit comprises two registers: the *accumulator* and the *multiplier-quotient* or *MQ*. The accumulator does all the addition and subtraction and participates in multiplication, division, and most other operations. It can hold eleven digits and sign. The MQ is involved in multiplication, division, some shift operation, and a few others. It holds ten digits and sign. TYDAC is assumed to be able to do floating decimal arithmetic (Chapter 10), i.e., keep track of decimal points during a calculation, if desired.

The control section has four registers: the current instruction register, the location counter, and two registers called index registers. As discussed in the previous section on general computer organization, each instruction from memory has to be placed in the control section before being interpreted and executed. The temporary storage in which each instruction is held after being brought from memory, and while it is being decoded, is called the *current instruction register*. The register which keeps a running record of the "location" in memory of the instruction of current interest is called the *location counter*. (The notion of location in memory has not been discussed yet; it will be clarified early in the next chapter.) The *index registers* have to do mostly with the automatic modification of instructions. Chapter 8 is devoted to their operation and use.

The output equipment of TYDAC is assumed to be punched cards, the special typewriter, and a paper-tape punch attached to the typewriter.

We may now draw a diagram of TYDAC, Figure 2, which is an expansion of the general diagram, Figure 1. The over-all information flow paths are the same as in Figure 1; the details will be presented in succeeding chapters.

## 1.3  History of Computing

The characteristics of present computers have been arrived at through a process of development, most of which has occurred since 1945. It may be instructive to trace, in broad outline, the course of these developments.

Devices to assist in working with numbers have been in existence as long as there have been numbers. The first was the abacus, which made use of the bi-quinary number system (page 49) some 5000 years before its application in several modern computers. The first mechanical computer was built by Pascal; a better device was built by Leibnitz in 1673. The first large computer was started in 1812 by Charles Babbage, a British mathematician. The machine was called

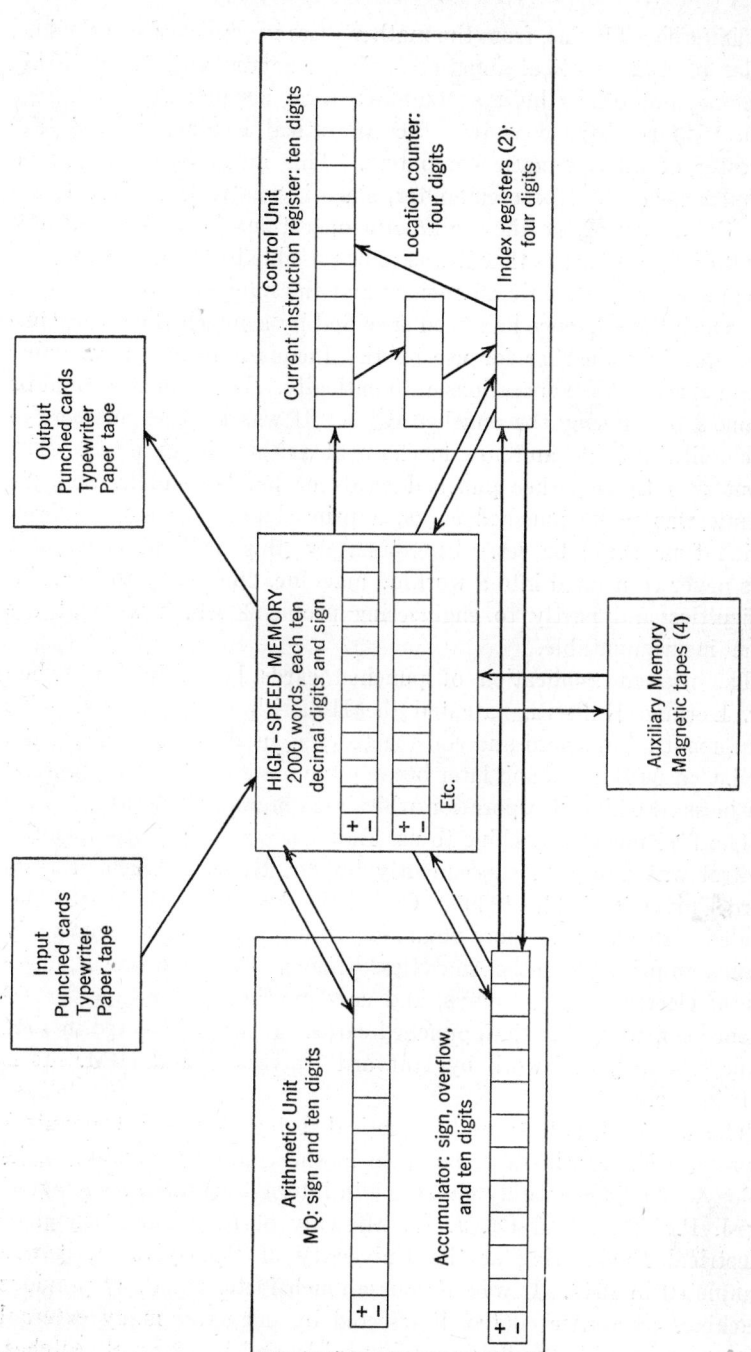

Figure 2. Functional diagram of TYDAC.

the Difference Engine, from the mathematics it employed to calculate tables of mathematical functions. Babbage did not complete his machine, but others built a computer from his plans.

In 1833 Babbage conceived the Analytical Engine, which is the ancestor of all automatic computers. This machine can fairly be called a general-purpose computer, since it was to have flexible sequential control over the arithmetic operations it performed. *Sequential control* means that it was to be possible to specify in advance a sequence of arithmetic operations and the numbers to be operated on. Once the sequence had been specified by a punched card mechanism developed earlier for use on the Jacquard loom, the machine would carry out the operations automatically. The sequence could be changed by altering the punched cards. It was to store numbers in mechanical wheels and use mechanical arithmetic elements. The input was to be either punched cards or hand-set dials, and the output was to be punched cards, a printed page, or a mold from which type could be set. Unfortunately, this brilliant conception was never translated into a working machine, due partly to financial difficulties and partly to engineering problems which were at the time insurmountable.

The present application of punched cards began in 1889 when Dr. Herman Hollerith patented the Hollerith punched card. The equipment he invented and constructed was used in his work for the U. S. Census Bureau, and later became the basis for the International Business Machines Corporation which was organized in 1911.

The first modern machine to use Babbage's principle of sequential control was described subsequently by Dr. Howard Aiken of Harvard University in the 1930's. Called the Automatic Sequence Controlled Calculator, or more commonly the Mark I, it is remarkably similar in principle to the Analytical Engine. It does, however, make use of electromagnetic relays, and uses punched paper tape for sequence control rather than punched cards. It was completed in 1944 after several years' work by Harvard University and IBM. It is still in use.

The ENIAC (Electronic Numerical Integrator and Computer) represented a considerable advance in the computer building technology, since it is entirely electronic in internal operation. Designed by J. P. Eckert and Dr. J. W. Mauchly of the Moore School of Electrical Engineering at the University of Pennsylvania, it was completed in 1946. It was of course much faster than any previous machine. Sequence control is effected by means of many external wires running between holes in plugboards, and by external switches.

Input and output are basically IBM cards, but dials may be used for the input of constants.

All these machines, and others along the same lines, use some external means of sequence control: punched cards, paper tape, wired plugboards. The memory is used only to store numbers. The fundamental idea of placing "instructions" in memory, which is basic to modern computers, did not emerge until 1945. This "stored program" idea, with which we shall have much contact, appeared in a report written by Dr. John von Neumann, proposing a computer quite different from the ENIAC. By storing the instructions internally and by using binary instead of decimal numbers (Chapter 3), much greater power could be achieved at considerably less expense of electronic equipment. The name EDVAC (Electronic Discrete Variable Automatic Computer) was suggested. In a further attempt to reduce the bulk of equipment, the memory of the EDVAC was built around the ultrasonic or mercury-delay type of memory. The EDSAC (Electronic Delay Storage Automatic Computer) was built along similar lines at Cambridge University. It first operated in 1949.

No radically new ideas, of the magnitude of the stored program principle, have appeared in the flood of computers designed and built since these early models. Great advances have been made, however, in speed, reliability, and ease of use.

The Univac, produced by what is now the Sperry Rand Corporation, was the first mass-produced computer placed on the market, in 1951. It is a decimal machine, has magnetic tapes, and uses the mercury memory. It and its successors are in wide use.

The IBM 701 appeared in 1953. It gained speed by using binary numbers and electrostatic storage.

The Whirlwind I, built at the Massachusetts Institute of Technology, was the first large machine to use magnetic cores for main memory. This development represented a gain of a factor of 2 or more in speed, and a great increase in reliability, over electrostatic memory. Production machines using magnetic cores include the Univac II and the IBM 704 and 705.

One of the problems plaguing computer designers for many years has been the great disparity in speed between the input-output equipment and the internal electronic circuitry. Significant advances have been made in improving the reading and writing devices, but no mechanical device can match arithmetic speeds of millions of operations per minute. A solution to this problem, which has been available since about 1954, is the use of separate high-speed tape reading and writing equipment. For instance, on a machine where punched cards are the primary input medium, it is highly uneconomical to tie up the entire machine while reading cards. What can be done is to read the cards in a separate machine and write the information onto magnetic tapes, at the usual card-reading speed; this, of course, while the main computer is doing something else. Then the information now on tape can be read by a tape reader connected to the computer, at the much higher tape-reading speeds. A similar saving can be effected on printing the output. Such equipment is available for the major production computers.

Many further advances are surely forthcoming. The foregoing is an outline of the trends of computers actually on the market, up to the time of writing. Computers now in development are said to be much faster, more flexible, and to have much larger memories.

## 1.4 Steps in Preparing a Problem for Computer Solution

There are several fairly distinct steps which must be carried out to solve a problem on a computer, some of which have been alluded to in previous sections. These steps are now outlined; details will be given later.

### NUMERICAL ANALYSIS

In all but the simplest problems, a considerable amount of work must be done before much *detailed* consideration of the computer is brought in. This is because computers, in a single step, can do only simple arithmetic and make only simple logical decisions. Most scientific and engineering problems are expressed in terms a computer cannot handle directly: integrals, cosines, differential equations, vectors. A numerical method must be found to translate continuous functions to arithmetic: finite difference methods, infinite series, continued fractions, iterative procedures, etc.

Although numerical analysis (and in business problems, procedures analysis) is a highly important part of the computing field, it is outside the scope of this book.

### PROGRAMMING

This is a classification which is often merged with the preceding or following. When interpreted strictly, it implies all the planning which comes after analysis and is related specifically to the computer. It involves primarily drawing a flow chart or block diagram (Chapter 7), planning memory allocation (Chapter 11), and planning for careful records of what is done during coding.

## CODING

This is the writing of detailed machine instructions which carry out the arithmetic operations called for above, whether in actual machine language or in some symbolic or abstract form (Chapters 14, 18). It is usually the first subject a newcomer to computing is taught. For most problems it is not the most demanding aspect of the work, but in others involving severe space or time restrictions it is crucial. It is the part of the job which really comes face to face with the details, not to say peculiarities, of the particular machine being used. Coding must to a certain extent be relearned in order to work on a new computer, although of course relearning will be much shorter than the original learning. It involves a great deal of detailed work and is the source of many errors. It is also at the center of many efforts to make the computer take over the detailed work and prepare its own programs (Chapter 18).

## CHECKOUT

There are so many opportunities to make mistakes in the steps outlined so far that most programs as originally written contain errors. Often these are of such a nature that the programs will not proceed far enough to get any answers; in other cases they will get wrong answers. The mistakes must of course be found and corrected, and initial answers checked against a calculation done by hand. There are systematic ways of finding the errors, and for that matter, of trying to avoid them. These are discussed in Chapter 13.

## PRODUCTION

After the program is known to be computing correct answers, it remains to obtain answers for all the sets of input data that may be required. This can often be set up as a fairly routine procedure and handled by an operator with less training than the programmer and others who may have worked on the problem.

## 1.5 Applications of Computing

Computer applications cover a wide variety of fields, which may be classified roughly as follows.

1. Speeding up the solution of simple problems. Some computing tasks, although not complex, are extremely long and cumbersome. A good example is the determination of prime numbers. This search, which is of considerable interest in number theory, requires tens of

thousands of arithmetic operations per prime number. The operations are of no complexity whatsoever, but 50,000 operations to find one prime number gets tiresome. The latest large machines can find several thousand primes per hour.

2. Taking into account more variables when solving mathematical and engineering problems. Many formulations must be greatly simplified before they can be solved by hand; a computer operates fast enough that much less simplification is required.

3. Doing "experiments" inside the machine. It is often possible to predict operation of equipment under study without ever building the device—thus saving years and millions of dollars in some cases. This is commonly called *simulation*.

4. Data reduction. In testing new equipment, literally millions of readings of temperature, pressure, force, strain, etc., may have to be taken. Reducing this mass of data to averages and meaningful answers is greatly accelerated by computers.

5. Optimizing designs. In designing complicated systems such as atomic reactors or jet engines, much time is spent trying to find the best combination of possibly dozens of design variables. Although present computers can by no means carry out the entire task, they can assist materially.

6. Commercial or business applications. Much of the detailed work of processing payrolls, inventory records, sales records, insurance billing, etc., can be done by computers. They may also be used to predict machine loading or market trends and thus assist in the planning phase of business. These business applications will eventually require a much larger use of computers than the engineering and scientific applications.

All of these areas share, to a greater or lesser extent, this characteristic: a certain basic calculation has to be carried out many times with different values of the input. For instance, the payroll operation has to be carried out for each man, each pay period. The basic calculations in the reduction of data from a jet engine test must be carried out thousands of times. The engineering analysis of a proposed design must be tried for many combinations of the design variables. It is almost never practical to set up a calculation for computer solution if the problem is to be done only once or only a few times. The reason for this will perhaps become clearer in the following chapters.

# 2 CODING FUNDAMENTALS

## 2.0 Introduction

To the newcomer to computing, this is probably the most important chapter in the book. Real problems may be more complex; later chapters will discuss many short cuts and elaborations; but the basic idea of what it takes to translate a problem into computer language is presented in this chapter.

## 2.1 Memory Identification

TYDAC has 2000 words of storage, which is roughly typical of existing computers. Each word consists of ten decimal digits and sign; TYDAC cannot handle alphabetic and other symbols as can many computers.

Since there are 2000 different locations where numbers or instructions can be located, some means must be provided for identifying each one uniquely. This is so that there will be some way of specifying an instruction, where to find data, where to put answers, or where to find the next instruction. The problem is solved by giving each of the 2000 locations an identification number, from 0 to 1999, which is called the *address* (synonyms for address: *cell, location, box, bucket*). A common analogy is to compare the computer memory with pigeonholes in a post office. Pigeonholes have name plates on them which serve as a reference identification. It is important to note that the name plate does not tell anything about the contents. The name "Smith" on the name plate does not tell where a letter came from or what it says. All it does is this: if you put a certain letter in the box labeled "Smith," you should subsequently be able to find that same letter, whatever it may be about, by going back to the pigeonhole marked "Smith."

That is really all the address of a memory location does: if we put a certain number in location 1507, we should be able to go back to 1507 later and find that same number. The *address* 1507 certainly does not mean that we can find the *number* 1507 stored there—except by accident. This may seem painfully obvious, perhaps, but it is a perennial source of difficulty to new coders.

Memory has two additional characteristics which unfortunately do not fit into the post office analogy. First, a memory location can hold only one word at a time, and placing a word in a location automatically and finally destroys whatever was there previously. On the one hand, this means that there is no problem of making sure a location is empty before putting something there; on the other hand, it means that we must be sure a cell does not contain anything we wish to keep before something else is put in it. Second, it is possible to read a number out of memory without destroying or removing it. It is as though the postal clerk, instead of removing a letter, simply made a quick copy of it on another piece of paper.

In TYDAC, instructions and numbers are of the same length and no special handling of instructions is required. Thus it is impossible to distinguish between numbers and instructions simply by inspecting the contents of a memory location, without information as to what is stored there.*

## 2.2 Instruction Format

Each TYDAC instruction consists of one word in memory. Instructions are always positive. The first two digits, from the left, are called the *operation part*, and tell the machine what to do. The next four digits are termed the *address part*, and usually refer to a location in memory, but may specify a number of shifts or an input or output unit. The last four digits are called the *index control* and used only occasionally, mostly in connection with the index registers (Chapter 8) ; if they are not used, nothing need be written in the four digits— which is the same as writing zeros. In writing instructions, we usually have an initial column showing where the instruction is in memory, which is called the location of the instruction. The location is not a part of the instruction proper, but must always be

---

* It is not essential to the stored program concept that this be so; all that is required is that it be possible to do arithmetic on instructions. Indeed, several machines distinguish between the two (although either can be stored in any location) and stop if an attempt is made to use data words as instructions.

known. We thus have these terms in connection with a TYDAC instruction:

| LOCATION | SIGN | OPERATION | ADDRESS | INDEX CONTROL (IF ANY) |
|----------|------|-----------|---------|------------------------|
| 4 digits | + | 2 digits | 4 digits | 4 digits |

The ten digits of an instruction are numbered from the left; thus the address part is digits 3–6 of the word.

The addresses of TYDAC memory registers run from 0 to 1999, yet the four digits allowed for the address of a TYDAC instruction could contain a number as large as 9999. What would happen if the machine encountered an instruction such as Clear add 3400? The answer is that we assume in TYDAC that only the odd-even character of the first digit of the address is sensed by the machine. Thus the address 3400 would be taken by the machine to be 1400; 6879 would be treated the same as 0879; 2000 would be treated the same as 0000. (Some actual computers handle the problem in this manner; others make some special use of the larger addresses.)

## 2.3 Examples

In the examples that follow, it will be assumed that the instructions and numbers are somehow loaded in storage, and that the location counter is just ready to proceed to the location of the first instruction in the illustrative program. This assumption is sometimes confusing to the student. It seems reasonable that since input is the first thing mentioned in connection with computer organization, it would also be the first topic under coding. It turns out, however, that input programming is an advanced topic which makes use of concepts which have not yet been introduced. The discussion of input and output coding must therefore be postponed until Chapter 11. The contents of the location counter at the start of these examples are somewhat similar. Actually, all of these illustrations would normally be simply small parts of larger programs; there would be other instructions both before and after those shown. We shall discuss only the effect of these few instructions by themselves.

The actual locations used for numbers and instructions are picked at random from one problem to the next. This is done to emphasize that a program can be located anywhere in memory. A few of the TYDAC instructions are used and described in these examples. Appendix 1 is a complete description of all instructions; the numerical code for each operation is given in tabular form on the page facing

Appendix 1. The instructions in the Appendix are in order of the operation codes. The description of each instruction should be read as it is encountered in the text.

*Example 1.  A + B*

Suppose it is required simply to add two numbers and store the result. Suppose the two numbers $A$ and $B$ (whatever their actual numerical values may be) are stored in locations 1000 and 1100, and that the result is to be stored in 1167. Assume further that the program, or sequence of instructions, is located in 500, 501, and 502. The program could be as follows:

| LOCATION | OPERATION CODE | OPERATION ABBREVIATION | ADDRESS |
|---|---|---|---|
| 500 | 10 | Clear add | 1000 |
| 501 | 11 | Add | 1100 |
| 502 | 40 | Store acc | 1167 |

This says that the first instruction, which is located in memory at address 500, consists of the operation part 10 and the address 1000, and that there is no index control. Thus the coded form of the first instruction as it would appear in memory is

$$1010000000$$

Clear add means to erase or clear the accumulator of whatever might have been there, and bring in (or, add to nothing) the number in the memory location specified by the address part. The details of the machine operation are as follows:

1. At the start of the cycle, the location counter contains 500, to show that the instruction now to be performed is located in cell 500 in memory.

2. The control circuits send signals to memory asking for the instruction at 500 to be sent over to the current instruction register. This would be the coded instruction 1010000000.

3. The control circuits analyze, or decode, the operation part (10) to discover what is to be done. This would be found to be Clear add.

4. As a result of 3, the accumulator is cleared by a signal from the control circuits, in keeping with the function of the Clear add operation.

5. The control circuits send a signal to memory, asking that the number in 1000 be sent to the accumulator. As pointed out above,

the number would be left unchanged in memory after it goes to the accumulator.

6. Since in this machine the instructions are taken from consecutive locations unless specified otherwise, the contents of the location counter are increased by one. This means that the next instruction comes from memory location 501. The control circuits proceed to deal with this next instruction.

Such a pattern must be carried out for each instruction in a program, with the pattern varying somewhat for different operations.

All we have accomplished so far is to get the first of the two numbers to be added from memory to the accumulator. The next instruction, at 501, brings the second number from memory location 1100 to the arithmetic unit and adds it to the number already there. To do this, the control unit has to go through steps similar to the six above, but we need not spell these out in detail for each instruction.

The third instruction, at 502, results in the sum of $A$ and $B$ being sent back to memory, to location 1167. In the TYDAC accumulator, this leaves the sum still in the accumulator. It destroys the previous contents of location 1167. The machine then proceeds to the instruction at 503, whatever it may be.

There have been two tacit assumptions here. The first is that the two numbers have the same decimal point location. This assumption will be made throughout this chapter; Chapter 4 deals with the more realistic situation of varying decimal points. The second assumption is that the sum of the two numbers of ten digits each can be contained in ten digits. It is quite possible in general for the sum to contain eleven digits. If so, the extra digit would *overflow* into the *overflow position* of the accumulator. This position obviously cannot be stored in a ten-digit memory location, so the program above would not give the correct answer if overflow occurred. The overflow possibility must be anticipated in writing real programs of this sort, unless other solutions such as floating decimal are available (Chapter 10). Methods for discovering and correcting overflow difficulties are discussed later.

*Example 2.* $-A - B + |C| - |D|$

Suppose it is required to form the sum indicated, i.e., the negative of $A$, the negative of $B$, the absolute value of $C$, and minus the absolute value of $D$. Assume that $A$ is in 231, $B$ in 232, $C$ in 1300, $D$ in 1350, and the sum is to go in 789. The following instructions would evaluate the formula, assuming that the first instruction is in 510.

| LOCATION | OPERATION CODE | OPERATION ABBREVIATION | ADDRESS |
|---|---|---|---|
| 510 | 13 | Clear sub | 231 |
| 511 | 14 | Sub | 232 |
| 512 | 12 | Add abs | 1300 |
| 513 | 15 | Sub abs | 1350 |
| 514 | 40 | Store acc | 789 |

There are several things to be pointed out about this program. The first and obvious reason for the example is to demonstrate the use of four new instructions. Clear subtract simply changes the sign of the number in memory before placing it in the accumulator. Subtract operates as might be expected. The other two new instructions simply allow for easy manipulation of absolute values. It may help to clarify some of these operations if a numerical example is given. First, observe that the numerical form of this program in memory would be:

$$510 + 1302310000$$
$$511 + 1402320000$$
$$512 + 1213000000$$
$$513 + 1513500000$$
$$514 + 4007890000$$

Next suppose that the numerical values of $A$, $B$, $C$, and $D$ are respectively 23, $-16$, $-40$, and $-12$. These could appear in a ten-digit memory location as 0000000023, etc. The contents of the accumulator after each instruction would then be:

| LOCATION | OPERATION | CONTENTS OF ACCUMULATOR AFTER OPERATION— TWO DIGITS ONLY |
|---|---|---|
| 510 | Clear sub | $-23$ |
| 511 | Sub | $-07$ |
| 512 | Add abs | $+33$ |
| 513 | Sub abs | $+21$ |
| 514 | Store acc | $+21$ |

This numerical example illustrates the second point: sign control is completely algebraic in the arithmetic unit.

The last observation on this example is that there is almost never a program which is uniquely the best possible program, or the *only* correct one. The following program would be just as short and give exactly the same answer, although it would arrive at it in a different order:

| 510 | 13 | Clear sub  | 232  |
|-----|----|-----------|------|
| 511 | 15 | Sub abs   | 1350 |
| 512 | 12 | Add abs   | 1300 |
| 513 | 14 | Sub       | 231  |
| 514 | 40 | Store acc | 789  |

It is also true that on many occasions there are alternative solutions which are *not* all equally good.  We shall have occasion from time to time to point out some of the criteria of what makes a program "good."

## 2.4 Details of Multiplication and Division

For complete understanding of some of the following material and especially parts of Chapter 4, it is necessary to have a fairly thorough grasp of how the computer handles multiplication and division.

The multiplication of two numbers is effected by having or placing one of them in the MQ register and giving the order multiply and specifying the address of the second.  Since multiplier and multiplicand each have ten digits (maximum), the product may have twenty digits (maximum) which appear in the accumulator and MQ combined, with the less significant ten in the MQ.  During the process of multiplication, the multiplicand is held in a register which has not been named or mentioned, since we have so little control over it in TYDAC.  For our purposes here we will call it the *memory register*.  Its function in this case is to provide a temporary storage register so that the multiplicand need be brought from memory to the arithmetic unit only *once*, even though it will ordinarily be needed many times during multiplication.  With these factors in mind, the multiplication process may be explained by means of an example.

Suppose the number 1111111111 (multiplicand) is to be multiplied by 0987654321 (multiplier), the latter number being already in the MQ as we begin.  After the control circuits discover the instruction calling for multiplication and giving the address of the number 1111111111, the steps are:

1. The number 1111111111 is brought from memory to the memory register, and the accumulator cleared.  The picture is now:

| + | Memory Register |
|---|---|

| 1 | 1 | 1 | 1 | 1 | 1 | 1 | 1 | 1 | 1 |
|---|---|---|---|---|---|---|---|---|---|

| + | Accumulator | | + | | MQ |
|---|---|---|---|---|---|

| 0 | 0 | 0 | 0 | 0 | 0 | 0 | 0 | 0 | 0 | 0 | 0 | 9 | 8 | 7 | 6 | 5 | 4 | 3 | 2 | 1 |
|---|---|---|---|---|---|---|---|---|---|---|---|---|---|---|---|---|---|---|---|---|

The accumulator and MQ are drawn together since that is the way they operate in multiplication.

2. The multiplicand is added into the accumulator as many times as the value of the digit standing in the tenth, or rightmost, position of the MQ:

| + | Accumulator | | | | | | | | | | | + | MQ | | | | | | | | |
|---|---|---|---|---|---|---|---|---|---|---|---|---|---|---|---|---|---|---|---|---|
| 0 | 1 | 1 | 1 | 1 | 1 | 1 | 1 | 1 | 1 | 1 | 1 | 0 | 9 | 8 | 7 | 6 | 5 | 4 | 3 | 2 | 1 |

(The memory register is unchanged throughout and will not be redrawn.)

3. The entire contents of the accumulator and MQ are shifted right one place, as though the accumulator and MQ were one register of twenty-one digits counting the overflow position:

| + | Accumulator | | | | | | | | | | | + | MQ | | | | | | | | |
|---|---|---|---|---|---|---|---|---|---|---|---|---|---|---|---|---|---|---|---|---|
| 0 | 0 | 1 | 1 | 1 | 1 | 1 | 1 | 1 | 1 | 1 | 1 | 1 | 0 | 9 | 8 | 7 | 6 | 5 | 4 | 3 | 2 |

4. The multiplicand is added into the accumulator as many times as the value of the digit in the tenth position of the MQ, which is now two:

| + | Accumulator | | | | | | | | | | | + | MQ | | | | | | | | |
|---|---|---|---|---|---|---|---|---|---|---|---|---|---|---|---|---|---|---|---|---|
| 0 | 2 | 3 | 3 | 3 | 3 | 3 | 3 | 3 | 3 | 3 | 1 | 0 | 9 | 8 | 7 | 6 | 5 | 4 | 3 | 2 |

5. The accumulator and MQ are shifted right one place:

| + | Accumulator | | | | | | | | | | | + | MQ | | | | | | | | |
|---|---|---|---|---|---|---|---|---|---|---|---|---|---|---|---|---|---|---|---|---|
| 0 | 0 | 2 | 3 | 3 | 3 | 3 | 3 | 3 | 3 | 3 | 3 | 1 | 0 | 9 | 8 | 7 | 6 | 5 | 4 | 3 |

6. The multiplicand is added into the accumulator as many times as the value of the digit in the last position of the MQ, which is now three:

| + | Accumulator | | | | | | | | | | | + | MQ | | | | | | | | |
|---|---|---|---|---|---|---|---|---|---|---|---|---|---|---|---|---|---|---|---|---|
| 0 | 3 | 5 | 6 | 6 | 6 | 6 | 6 | 6 | 6 | 6 | 3 | 1 | 0 | 9 | 8 | 7 | 6 | 5 | 4 | 3 |

Following the same pattern, the successive contents of these two registers are:

| | + | | | | | | | | | | | | + | | | | | | | | |
|---|---|---|---|---|---|---|---|---|---|---|---|---|---|---|---|---|---|---|---|---|---|
| Shift | 0 | 0 | 3 | 5 | 6 | 6 | 6 | 6 | 6 | 6 | 6 | 3 | 1 | 0 | 9 | 8 | 7 | 6 | 5 | 4 |

Add   | 0 | 4 | 8 | 0 | 1 | 1 | 1 | 1 | 1 | 1 | 0 | 6 | 3 | 1 | 0 | 9 | 8 | 7 | 6 | 5 | 4 |

Shift | 0 | 0 | 4 | 8 | 0 | 1 | 1 | 1 | 1 | 1 | 1 | 0 | 6 | 3 | 1 | 0 | 9 | 8 | 7 | 6 | 5 |

Add   | 0 | 6 | 0 | 3 | 5 | 6 | 6 | 6 | 6 | 6 | 6 | 0 | 6 | 3 | 1 | 0 | 9 | 8 | 7 | 6 | 5 |

Shift | 0 | 0 | 6 | 0 | 3 | 5 | 6 | 6 | 6 | 6 | 6 | 6 | 0 | 6 | 3 | 1 | 0 | 9 | 8 | 7 | 6 |

Add   | 0 | 7 | 2 | 7 | 0 | 2 | 3 | 3 | 3 | 3 | 3 | 2 | 6 | 0 | 6 | 3 | 1 | 0 | 9 | 8 | 7 | 6 |

Shift | 0 | 0 | 7 | 2 | 7 | 0 | 2 | 3 | 3 | 3 | 3 | 3 | 2 | 6 | 0 | 6 | 3 | 1 | 0 | 9 | 8 | 7 |

Add   | 0 | 8 | 5 | 0 | 4 | 8 | 0 | 1 | 1 | 1 | 0 | 2 | 6 | 0 | 6 | 3 | 1 | 0 | 9 | 8 | 7 |

Shift | 0 | 0 | 8 | 5 | 0 | 4 | 8 | 0 | 1 | 1 | 1 | 0 | 2 | 6 | 0 | 6 | 3 | 1 | 0 | 9 | 8 |

Add   | 0 | 9 | 7 | 3 | 9 | 3 | 6 | 8 | 9 | 9 | 9 | 0 | 2 | 6 | 0 | 6 | 3 | 1 | 0 | 9 | 8 |

Shift | 0 | 0 | 9 | 7 | 3 | 9 | 3 | 6 | 8 | 9 | 9 | 9 | 0 | 2 | 6 | 0 | 6 | 3 | 1 | 0 | 9 |

Add   | 1 | 0 | 9 | 7 | 3 | 9 | 3 | 6 | 8 | 9 | 8 | 9 | 0 | 2 | 6 | 0 | 6 | 3 | 1 | 0 | 9 |

Shift | 0 | 1 | 0 | 9 | 7 | 3 | 9 | 3 | 6 | 8 | 9 | 8 | 9 | 0 | 2 | 6 | 0 | 6 | 3 | 1 | 0 |

Add   | 0 | 1 | 0 | 9 | 7 | 3 | 9 | 3 | 6 | 8 | 9 | 8 | 9 | 0 | 2 | 6 | 0 | 6 | 3 | 1 | 0 |

Shift | 0 | 0 | 1 | 0 | 9 | 7 | 3 | 9 | 3 | 6 | 8 | 9 | 8 | 9 | 0 | 2 | 6 | 0 | 6 | 3 | 1 |

The multiplication is now complete. The product has been developed in the accumulator and the MQ taken as one long register. The multiplier in the MQ has been lost. The multiplicand is still in memory. If either or both numbers had been negative, algebraic sign control would have given the correct sign to the product, with the sign appearing in the sign position of both the accumulator and MQ. All of this is effected by the single instruction, multiply.

In the multiply-round order, multiplication is automatically followed by a round operation as described in Appendix 1.

All of this may be seen to be simply a mechanization of the ordinary process of multiplying with paper and pencil. Details vary from one machine to the next, as regards the actual multiplication of the multiplicand by one digit of the multiplier and the placement of operands in arithmetic registers, but the adding-and-shifting scheme is the same.

If multiplication is effected by using one digit of the multiplier in an adding-and-shifting routine, division is accomplished by building up the quotient one digit at a time in a *subtracting*-and-shifting system. Only a few steps of an example need be followed through, since the process is similar to multiplication and is almost exactly analogous to paper-and-pencil long division.

The dividend must be in the accumulator and MQ, as a twenty-digit number. The *twenty* comes from comparison with multiplication: two ten-digit factors give a twenty-digit product. Conversely, division of a twenty-digit dividend by a ten-digit divisor gives a ten-digit quotient. If, as is usually the case, the dividend at hand has only ten digits, then the last ten digits may be made zero by simply clearing the MQ. Division is effected by giving the operation divide and specifying the address of the divisor.

Suppose the number 1045203973 is to be divided by 1111111111. The first number is in the accumulator, the MQ has been cleared, and the divide order given. The first few steps would be:

1. The divisor is brought from memory and placed in the memory register. The picture:

| + | Memory Register |
|---|---|

| 1 | 1 | 1 | 1 | 1 | 1 | 1 | 1 | 1 | 1 |
|---|---|---|---|---|---|---|---|---|---|

| + | Accumulator | | | | | | | | | | + | MQ |
|---|---|---|---|---|---|---|---|---|---|---|---|---|

| 0 | 1 | 0 | 4 | 5 | 2 | 0 | 3 | 9 | 7 | 3 | 0 | 0 | 0 | 0 | 0 | 0 | 0 | 0 | 0 | 0 |
|---|---|---|---|---|---|---|---|---|---|---|---|---|---|---|---|---|---|---|---|---|

2. The divisor is compared with the number in the accumulator. If the divisor is now *larger* (in absolute value, sign control being

automatic as usual), the division continues. If not, i.e., if the divisor is equal or smaller, the machine stops in what is called the *divide stop* condition. A little experimentation with paper and pencil or a desk calculator will show that if this condition is not met, the quotient will have to contain eleven digits—and the MQ has room for only ten. Of course, attempted division by zero will always result in a divide stop.

3. The contents of the accumulator and MQ together are shifted left one place:

| + | | Accumulator | | | | | | | | | + | | | | | MQ | | | | | |
|---|---|---|---|---|---|---|---|---|---|---|---|---|---|---|---|---|---|---|---|---|---|
| 1 | 0 | 4 | 5 | 2 | 0 | 3 | 9 | 7 | 3 | 0 | 0 | 0 | 0 | 0 | 0 | 0 | 0 | 0 | 0 | 0 | 0 |

(Memory register again omitted.)

4. The divisor is subtracted from the accumulator as many times as possible without changing the sign of the accumulator. This is just the long-division process of "seeing how many times it will go." The number of times is entered into the last position of the MQ:

| + | | | | | | | | | | | + | | | | | | | | | | |
|---|---|---|---|---|---|---|---|---|---|---|---|---|---|---|---|---|---|---|---|---|---|
| 0 | 0 | 4 | 5 | 2 | 0 | 3 | 9 | 7 | 3 | 1 | 0 | 0 | 0 | 0 | 0 | 0 | 0 | 0 | 0 | 0 | 9 |

5. The accumulator and MQ are shifted one place left:

| + | | | | | | | | | | | + | | | | | | | | | | |
|---|---|---|---|---|---|---|---|---|---|---|---|---|---|---|---|---|---|---|---|---|---|
| 0 | 4 | 5 | 2 | 0 | 3 | 9 | 7 | 3 | 1 | 0 | 0 | 0 | 0 | 0 | 0 | 0 | 0 | 0 | 0 | 9 | 0 |

6. The divisor in the memory register is subtracted from the accumulator as many times as possible and this number entered into the last position of the MQ:

| + | | Accumulator | | | | | | | | | + | | | | | MQ | | | | | |
|---|---|---|---|---|---|---|---|---|---|---|---|---|---|---|---|---|---|---|---|---|---|
| 0 | 0 | 0 | 7 | 5 | 9 | 5 | 2 | 8 | 6 | 6 | 0 | 0 | 0 | 0 | 0 | 0 | 0 | 0 | 0 | 9 | 4 |

The process is continued. The last three steps are:

Subtract

| + | | Accumulator | | | | | | | | | + | | | | | MQ | | | | | |
|---|---|---|---|---|---|---|---|---|---|---|---|---|---|---|---|---|---|---|---|---|---|
| 0 | 0 | 8 | 8 | 2 | 2 | 9 | 8 | 1 | 7 | 5 | 0 | 9 | 4 | 0 | 6 | 8 | 3 | 5 | 7 | 5 |

Shift

| + | | Accumulator | | | | | | | | | + | | | | | MQ | | | | | |
|---|---|---|---|---|---|---|---|---|---|---|---|---|---|---|---|---|---|---|---|---|---|
| 0 | 8 | 8 | 2 | 2 | 9 | 8 | 1 | 7 | 5 | 0 | 9 | 4 | 0 | 6 | 8 | 3 | 5 | 7 | 5 | 0 |

Subtract

| + | | Accumulator | | | | | | | | | + | | | | | MQ | | | | | |
|---|---|---|---|---|---|---|---|---|---|---|---|---|---|---|---|---|---|---|---|---|---|
| 0 | 1 | 0 | 4 | 5 | 2 | 0 | 3 | 9 | 7 | 3 | 9 | 4 | 0 | 6 | 8 | 3 | 5 | 7 | 5 | 7 |

Thus the quotient is developed a digit at a time in the MQ. After the process is finished, the accumulator contains the remainder, which, because of the numbers used, happens in this case to be the same as the dividend.

*Example 3.* $A \cdot B$

$A$ is stored in 1803, $B$ in 1812, the result to go in 1837. Suppose this program starts at 1787.

| LOCATION | OPERATION CODE | OPERATION ABBREVIATION | ADDRESS |
|---|---|---|---|
| 1787 | 42 | Load MQ | 1803 |
| 1788 | 17 | Mult round | 1812 |
| 1789 | 40 | Store acc | 1837 |

The first instruction places the multiplier in the MQ, destroying whatever was there, the second forms the ten-digit rounded product in the accumulator, and the third stores this product. Whether multiply or multiply-round is used depends on the particular situation; there was not enough information given to specify the choice here, which was made arbitrarily.

*Example 4.* $A \div B$

$A$ is assumed to be in 1103, $B$ in 1196, 25 contains zero, and the result is to go in 1200.

| LOCATION | OPERATION CODE | OPERATION ABBREVIATION | ADDRESS |
|---|---|---|---|
| 401 | 42 | Load MQ | 0025 |
| 402 | 10 | Clear add | 1103 |
| 403 | 18 | Divide | 1196 |
| 404 | 43 | Store MQ | 1200 |

The first instruction simply clears the MQ register, which is necessary because the accumulator plus MQ is considered to be one long twenty-digit register. On the other hand, this will ordinarily have a rather small effect and is often not done. The second instruction places the dividend in the accumulator. The number in memory is as usual unchanged. The last instruction simply stores the quotient in 1200.

*Example 5.   Adding Ten Numbers*

Suppose that the ten numbers in 200 to 209 are to be added and the sum placed in 210. The only way available at this point is:

| LOCATION | OPERATION CODE | OPERATION ABBREVIATION | ADDRESS |
|---|---|---|---|
| 1600 | 10 | Clear add | 200 |
| 1601 | 11 | Add | 201 |
| 1602 | 11 | Add | 202 |
| 1603 | 11 | Add | 203 |
| 1604 | 11 | Add | 204 |
| 1605 | 11 | Add | 205 |
| 1606 | 11 | Add | 206 |
| 1607 | 11 | Add | 207 |
| 1608 | 11 | Add | 208 |
| 1609 | 11 | Add | 209 |
| 1610 | 40 | Store acc | 210 |

This example is intended to provoke some thought about the inconvenience of writing out so many nearly similar instructions. If there were very many more numbers in the list, the problem would become intolerable. Such is the basic problem solved by loops, discussed in Chapter 6.

*Example 6. Determining Larger of Two Numbers*

Suppose the number $A$ is in location 507, the number $B$ in 508. It is required to put the larger (algebraically) in location 600. If they are equal, either may be placed in 600 and no signal need be given.

| LOCATION | OPERATION CODE | OPERATION ABBREVIATION | ADDRESS |
|---|---|---|---|
| 1000 | 10 | Clear add | 507 |
| 1001 | 14 | Sub | 508 |
| 1002 | 03 | Acc plus-jump | 1005 |
| 1003 | 10 | Clear add | 508 |
| 1004 | 01 | Un jump | 1006 |
| 1005 | 10 | Clear add | 507 |
| 1006 | 40 | Store acc | 600 |

This is the first contact with a *jump* instruction. The various jumps have the function of breaking the usual one-after-the-other sequence of instructions. The Unconditional jump simply breaks the sequence by taking the next instruction from the location specified by the address of the jump instruction—which is a new use for the address. The various conditional jumps break out of sequence only if some condition in the machine is met. For instance, the Accumulator plus-jump breaks the sequence, i.e., executes the jump, *only* if the accumulator has a plus sign at the time. If not, the next instruction in normal sequence is taken.

The problem in the example is to instruct the computer how to determine which of the two numbers is larger, and then choose one of two alternatives. The seven-word program consists basically of four parts. The first three instructions determine which of the numbers stored in 507 and 508 is larger, by subtracting them and executing a conditional jump based on the difference. The Accumulator plus-jump at 1002 decides whether the instruction at 1003 or 1005 is to be carried out.

If the difference is positive, indicating that the number in 507 is larger, the plus jump goes down to 1005 which brings in the number in 507. If the conditional jump is not executed, the number in 508 must be larger, and the program goes on to 1003 which brings in the number in 508. The last of the four parts is step 1006, which stores whichever number was brought into the accumulator by step 1003 or 1005. Step 1004 was necessary, since without it the number brought into the accumulator by step 1003 would have been replaced at step 1005—either way, we would get the contents of 507 going into 600.

We have here the first of many illustrations of the computer making a choice of two or more alternatives on the basis of a fairly simple test.

*Example 7.* $(10 \cdot A + B) \cdot C$

$A$ is stored in 0804, $B$ in 0805, $C$ in 0806, result to go in 0807. The problem here is to obtain the product $10A$ as simply as possible and to get the numbers into the right registers at the right time.

By far the simplest way to multiply by ten in a decimal machine is to shift left one place. Multiplication by any power of ten, positive or negative, can be carried out by shifting the appropriate number of places to the left or right respectively.*

The program could look like this:

| LOCATION | OPERATION CODE | OPERATION ABBREVIATION | ADDRESS |
|---|---|---|---|
| 1200 | 10 | Clear add | 804 |
| 1201 | 30 | Acc left | 1 |
| 1202 | 11 | Add | 805 |
| 1203 | 33 | Long right | 10 |
| 1204 | 17 | Mult round | 806 |
| 1205 | 40 | Store acc | 807 |

The first two instructions bring the number $A$ into the accumulator and multiply it by ten. Note that the "address" of a shift instruction

* In a binary machine, multiplication by powers of two is similarly easy.

is not an address at all, but simply a number of shifts. The "address" is *not* a location in memory where the number of shifts may be found. The next step adds $B$. The sum is in the accumulator, whereas the multiplication step requires it to be in the MQ. The most direct attack is simply to call for a long right shift of ten.* This shifts the contents of the accumulator into the MQ. The sign of the accumulator becomes the sign of both and whatever was in the MQ is lost. Multiplication and storing are as usual.

## 2.5 Arithmetic Speeds

Table 1 gives some approximate idea of the arithmetic speeds of three representative types of computers. The first type is a magnetic drum machine of medium size. The second is a large magnetic core computer intended primarily for commercial applications, and which

### TABLE 1

OPERATIONS PER SECOND

| TYPE OF OPERATION | Magnetic drum, medium size | Magnetic core, commercial, alphabetic | Magnetic core, scientific, binary |
|---|---|---|---|
| Add, subtract, store, shift, jump, etc. | 400 | 6,000 | 40,000 |
| Multiply | 100 | 500 | 5,000 |
| Divide | 80 | 200 | 5,000 |

can handle alphabetic characters with no special effort. The third is a magnetic core machine intended for scientific work, operating in binary where the others are decimal. The speeds in each case include the average time required to get the necessary numbers from memory, which can be reduced considerably in the case of the magnetic drum machine by careful programming. All are for single address machines like TYDAC, operating on numbers equivalent to ten decimal digits.

## Exercises

For exercises 1 through 10, $a$ is in 500, $b$ is in 501, $c$ is in 1400, and $d$ is in 1450; place $x$ in 600. Each exercise should be written as a separate program.

* In some computers it is faster to store the accumulator and then load the MQ. This would probably hold where memory is random-access, as electrostatic or magnetic cores; it would decidedly not be true for a delay line or magnetic drum memory. In other machines this consideration might not apply at all, since the functions of the arithmetic registers can be quite different.

1. $x = a + b + c$

2. $x = a + 2b + 3c$

3. $x = b - c$

4. $x = 2b - d$

5. $x = ab$

6. $x = ab + c$

7. $x = ad - cd$

8. $x = (a + c)/d$

9. $x = \dfrac{abc + d}{4(a + b)}$

10. $x = a - |b| + |d|$

11. The three numbers in 100, 200, and 300 *should* all be nonzero. If so, form the sum of the three and place it in 400. Test each number separately, and *halt* if any of the numbers *is* zero. This will require the halt order described in the instruction summary. *Hint:* Be sure your program stops *only* if one of the numbers is zero, i.e., be careful the halt is not placed in such a way that the program will *always* stop.

12. Program the evaluation of $a + b \pm c$. $a$ is in 50, $b$ in 51, $c$ in 52; place result in 53. $a$ and $b$ are both known to be positive. If $c$, as found in memory, is positive, take the plus sign in the formula; if negative, the minus sign.

13. Three numbers which may be positive or negative are stored in 100, 101, and 102. Change the sign of any negative numbers so that after the program has been executed the numbers *in memory* are all positive.

14. Three numbers are stored in 1500, 1547, and 1609. Place the number which is algebraically largest in 1900.

15. An angle in radian measure is in 500, $2\pi$ is in 600. The angle is known to be between 0 and $+20$ radians. Subtract $2\pi$ as many times as needed to reduce the angle to less than $2\pi$, and place the reduced angle in 501.

16. Program the evaluation of $a + bx + cx^2 + dx^3$. $a$ is in 1000, $b$ in 1001, $c$ in 1002, $d$ in 1003, $x$ in 1100; place result in 1200. *Hint:* The program can be shortened somewhat by rewriting the formula as $a + x [b + x (c + dx)]$.

17. Program the evaluation of $(a + bx + 10c)/(x^2 - d)$. $a$ is in 800, $b$ in 801, $c$ in 802, $d$ in 803, $x$ in 405; place result in 500. Divide stop might occur, depending on size of $x$. Evaluate numerator and denominator, then program a test to anticipate divide stop. If divide stop *would* happen, halt instead of finishing evaluation.

18. The "number" in 500 consists of three positive numbers placed in that one location by a special loading program. $a$ consists of the first four

digits, $b$ of the next three, and $c$ of the last three, so that the word looks like:

| | 1 2 3 4 | 5 6 7 | 8 9 10 |
|---|---|---|---|
| | a | b | c |

By shifting and manipulating the arithmetic registers, separate these three numbers and place $a$ in 501, $b$ in 502, $c$ in 503. Each number should be placed to the far right of the specified location. For instance, $a$ should appear in 501 as

| 0 | 0 | 0 | 0 | 0 | 0 | X | X | X | X |
|---|---|---|---|---|---|---|---|---|---|

# 3 BINARY AND OCTAL NUMBER SYSTEMS

## 3.0 Introduction*

The binary number system, which is at the heart of all digital computers, is built around only two (hence, *binary*) digits, zero and one. The system is used explicitly in many present computers, i.e., numbers and instructions must be *entered into* the machine in binary form. Usually the computer is programmed to make the conversion from decimal to binary, concurrent with reading the numbers from an input medium which is prepared in decimal form. For instance, cards may be punched in standard decimal format, read as though they were binary by the computer, and the pattern of binary digits then converted to the actual binary representation. Output is handled similarly. Thus, although the computer is completely binary in operation, it can be programmed to accept and interpret decimal information and give decimal answers. (Binary digit is usually abbreviated to bit.)

Many other computers, although still basically binary in electronics, do the conversion from decimal to binary and back electronically. This is inherently wasteful of electronic circuitry, but is felt by many to be enough of a simplification in programming and operation to justify the additional cost.

The reason the binary number system lies at the heart of all computers, whether of binary or decimal input and output, is that a binary variable is so simple to represent physically. Common examples are: a particular location on a punched card which either has a hole or does not; an electric switch which is either on or off; an electron tube which is either conducting or not; a track on a magnetic tape which either has a change in magnetization at a given point or does not; a magnetic core which is magnetized in one direction or the other. In each case, the device or state has just two stable, mutually exclusive conditions. The digit value 0 is assigned to one of these conditions and 1 to the other; the circuits of the computer are built

---

* The entire chapter may be omitted without loss of continuity.

to act according to the rules of binary arithmetic on combinations of the two states.

It might seem reasonable to try to discover computing elements which have three—or ten—stable states. There are indeed such devices, but it turns out that they are still basically binary, and nothing has been gained. Take, for instance, an electromechanical wheel with ten electric contacts around a circle with a wiping arm to touch just one of them and some sort of spring to maintain the position. This could be used, in conjunction with some type of actuating device, to store a decimal digit. But observe that what we have here is a system of ten binary digits: each position of the contact arm is either on or off! We see, then, that basic decision elements in computers are always binary.

In use, binary numbers are quite cumbersome, since about $3\frac{1}{3}$ binary digits are required to represent a decimal digit. By combining binary digits into groups of three or four or five, we get the octal, hexadecimal, or duotricenary number systems. Since the conversions between these systems and binary are so simple, wide use is made of them in reducing the number of symbols required to write down binary numbers.

### 3.1 Number Representation

The central feature of the Arabic number system is the fact that a given digit can have more or less value depending on where it is written. For instance, the symbol 2 may mean 2.0, 200, or 0.00002 depending on where it is written. (Recall that there is no such general place value in the Roman number system; also no zero, decimals, or convenient fractions.) This is so familiar to us as to be overlooked in everyday use of decimal numbers. What we really mean by 744.819 is of course

$$700 + 40 + 4 + 0.8 + 0.01 + 0.009$$

or

$$7 \cdot 10^2$$
$$+ 4 \cdot 10^1$$
$$+ 4 \cdot 10^0$$
$$+ 8 \cdot 10^{-1}$$
$$+ 1 \cdot 10^{-2}$$
$$+ 9 \cdot 10^{-3}$$

Another way of saying the same thing: the first 4 is worth ten times as much for being written where it is as is the second 4.

The question we must ask is, why this number ten, or why just ten digits? Why not six, or twenty—or two? The answer, in all probability, arose from our having ten fingers. If we use some other place value, we will of course need the same number of digits as the number base, which will require invention of some new ones if there are to be more than ten.

In the case of binary numbers we need only two—zero and one—and the place value between adjacent digits is just two. For instance, in binary the number 1101 means:

$$1 \cdot 2^3$$
$$+ 1 \cdot 2^2$$
$$+ 0 \cdot 2^1$$
$$+ 1 \cdot 2^0$$

Again, the first 1 is worth twice as much as the second 1, and eight times as much as the last. The basic idea of place value is unchanged: the amount of the place values is now *two* instead of the familiar ten.

Since a number involving only zeros and ones could be taken as either binary or decimal, we must be careful to specify the base (place value) wherever there could be confusion. This is usually indicated by enclosing the number in parentheses and writing the base as a subscript, in decimal. Thus:

$$(1101)_2, \quad (1101)_{10}$$

As an exercise in interpreting the meaning of binary numbers, we may take a direct method of conversion from binary to decimal. The number $(11101.101)_2$ means:

$$1 \cdot 2^4 \; = \; (16)_{10}$$
$$+ 1 \cdot 2^3 \; = \; (8)_{10}$$
$$+ 1 \cdot 2^2 \; = \; (4)_{10}$$
$$+ 0 \cdot 2^1 \; = \; (0)_{10}$$
$$+ 1 \cdot 2^0 \; = \; (1)_{10}$$
$$+ 1 \cdot 2^{-1} = \; (0.5)_{10}$$
$$+ 0 \cdot 2^{-2} = \; (0)_{10}$$
$$+ 1 \cdot 2^{-3} = \; (0.125)_{10}$$

or, $(11101.101)_2 = (29.625)_{10}$. Binary fractions may be confusing at first. It may help to observe that:

$$(0.1)_2 = 1 \cdot 2^{-1} = \tfrac{1}{2} = \tfrac{5}{10} = (0.5)_{10}$$

Octal numbers fit into the same pattern; here the place value is eight, and only eight digits, zero through seven, are needed. For example:

$$
\begin{aligned}
(327.41)_8 = \quad 3 \cdot 8^2 &= (192)_{10} \\
+ 2 \cdot 8^1 &= (16)_{10} \\
+ 7 \cdot 8^0 &= (7)_{10} \\
+ 4 \cdot 8^{-1} &= (0.5)_{10} \\
+ 1 \cdot 8^{-2} &= \underline{(0.015625)_{10}} \\
&\phantom{=} (215.515625)_{10}
\end{aligned}
$$

The simple reason for the use of octal (also sometimes called octonary) numbers is that the conversion from binary to octal can be carried out mentally, and only a third as many digits are required to carry the same information. All that is necessary to convert from binary to octal is to group the binary digits in groups of three's from the binary point, and write down the decimal value of each group taken as an integer. Thus:

$$(11/011/010/110.110/001/110)_2 = (3326.616)_8$$

The basis for this may be seen readily with an example:

$$
(101011)_2 = \quad
\begin{aligned}
&1 \cdot 2^5 \\
&+ 0 \cdot 2^4 \\
&+ 1 \cdot 2^3 \\
&+ 0 \cdot 2^2 \\
&+ 1 \cdot 2^1 \\
&+ 1 \cdot 2^0
\end{aligned}
\; = \;
\begin{aligned}
&\left.\begin{aligned} 4 \cdot 2^3 \\ + 0 \cdot 2^3 \\ + 1 \cdot 2^3 \end{aligned}\right\} = 5 \cdot 2^3 = 5 \cdot 8^1 \\
&\left.\begin{aligned} + 0 \cdot 2^0 \\ + 2 \cdot 2^0 \\ + 1 \cdot 2^0 \end{aligned}\right\} = 3 \cdot 2^0 = 3 \cdot 8^0
\end{aligned}
$$

or, $(101011)_2 = 5 \cdot 8^1 + 3 \cdot 8^0 = (53)_8$

The same simplicity of conversion could be accomplished using any base which is a power of two. Four would be the quaternary system, which would have no particular advantage over octal and would indeed require more digits to represent the same number. Bases 16 and 32 are both in use by at least one computing installation. They accomplish a further reduction in number of digits at the expense of requiring new symbols for the extra six or twenty-two digits. In the balance, the disadvantages of these latter outweigh the gains, unless there are overriding factors such as the characteristics of input-output equipment.

### 3.2 Arithmetic in Binary and Octal

Addition of integers may be regarded as an extension of the idea of counting. Before proceeding we should therefore be sure that the formation of the symbols for the integers is clear.

When counting in decimal, we first write the ten digits in order.

Then we begin writing a 1 to the left, giving it a place value of ten—the base of the number system. The process is similar for counting in any other number system: we write the digit symbols until we run out, then start writing a 1 to the left, giving it the place value of the system. As soon as we run out using two digits, we write another 1, giving it the value of the number base squared. This, of course, is nothing more than we have already discussed, but the difference in viewpoint may make the scheme clearer. Counting in decimal, octal, and binary, we have:

| DECIMAL | OCTAL | BINARY |
|---|---|---|
| 0 | 0 | 0 |
| 1 | 1 | 1 |
| 2 | 2 | 10 |
| 3 | 3 | 11 |
| 4 | 4 | 100 |
| 5 | 5 | 101 |
| 6 | 6 | 110 |
| 7 | 7 | 111 |
| 8 | 10 | 1000 |
| 9 | 11 | 1001 |
| 10 | 12 | 1010 |
| 11 | 13 | 1011 |
| 12 | 14 | 1100 |
| 13 | 15 | 1101 |
| 14 | 16 | 1110 |
| 15 | 17 | 1111 |
| 16 | 20 | 10000 |
| 17 | 21 | 10001 |
| 18 | 22 | 10010 |
| 19 | 23 | 10011 |
| 20 | 24 | 10100 |

Coming back to the relation between addition and counting, we may begin by laying out a numbered scale, thus:

```
┌─┬─┬─┬─┬─┬─┬─┬─┬─┬─┬─┬─┬─┬─┬─┬─┬─┬─┬─┬─┬─┬─┬─┬─┬─┐
0 1 2 3 4 5 6 7 8 9 10 11 12 13 14 15 16 17 18 19 20 21 22 23 24 25
```

If two integers $m$ and $n$ are to be added, we count $n$ places beyond $m$ to find the sum of $m$ and $n$. The scale may be labeled in any number system we please.

This would, of course, be a cumbersome way of actually adding, and would have to be extended to cover fractions. The rules of addition may be summarized in small tables, such as Table 1 (in decimal).

## TABLE 1

|   | 0 | 1 | 2 | 3 | 4 | 5 | 6 | 7 | 8 | 9 |
|---|---|---|---|---|---|---|---|---|---|---|
| 0 | 0 | 1 | 2 | 3 | 4 | 5 | 6 | 7 | 8 | 9 |
| 1 |   | 2 | 3 | 4 | 5 | 6 | 7 | 8 | 9 | 0 + C |
| 2 |   |   | 4 | 5 | 6 | 7 | 8 | 9 | 0 + C | 1 + C |
| 3 |   |   |   | 6 | 7 | 8 | 9 | 0 + C | 1 + C | 2 + C |
| 4 |   |   |   |   | 8 | 9 | 0 + C | 1 + C | 2 + C | 3 + C |
| 5 |   |   |   |   |   | 0 + C* | 1 + C | 2 + C | 3 + C | 4 + C |
| 6 |   |   |   |   |   |   | 2 + C | 3 + C | 4 + C | 5 + C |
| 7 |   |   |   |   |   |   |   | 4 + C | 5 + C | 6 + C |
| 8 |   |   |   |   |   |   |   |   | 6 + C | 7 + C |
| 9 |   |   |   |   |   |   |   |   |   | 8 + C |

*C = 1 carry, or 1 added to next most significant position.

In octal the table is smaller, as shown by Table 2.

## TABLE 2          *1019557*

|   | 0 | 1 | 2 | 3 | 4 | 5 | 6 | 7 |
|---|---|---|---|---|---|---|---|---|
| 0 | 0 | 1 | 2 | 3 | 4 | 5 | 6 | 7 |
| 1 |   | 2 | 3 | 4 | 5 | 6 | 7 | 0 + C |
| 2 |   |   | 4 | 5 | 6 | 7 | 0 + C | 1 + C |
| 3 |   |   |   | 6 | 7 | 0 + C | 1 + C | 2 + C |
| 4 |   |   |   |   | 0 + C | 1 + C | 2 + C | 3 + C |
| 5 |   |   |   |   |   | 2 + C | 3 + C | 4 + C |
| 6 |   |   |   |   |   |   | 4 + C | 5 + C |
| 7 |   |   |   |   |   |   |   | 6 + C |

In binary the table is simplicity itself:

|   | 0 | 1 |
|---|---|---|
| 0 | 0 | 1 |
| 1 | 1 | 0 + C |

Using these tables we may carry out some additions.

*Octal*

```
   1            1  11
  12743        770146
+  4701      + 11135
  17644       1001303
```

*Binary*

```
     111          111             111
    1011       10111000         1001100
+    101      +  101011        +  10101
   10000       11100011         1100001
```

Subtraction may also be related to counting, going backwards this time. Again we may develop simple tables, such as the octal one shown in Table 3, where the number on the side (subtrahend) is subtracted from the number at the top (minuend).

## TABLE  3

|   | 0 | 1 | 2 | 3 | 4 | 5 | 6 | 7 |
|---|---|---|---|---|---|---|---|---|
| 0 | 0 | 1 | 2 | 3 | 4 | 5 | 6 | 7 |
| 1 | 7 + b* | 0 | 1 | 2 | 3 | 4 | 5 | 6 |
| 2 | 6 + b | 7 + b | 0 | 1 | 2 | 3 | 4 | 5 |
| 3 | 5 + b | 6 + b | 7 + b | 0 | 1 | 2 | 3 | 4 |
| 4 | 4 + b | 5 + b | 6 + b | 7 + b | 0 | 1 | 2 | 3 |
| 5 | 3 + b | 4 + b | 5 + b | 6 + b | 7 + b | 0 | 1 | 2 |
| 6 | 2 + b | 3 + b | 4 + b | 5 + b | 6 + b | 7 + b | 0 | 1 |
| 7 | 1 + b | 2 + b | 3 + b | 4 + b | 5 + b | 6 + b | 7 + b | 0 |

*b = 1 borrowed from adjacent digit.

Again the binary table is very simple:

|   | 0 | 1 |
|---|---|---|
| 0 | 0 | 1 |
| 1 | 1 + b | 0 |

*Illustrations*
Octal

$$
\begin{array}{r}
40 \\
12\not5\not\!13 \\
-\ 12642 \\
\hline
112251
\end{array}
\qquad
\begin{array}{r}
57706 \\
4\not0\not0\not0 1\not7 5 \\
-\ 123456 \\
\hline
4454517
\end{array}
$$

*Binary*

$$
\begin{array}{r}
0 \\
\not1 01111 \\
-\ 10011 \\
\hline
11100
\end{array}
\qquad
\begin{array}{r}
0\ 001 \\
\not1 0\not1\not1\not0 0010 \\
-\ 10101010 \\
\hline
10111000
\end{array}
$$

Subtractions which give negative answers can be handled as usual by subtracting in reverse order and attaching a minus sign to the difference.

Subtractions are actually carried out in computer electronics by the addition of complements. This method is based on the following, illustrated with a six-digit decimal number:

$$493{,}201 - 126{,}944 = 493201 + (1{,}000{,}000 - 126{,}944) - 1{,}000{,}000$$

The subtraction $1{,}000{,}000 - 126{,}944$ can be very simply performed by subtracting each digit from 9 except the last, which is subtracted from 10 (if the last digit is 0, the next to the last is subtracted from 10, etc.). This is then called the ten's complement. Thus

$$1{,}000{,}000 - 126{,}944 = 873{,}056$$

Now adding:

$$
\begin{array}{r}
493{,}201 \\
873{,}056 \\
\hline
1{,}366{,}257
\end{array}
$$

The 1,000,000 is subtracted off again simply by deleting the 1 at the beginning.

An alternative method uses the nine's complement, which is formed by subtracting each digit from nine, including the last. After the addition of the complement, the leading 1 is deleted and a 1 is added to the units position. This is sometimes called "end-around-carry." In either method, a negative difference will be in complement form, and must be reconverted. Also, no end-around-carry is required. A negative difference may be recognized by complementing one more digit than necessary, i.e., adding a 0 at the front; a negative difference will be signaled by a 9 in the first position, instead of a 0.

*Examples*

| | | | |
|---|---|---|---|
| 0456789 | becomes | 0456789 | |
| −0123456 | | 9876543 | 9's complement |
| | | ⟨1⟩0333332 | |
| | | ⟶1 | |
| | | 0333333 | |

| | | | |
|---|---|---|---|
| 0123456 | becomes | 0123456 | |
| −0456789 | | 9543210 | |
| | | 9666666 | which becomes |
| | | −333333 | on reconversion |

This may seem to be an exceedingly difficult way of subtracting two numbers. It is used (or the equivalent thing in binary) because it is far simpler to form a digit-by-digit complement than to build circuits or devices to "borrow." This is especially true in binary, where the one's complement is formed simply by changing ones to zeros and zeros to ones, which can be done with great ease electronically.

In fact, in some machines (Univac Scientific, JOHNIAC, ENIAC, and others) negative numbers are represented entirely by complements rather than by the use of minus signs. Again circuit simplicity makes for programming difficulty. This is the reverse of the current trend.

## MULTIPLICATION

Multiplication is simply a process of repeated addition. We can multiply in octal or binary simply by developing an appropriate multiplication table and following a process similar to decimal multiplication.

In binary we have:

$$0 \cdot 0 = 0$$
$$0 \cdot 1 = 0$$
$$1 \cdot 0 = 0$$
$$1 \cdot 1 = 1$$

*Example*

```
1011011
   1101
1011011
0000000
1011011
1011011
10010011111
```

The octal table is given in Table 4.

### TABLE  4

|   | 0 | 1 | 2 | 3 | 4 | 5 | 6 | 7 |
|---|---|---|---|---|---|---|---|---|
| 0 | 0 | 0 | 0 | 0 | 0 | 0 | 0 | 0 |
| 1 |   | 1 | 2 | 3 | 4 | 5 | 6 | 7 |
| 2 |   |   | 4 | 6 | 10 | 12 | 14 | 16 |
| 3 |   |   |   | 11 | 14 | 17 | 22 | 25 |
| 4 |   |   |   |   | 20 | 24 | 30 | 34 |
| 5 |   |   |   |   |   | 31 | 36 | 43 |
| 6 |   |   |   |   |   |   | 44 | 52 |
| 7 |   |   |   |   |   |   |   | 61 |

*Example*

```
1247
 305
6503
3765
405203
```

In a binary computer, no multiplication table need be stored since the table is so simple. Each digit of the multiplier is examined in turn: if it is a 1, the multiplicand is added; if it is a 0, no addition takes place. This is all done quite simply electronically, and is another reason the binary number system is so attractive to computer designers.

In most decimal machines, no table is stored, but multiplication is carried out by adding the multiplicand as many times as the digit value of the multiplier.

*Example*

$$12345 \cdot 123 = \begin{array}{r} 1234500 \\ +\ 123450 \\ +\ 123450 \\ +\ 12345 \\ +\ 12345 \\ +\ 12345 \\ \hline 1518435 \end{array}$$

Advanced machines do, however, have multiplication tables "built into" the electronic circuitry, gaining speed at the expense of circuit complexity.

## DIVISION

Division can be carried out in binary or octal by the same process as in decimal: repeated subtraction.

*Examples*
*Octal*

$$\begin{array}{r} 114 \\ 126\overline{)14723} \\ 126 \\ \hline 0212 \\ 126 \\ \hline 643 \\ 530 \\ \hline 113 \quad \text{remainder} \end{array}$$

*Binary*

$$\begin{array}{r} 1001 \\ 1011\overline{)1101101} \\ 1011 \\ \hline 0010101 \\ 1011 \\ \hline 1010 \quad \text{remainder} \end{array}$$

For most work in computer programming it is not necessary to be *expert* at nondecimal arithmetic, but it is often useful to *know how* it is done.

## 3.3 Number Base Conversion

It is often necessary to know what is the equivalent, in one number base, of a number expressed in a different base. For instance, it may be desired to enter a decimal number into the memory of a binary machine directly, without using the conversion system programmed for usual data loading. Although it is possible to use methods based on experimentation, with the principles presented so far, or to use prepared tables, systematic methods are available.

## CONVERSION OF DECIMAL INTEGERS TO BINARY

The basis of the method may be presented as a series of algebraic manipulations with an example. All arithmetic will be carried out in decimal.

*Example.* $(27)_{10}$ *to binary.*

$$27 = \frac{27}{2} \cdot 2 = (13 + \tfrac{1}{2})2 = 13 \cdot 2^1 + 1 \cdot 2^0$$

But
$$13 = \frac{13}{2} \cdot 2 = (6 + \tfrac{1}{2})2 = 6 \cdot 2^1 + 1 \cdot 2^0$$

So
$$27 = (6 \cdot 2^1 + 1 \cdot 2^0)2 + 1 \cdot 2^0 = 6 \cdot 2^2 + 1 \cdot 2^1 + 1 \cdot 2^0$$

Again
$$6 = \frac{6}{2} \cdot 2 = (3 + 0)2 = 3 \cdot 2^1 + 0 \cdot 2^0$$

So
$$27 = (3 \cdot 2^1 + 0 \cdot 2^0) \cdot 2^2 + 1 \cdot 2^1 + 1 \cdot 2^0$$
$$= 3 \cdot 2^3 + 0 \cdot 2^2 + 1 \cdot 2^1 + 1 \cdot 2^0$$

Finally
$$3 = \frac{3}{2} \cdot 2 = (1 + \tfrac{1}{2})2 = 1 \cdot 2^1 + 1 \cdot 2^0$$

So
$$27 = (1 \cdot 2^1 + 1 \cdot 2^0)2^3 + 0 \cdot 2^2 + 1 \cdot 2^1 + 1 \cdot 2^0$$
$$= 1 \cdot 2^4 + 1 \cdot 2^3 + 0 \cdot 2^2 + 1 \cdot 2^1 + 1 \cdot 2^0$$

This last is precisely the meaning of the binary number **11011** so we have effected the conversion.

The procedure may be summarized in the following rule:

To convert a decimal integer to binary, divide repeatedly by 2. Each time write down the remainder, starting from the right, and divide the quotient by two to get the next digit. The sequence of remainders will be the binary number.

It may be noted that this process is inherent in the definition of the binary form. If an integer $N$ is to be converted to the form

$$N = a_n 2^n + a_{n-1} 2^{n-1} + \cdots + a_1 2^1 + a_0 2^0$$

it is obvious that $a_0$ is the remainder on division of $N$ by 2, $a_1$ is the remainder on division of this quotient by 2, etc.

*Example.* $(27)_{10}$ *to binary.*

$$\begin{array}{r} 13 \\ 2\overline{)27} \\ 26 \\ \hline 1 \end{array}$$   1 (First remainder)

$$\begin{array}{r} 6 \\ 2\overline{)13} \\ 12 \\ \hline 1 \end{array}$$   11 (First two remainders)

$$\begin{array}{r} 3 \\ 2\overline{)6} \\ 6 \\ \hline 0 \end{array}$$   011 (First three remainders)

$$\begin{array}{r} 1 \\ 2\overline{)3} \\ 2 \\ \hline 1 \end{array}$$   1011 (First four remainders)

$$\begin{array}{r} 0 \\ 2\overline{)1} \\ 0 \\ \hline 1 \end{array}$$   11011 (All remainders)

and as before, $(27)_{10} = (11011)_2$

Since division by 2 can be done mentally, the process can be condensed to writing down only the quotient:

$$\begin{array}{cc} 27 & 1 \\ 13 & 11 \\ 6 & 011 \\ 3 & 1011 \\ 1 & 11011 \end{array}$$

Conversion of a decimal integer to octal can be carried out similarly, except, of course, division is by eight (again all arithmetic is in decimal).

*Example.* $(1809)_{10}$ *to octal.*

$$\begin{array}{r} 226 \\ 8\overline{)1809} \\ 1808 \\ \hline 1 \end{array}$$   1 (First remainder)

$$\begin{array}{r} 28 \\ 8\overline{)226} \\ 224 \\ \hline 2 \end{array}$$   21 (First two remainders)

$$8 \overline{\smash{)}\ \begin{array}{c} 3 \\ 28 \\ 24 \end{array}}$$

$$\overline{\phantom{8)}\ 4} \qquad 421 \text{ (First three remainders)}$$

$$8 \overline{\smash{)}\ \begin{array}{c} 0 \\ 3 \\ 0 \end{array}}$$

$$\overline{\phantom{8)}\ 3} \qquad 3421 \text{ (All remainders)}$$

So $\qquad\qquad (1809)_{10} = (3421)_8$

## CONVERSION OF DECIMAL FRACTIONS TO BINARY AND OCTAL

A somewhat similar process is used for conversion of fractions.

*Example.* (0.62) *to binary.*

$$0.62 = \frac{0.62}{2} \cdot 2 = \frac{1.24}{2} = 1 \cdot 2^{-1} + (0.24)2^{-1}$$

$$0.24 = \frac{0.24}{2} \cdot 2 = \frac{0.48}{2} = 0 \cdot 2^{-1} + (0.48)2^{-1}$$

So $\quad 0.62 = 1 \cdot 2^{-1} + (0 \cdot 2^{-1} + 0.48 \cdot 2^{-1})2^{-1}$

$\qquad\qquad = 1 \cdot 2^{-1} + 0 \cdot 2^{-2} + (0.48)2^{-2}$

$$0.48 = \frac{0.48}{2} \cdot 2 = \frac{0.96}{2} = 0 \cdot 2^{-1} + 0.96 \cdot 2^{-1}$$

So $\quad 0.62 = 1 \cdot 2^{-1} + 0 \cdot 2^{-2} + (0 \cdot 2^{-1} + 0.96 \cdot 2^{-1})2^{-2}$

$\qquad\qquad = 1 \cdot 2^{-1} + 0 \cdot 2^{-2} + 0 \cdot 2^{-3} + 0.96 \cdot 2^{-3}$

$$0.96 = \frac{0.96}{2} \cdot 2 = \frac{1.92}{2} = 1 \cdot 2^{-1} + 0.92 \cdot 2^{-1}$$

So $\quad 0.62 = 1 \cdot 2^{-1} + 0 \cdot 2^{-2} + 0 \cdot 2^{-3} + (1 \cdot 2^{-1} + 0.92 \cdot 2^{-1})2^{-3}$

$\qquad\qquad = 1 \cdot 2^{-1} + 0 \cdot 2^{-2} + 0 \cdot 2^{-3} + 1 \cdot 2^{-4} + 0.92 \cdot 2^{-4}$

$\qquad\qquad = (0.1001)_2$

This may be continued as long as we wish; in general, the binary fraction will be infinite. This is an unfortunate quirk of number base conversion, that finite fractions in one base do not usually have finite forms in another base. [We are familiar with this in such cases as the fraction $\frac{1}{3}$, which as a decimal fraction is nonterminating while in base three it would be $(0.1)_3$.]

The binary expression above is just what we mean by $(0.1001)_2$, and is the equivalent, to four digits, of the decimal number $(0.62)$.

There is of course a systematic way of doing the conversion, expressed in this rule:

To convert a decimal fraction to binary, multiply the fraction (in decimal) by 2. Write down whatever appears to the left of the decimal point, as the first binary digit. Multiply the *fractional* part of the product by 2 again, etc.

*Example.* $(0.79)_{10}$ *to binary.*

$$
\begin{array}{ll}
0.79 & \\
\underline{\phantom{0}2} & \\
1.58 & 0.1 \\
\underline{\phantom{0}2} & \\
1.16 & 0.11 \\
\underline{\phantom{0}2} & \\
0.32 & 0.110 \\
\underline{\phantom{0}2} & \\
0.64 & 0.1100 \\
\underline{\phantom{0}2} & \\
1.28 & 0.11001, \text{ etc.}
\end{array}
$$

Since multiplication by 2 can be done mentally, the binary equivalent can be written down quite rapidly.

The problem of converting a number which is part integral and part fractional can be handled several ways. The most obvious is to convert the two parts separately:

$$
\begin{aligned}
91.42 &= 91 + 0.42 \\
&= (1011011)_2 + (0.0110110)_2 \\
&= (1011011.0110110)_2
\end{aligned}
$$

Another way is to convert the entire number as if it were an integer, then multiply, in binary, by the binary equivalent of the required power of ten:

$$
\begin{aligned}
91.42 &= 9142 \cdot 10^{-2} \\
&= (10001110110110) \cdot (0.00000010100011) \\
&= (1011011.0110110)_2
\end{aligned}
$$

Similarly, we can convert the number as if it were entirely fractional, then multiply by the required power of ten:

$$
91.42 = (0.9142)(10^2)
$$

Exactly analogous methods may be used to convert to octal.

## CONVERSION FROM BINARY OR OCTAL TO DECIMAL

The same techniques may be used to reverse the process, except that we must now use the binary or octal representation of decimal ten, and of course all arithmetic must be done in binary or octal.

Also, as the decimal digits are developed, they will appear in binary or octal and must be converted.

*Example.* $(10110111)_2$ *to Decimal*

$$(10)_{10} = (1010)_2$$

```
            10010
     1010|10110111
          1010
          ‾‾‾‾
           1011
           1010
           ‾‾‾‾
             11   remainder = (3)₁₀ = unit's digit
```

remainder = $(3)_{10}$ = unit's digit

```
              1
     1010|10010
          1010
          ‾‾‾‾
          1000   remainder = (8)₁₀ = ten's digit
```

remainder = $(8)_{10}$ = ten's digit

```
            0
     1010|1
          1   remainder = (1)₁₀ = hundred's digit
```

remainder = $(1)_{10}$ = hundred's digit

So
$$(10110111)_2 = (183)_{10}$$

*Example.* $(1705)_8$ *to Decimal*

$$(10)_{10} = (12)_8$$

```
          140
     12|1705              (All arithmetic in octal)
        12
        ‾‾
        50
        50
        ‾‾
        05   remainder = (5)₁₀
```

remainder = $(5)_{10}$

```
          11
     12|140
        12
        ‾‾
        20
        12
        ‾‾
         6   remainder = (6)₁₀
```

remainder = $(6)_{10}$

```
          0
     12|11
        11   remainder = (9)₁₀
```

remainder = $(9)_{10}$

So
$$(1705)_8 = (965)_{10}$$

*Example.*   $(0.1101110)_2$ *to Decimal*

$$0.1101110$$
$$\underline{1010}$$
$$11011100$$
$$1101110$$
$$\overline{1000.1001100}$$   $(1000)_2 = (8)_{10}$, so first decimal digit is 8

$$0.1001100$$
$$\underline{1010}$$
$$10011000$$
$$1001100$$
$$\overline{0101.1111000}$$   $(0101)_2 = (5)_{10}$

$$0.1111000$$
$$\underline{1010}$$
$$11110000$$
$$1111000$$
$$\overline{1001.0110000}$$   $(1001)_2 = (9)_{10}$

So                            $(0.1101110)_2 = (0.859)_{10}$

*Example.*   $(0.7235)_8$ *to Decimal*

$$0.7235$$
$$\underline{12}$$
$$16472$$
$$7235$$     (All arithmetic in octal)
$$\overline{11.1042}$$   $(11)_8 = (9)_{10}$

$$0.1042$$
$$\underline{12}$$
$$2104$$
$$1042$$
$$\overline{1.2524}$$   $(1)_8 \; = (1)_{10}$

$$0.2524$$
$$\underline{12}$$
$$5250$$
$$2524$$
$$\overline{3.2510}$$   $(3)_8 \; = (3)_{10}$

$$0.2510$$
$$\underline{12}$$
$$5220$$
$$2510$$
$$\overline{3.2320}$$   $(3)_8 \; = (3)_{10}$

$$(0.7235)_8 = (0.9133)_{10}$$

## RECONVERSION

Suppose we were to convert a decimal fraction to binary, then convert the binary fraction to decimal. Would we get the same decimal fraction? Testing the first example above:

$$(0.62)_{10} = (0.1001)_2$$

$$
\begin{array}{l}
0.1001 \\
\underline{\phantom{0}1010} \\
10010 \\
\underline{1001} \\
101.1010 \qquad (101)_2 = (5)_{10}
\end{array}
$$

$$
\begin{array}{l}
0.1010 \\
\underline{\phantom{0}1010} \\
10100 \\
\underline{1010} \\
110.0100 \qquad (110)_2 = (6)_{10}
\end{array}
$$

We seem to get $(0.62)_{10} = (0.1001)_2 = (0.56)_{10}$?

The problem is that four binary digits cannot carry as much information as two decimal digits. If we had continued the conversion to binary to get seven places:

$(0.62)_{10} = (0.1001111)$, then reconversion would have given:

$$
\begin{array}{l}
0.1001111 \\
\underline{\phantom{000}1010} \\
10011110 \\
\underline{1001111} \\
110.0010110 \qquad (110)_2 = (6)_{10}
\end{array}
$$

$$
\begin{array}{l}
0.0010110 \\
\underline{\phantom{000}1010} \\
00101100 \\
\underline{0010110} \\
001.1011100 \qquad \text{which rounds off to} \\
\phantom{001.1011100 \qquad} (010)_2 = (2)_{10}
\end{array}
$$

$$(0.1001111)_2 = (0.62)_{10} \text{ as before}$$

The number of binary places necessary to give exact reconversion to decimal may be presented in a table, as illustrated in Table 5.

## OTHER METHODS

There are other techniques for number base conversion. Some provide short cuts for special uses; others are dictated by equipment design or input format, such as punched cards. The methods presented here are simple and general; they provide a basic technique.

### TABLE 5

| NUMBER OF DECIMALS | NUMBER OF BINARY PLACES TO GIVE EXACT RECONVERSION |
|---|---|
| 0 | 0 |
| 1 | 4 |
| 2 | 7 |
| 3 | 10 |
| 4 | 14 |
| 5 | 17 |
| 6 | 20 |
| 7 | 24 |
| 8 | 27 |
| 9 | 30 |
| 10 | 34 |

## 3.4 Binary Coding of Decimal Digits

Machines which operate in decimal require that each decimal digit be coded in binary. The arithmetic and control circuits then operate on the *groups* of bits which represent the decimal digits. There are many ways of "coding" the decimal digits, i.e., of combining several binary digits to represent one decimal digit. All the methods require at least four bits, and involve assigning some value or "weight" to each. There are about five systems in common use, namely the 8-4-2-1, the 2-4-2*-1, the excess-three, the two-out-of-five, and the bi-quinary systems.

### TABLE 6

| DECIMAL DIGIT | Weights | 8 | 4 | 2 | 1 |
|---|---|---|---|---|---|
| | | | BINARY VARIABLES | | |
| 0 | | 0 | 0 | 0 | 0 |
| 1 | | 0 | 0 | 0 | 1 |
| 2 | | 0 | 0 | 1 | 0 |
| 3 | | 0 | 0 | 1 | 1 |
| 4 | | 0 | 1 | 0 | 0 |
| 5 | | 0 | 1 | 0 | 1 |
| 6 | | 0 | 1 | 1 | 0 |
| 7 | | 0 | 1 | 1 | 1 |
| 8 | | 1 | 0 | 0 | 0 |
| 9 | | 1 | 0 | 0 | 1 |

The 8-4-2-1 system† assigns the same weights as in ordinary binary notation. The coding is simply the binary representation of the decimal digits; see Table 6.

† IBM 604, 605, 702, 705; NORC; National 102-D; Mark II; MONROBOT; MINIAC; DATATRON.

The next two systems share several features which are desirable in design. They have these two characteristics: 1. The nine's complement of a decimal digit can be formed by complementing each binary digit, which is easily done electronically. 2. When two binary coded digits are added in binary, the sum contains five binary digits if it is ten or greater, four if less.

The first of these is the 2-4-2\*-1 system,† the second 2 being starred to remind us that there are two two's. The representations are given in Table 7.

### TABLE 7

| DECIMAL DIGIT | BINARY VARIABLES Weights 2 4 2 1 | | | |
|:---:|:---:|:---:|:---:|:---:|
| 0 | 0 | 0 | 0 | 0 |
| 1 | 0 | 0 | 0 | 1 |
| 2 | 0 | 0 | 1 | 0 |
| 3 | 0 | 0 | 1 | 1 |
| 4 | 0 | 1 | 0 | 0 |
| 5 | 1 | 0 | 1 | 1 |
| 6 | 1 | 1 | 0 | 0 |
| 7 | 1 | 1 | 0 | 1 |
| 8 | 1 | 1 | 1 | 0 |
| 9 | 1 | 1 | 1 | 1 |

The two characteristics mentioned above may be checked. The nine's complement of seven is two; the representations are respectively 1101 and 0010, which are seen to have binary zeros and ones reversed. Adding two and seven in decimal causes no carry; adding 0010 and 1101 in binary does not. Adding six and five does; adding 1100 and 1011 does.

The other is the excess-three system, so called because it is just like the 8-4-2-1 system but with binary three added to each representation,‡ as Table 8 illustrates.

The two considerations above are also seen to apply. This system has the additional advantage that combinations 0000 and 1111 are illegal. Since these are easy to check for electronically, a simple test of machine reliability is available.

The next system is based on checking machine reliability, to which is sacrificed the cost of an additional binary variable. Sometimes called the two-out-of-five system, it requires that exactly two binary variables be "on" in the representation of each digit. The weights

† Mark III.
‡ Univac.

assigned are 0, 1, 2, 3, 6. Each decimal digit can be made up of *exactly* two of these, which provides a simple check of machine operation. There are two ways of coding the digit three; one of these is used for zero.

TABLE 8

| DECIMAL DIGIT | BINARY VARIABLES Weights 8 4 2 1 (Three added to each) |
|---|---|
| 0 | 0 0 1 1 |
| 1 | 0 1 0 0 |
| 2 | 0 1 0 1 |
| 3 | 0 1 1 0 |
| 4 | 0 1 1 1 |
| 5 | 1 0 0 0 |
| 6 | 1 0 0 1 |
| 7 | 1 0 1 0 |
| 8 | 1 0 1 1 |
| 9 | 1 1 0 0 |

In the machine where this last finds widest application, the IBM 650, the representations on the drum and on the console are different. The two-out-of-five scheme is used on the drum, but the bi-quinary ("two-five") system is used on the console.* This method requires

TABLE 9

| DECIMAL | 5 | 0 | 4 | 3 | 2 | 1 | 0 |
|---|---|---|---|---|---|---|---|
| 0 | 0 | 1 | 0 | 0 | 0 | 0 | 1 |
| 1 | 0 | 1 | 0 | 0 | 0 | 1 | 0 |
| 2 | 0 | 1 | 0 | 0 | 1 | 0 | 0 |
| 3 | 0 | 1 | 0 | 1 | 0 | 0 | 0 |
| 4 | 0 | 1 | 1 | 0 | 0 | 0 | 0 |
| 5 | 1 | 0 | 0 | 0 | 0 | 0 | 1 |
| 6 | 1 | 0 | 0 | 0 | 0 | 1 | 0 |
| 7 | 1 | 0 | 0 | 0 | 1 | 0 | 0 |
| 8 | 1 | 0 | 0 | 1 | 0 | 0 | 0 |
| 9 | 1 | 0 | 1 | 0 | 0 | 0 | 0 |

that each digit be represented by one of two (binary) variables, assigned weights 5 and 0, and one of five (quinary) variables, assigned weights of 4, 3, 2, 1, and 0. The codings are given in Table 9.

* Bell Computer, Models IV and VI; IBM 650.

The main advantage here seems to be that it can be presented in a very readable form on the console:

```
      0          5
      ●          ●

          0
          ●

          1
          ●

          2
          ●

          3
          ●

          4
          ●
```

Of some historical interest is the fact that the first large electronic (but not stored program) machine, the ENIAC, uses ten binary variables, one for each decimal digit. No other electronic machine has ever been built this way.

### 3.5 Conversion Tables

In practice, such conversions as must be done by hand are usually done with the aid of prepared tables. Two are appended, one for integers (Appendix 4), and one for fractions (Appendix 5). The integer table is self-explanatory. Two points may be mentioned about the fraction table. First, only numbers less than $(0.5)_{10}$ are included; larger numbers are handled by subtracting $(0.5)_{10}$, converting, and adding $(0.4)_8$ [since $(0.5)_{10} = (0.4)_8$]. Second, the conversion must be done in two parts, once to get the equivalent of the first three digits, and again to get the equivalent of the last three.

### Exercises

Perform the indicated arithmetic operations:

| | | | | | | | |
|---|---|---|---|---|---|---|---|
| 1. | 1010<br>+0101 | 2. | 1101<br>+0001 | 3. | 1101<br>+0011 | 4. | 1011010<br>+ 111011 |
| 5. | 10010111<br>+11111111 | 6. | 111111<br>+111111 | 7. | 1010<br>−0001 | 8. | 1010<br>−0001 |
| 9. | 100<br>−001 | 10. | 1010<br>−101 | 11. | 101110<br>− 10101 | 12. | 101111001<br>−110101110 |

13. $\begin{array}{r} 1010 \\ \times\ 11 \\ \hline \end{array}$    14. $\begin{array}{r} 10111 \\ \times\ 10 \\ \hline \end{array}$    15. $\begin{array}{r} 1011101 \\ \times\ 1011 \\ \hline \end{array}$    16. $\begin{array}{r} 10111 \\ \times 10001 \\ \hline \end{array}$

17. $\begin{array}{r} 101101 \\ \times\ 10111 \\ \hline \end{array}$    18. $\begin{array}{r} 11101101 \\ \times\ 11111 \\ \hline \end{array}$    19. $10\overline{)1010}$    20. $101\overline{)1010}$

21. $110\overline{)10010}$                          22. $1010\overline{)1100100}$

23. $1011\overline{)10000000}$                     24. $11010\overline{)10101110001}$

Perform the indicated base conversions:

25. $(5)_{10} = (\ \ )_8 = (\ \ )_2$

26. $(8)_{10} = (\ \ )_8 = (\ \ )_2$

27. $(10)_{10} = (\ \ )_8 = (\ \ )_2$

28. $(32)_{10} = (\ \ )_8 = (\ \ )_2$

29. $(100)_{10} = (\ \ )_8 = (\ \ )_2$

30. $(1125)_{10} = (\ \ )_8 = (\ \ )_2$

31. $(0.25)_{10} = (\ \ )_8 = (\ \ )_2$

32. $(0.729)_{10} = (\ \ )_8 = (\ \ )_2$

33. $(0.110986)_{10} = (\ \ )_8 = (\ \ )_2$

34. $(0.997)_{10} = (\ \ )_8 = (\ \ )_2$

35. $(0.2)_{10} = (\ \ )_8 = (\ \ )_2$

36. $(14.65)_{10} = (\ \ )_8 = (\ \ )_2$

37. $(173.409)_{10} = (\ \ )_8 = (\ \ )_2$

38. $(11010)_2 = (\ \ )_8 = (\ \ )_{10}$

39. $(1011110111)_2 = (\ \ )_8 = (\ \ )_{10}$

40. $(11111111)_2 = (\ \ )_8 = (\ \ )_{10}$

41. $(100000000)_2 = (\ \ )_8 = (\ \ )_{10}$

42. $(11011.110)_2 = (\ \ )_8 = (\ \ )_{10}$

43. $(10001.11010)_2 = (\ \ )_8 = (\ \ )_{10}$

44. $(1.1)_2 = (\ \ )_8 = (\ \ )_{10}$

45. $(1.4)_8 = (\ \ )_2 = (\ \ )_{10}$

46. $(177.45)_8 = (\ \ )_2 = (\ \ )_{10}$

47. $(100.01)_8 = (\ \ )_2 = (\ \ )_{10}$

48. $(25.111)_8 = (\ \ )_2 = (\ \ )_{10}$

# 4 DECIMAL POINT LOCATION METHODS

## 4.0 Introduction

One of the problems requiring most careful attention in programming is decimal point or binary point location.* This may not be readily apparent to the person who has not used a computer before: the ordinary arithmetic of balancing a checkbook or doing engineering calculations by paper and slide rule does not seem to present great problems involving decimal point location. The difference is that in a stored program calculator, and to a lesser extent with any computer, all of the planning must be done *in advance*. In writing a program, provision must be made for contingencies which may only arise under certain unlikely circumstances. All this is done, not in terms of actual numbers, but in terms of quantities about which no more can be specified than the maximum and minimum sizes.

Considerable simplification could be made in the techniques to be described if it were not for the fact that it is usually necessary to retain as many significant figures as possible throughout a calculation. Even though the accuracy of the data does not justify it, considerations from numerical analysis may demand that there be as few nonsignificant zeros at the left of the numbers as possible. But if this is done, the addition of two numbers may produce a sum with more digits than can be stored in memory. Add to these considerations the fact that there are always precautions to be observed regarding division, and we see that decimal point planning is not trivial.

In the sections which follow, various devices are presented which assist in planning and keeping records of what goes on inside the machine. It is quite important to observe, however, that all of these are simply conveniences to the programmer, not rules which govern the operation of the calculator. Multiplication of the two sets of digits 1234 and 9876 always gives the result 12186984, regardless of whether we are thinking of the result as

---

* Most of the chapter applies equally to decimal and binary, with appropriate changes in terms and notation.

$$(1.234) \cdot (9.876) = 12.186984$$
or $$(1234.) \cdot (.9876) = 1218.6984$$
or $$(0.0001234) \cdot (98760) = 12.186984$$
or whatever.

Similarly, if 1.234 and 987.6 are to be added in a computer, it is the responsibility of the programmer to shift the numbers so that the decimal points line up. After all, there is no decimal point in memory (with minor exceptions in the case of one or two machines): all that is in memory is a collection of digits. If the programmer is thinking of the digits 1234 and 9876 as 1.234 and 987.6, but forgets and programs the addition as

$$\begin{array}{r} 1.234 \\ +987.6 \\ \hline \end{array}$$

the mistake is of no concern to the machine. The digits of the sum will be 11110, with no warning that to the programmer this is a meaningless result.

This is intended to emphasize that the decimal point problem is a matter of how to *think* about numbers in memory and the operations performed on them. The following sections present different ways of thinking about the numbers and different notations for keeping records, but the functioning of the arithmetic unit is the same in all cases.

It is likely that the reader will find one of the three methods more pertinent to his area of interest than the others. No loss of continuity will result if these sections are merely skimmed.

## 4.1 Decimal Point Fixed in the Middle of the Word

This technique is useful under the following conditions:

1. The significance requirements of the numbers are not severe, or,
2. The numbers actually are all the same size, which is seldom, or,
3. It is impossible to predict the sizes of intermediate values and floating point methods are not feasible (Chapter 10).

If any of these conditions are met, it is possible to write a simpler program, with much less effort, than with the two following methods.*

* One small machine, the MONROBOT V, is built on this principle. Words are twenty digits long, with a decimal point fixed in the middle. All results of arithmetic operations are in this form, and the manual makes little mention of the point location problem. The machine has no shift orders. This simplicity, however, is gained at the expense of extra equipment. Twenty-digit word length would be a high price to pay in a machine with a large memory.

Suppose we are again dealing with TYDAC with its ten digit numbers, and we locate the decimal point between the fifth and sixth digits, such as:

$$12345.67890$$
$$04960.12000$$
$$-00001.00047$$
$$-00000.02394$$

This is the form in which all data and constants are entered into the problem, the form in which all intermediate answers appear, and the form of all final answers. Perhaps it is obvious, but note that this means that no data, intermediate results, or answers may be larger in absolute value than **99999.99999** or smaller than 00000.00001. (It is possible, however, to generalize the method somewhat by observing that a similar set of rules could be built around *any* fixed point location—at the left end of the word, at the right end, or anywhere else.)

Since in this system all numbers in memory have the same decimal point, addition and subtraction can be carried out without any preliminaries. Furthermore, if the maximum-size limitation is valid, there can never be overflow in this system. If overflow did occur, it would mean that the sum was larger than **99999.99999**, and all numbers have been assumed to be smaller than this. This fact is essential, for if overflow were to occur, nothing could be done—within the framework of this system—to rectify the trouble. There is no way to shift the sum and store the extra digit, without also shifting the decimal point and thus destroying the whole system.

In multiplication, we are multiplying two numbers each of which has five places to the right of the decimal point; the result, by the ordinary rules of arithmetic, will have ten places to the right of the point. The before and after pictures of the arithmetic registers, in terms of an example, are:

| Before: | Memory | Accumulator | MQ |
|---|---|---|---|
|  | 00147.05100 | XXXXXXXXXX | 00098.46123 |

The contents of the accumulator are immaterial, since the accumulator is cleared before multiplication in TYDAC.

| After: | Memory | Accumulator | MQ |
|---|---|---|---|
|  | 00147.05100 | 0000014478 | 8223327300 |

As may be seen, the result is split up between the accumulator and MQ, with the decimal point between the two; in order to make use of the product, it is usually necessary to shift into the accumulator and, if desired, round off.

In the division of a twenty-digit dividend by a ten-digit divisor to get a ten-digit quotient, there will be as many places to the right of the point in the quotient as the difference of the number of decimal places in the dividend and in the divisor. Thus to get five to the right of the point in the quotient, with five to the right in the divisor, we must arrange to have ten in the dividend. The before and after pictures are almost the reverse of multiplication, although the numerical example is different:

| Before: | Memory | Accumulator | MQ |
|---------|--------|-------------|-----|
|         | 00057.19447 | 0000010973 | 4002700000 |

The dividend has been shifted right five places, as required.

| After: | Memory | Accumulator | MQ |
|--------|--------|-------------|-----|
|        | 00057.19447 | 0000504913 | 00191.86121 |
|        |        | (Remainder) | (Quotient) |

The difference between multiplication and division, of course, is that the accumulator contains the remainder after division, whereas before multiplication the contents of the accumulator were immaterial. Observe that we have legislated the divide stop possibility out of existence, just as we did overflow, by assuming that the numbers would be of such size that it could not occur. If two numbers are simply to be divided and the result stored, the dividend must be shifted right five places before division, as noted above. If two numbers are to be multiplied and the product divided by a third, it is clearly better to perform the multiplication first, since there will then be no shifting required.

*Example 1.* $y = \dfrac{a + bx}{c + dx} + \dfrac{x^2}{2}$

| QUANTITY | LOCATION |
|----------|----------|
| $a$ | 1000 |
| $b$ | 1001 |
| $c$ | 1002 |
| $d$ | 1003 |
| 2 | 1004 |
| $x$ | 1005 |
| $y$ | 1006 |
| Temporary storage | 1100, 1101 |

| LOCATION | OPERATION CODE | OPERATION ABBREVIATION | ADDRESS | COMMENTS |
|---|---|---|---|---|
| 500 | 42 | Load MQ | 1005 | $x$ into MQ |
| 501 | 16 | Mult | 1005 | $x^2$ |
| 502 | 18 | Divide | 1004 | $x^2/2$ in MQ |
| 503 | 43 | Store MQ | 1100 | Store temporarily |
| 504 | 42 | Load MQ | 1005 | $x$ into MQ |
| 505 | 16 | Mult | 1003 | $dx$ |
| 506 | 32 | Long left | 5 | Into acc |
| 507 | 35 | Round | | |
| 508 | 11 | Add | 1002 | $c + dx$ |
| 509 | 40 | Store acc | 1101 | Store temporarily |
| 510 | 42 | Load MQ | 1005 | $x$ into MQ |
| 511 | 16 | Mult | 1001 | $bx$ |
| 512 | 32 | Long left | 5 | Into acc |
| 513 | 11 | Add | 1000 | $a + bx$ |
| 514 | 33 | Long right | 5 | Prepare to divide |
| 515 | 18 | Divide | 1101 | $\dfrac{a + bx}{c + dx}$ |
| 516 | 43 | Store MQ | 1101 | Move quotient into |
| 517 | 10 | Clear add | 1101 | acc and clear remainder |
| 518 | 11 | Add | 1100 | Form $y$ |
| 519 | 40 | Store acc | 1006 | Store result |

It is instructive to note how these twenty steps were used. Four were utilized to shift numbers and round. Eight were used to move numbers to and from memory. Only eight called for actual arithmetic operations; if anything, this is a high proportion of "productive" steps. It is an unfortunate fact that the bulk of most programs is mere manipulation of numbers.

## 4.2 Graphic Method

This method is so called because it is simply a generalization of the technique we use in doing arithmetic by hand. It provides a fairly simple notation for keeping track of the decimal point throughout planning and coding. As compared with the other methods presented, the graphic method is slightly more general than the middle-of-the-word technique; since it is quite similar to methods we are familiar with, it is easy to learn and use; it is applicable with slight changes to machines which have registers of different lengths and to variable word length machines, whereas the scale factor method is somewhat inflexible for such situations.

The rules of the method are just those of ordinary arithmetic.

1. In addition or subtraction, the decimal point location of both

numbers must be the same. In TYDAC and other fixed word length machines, this may be made more specific by saying that the two numbers must have the same number of places to the right or *left* of the point.

2. In multiplication, the product has as many places to the right of the point as the sum of the number of places to the right of the multiplier and multiplicand. In TYDAC, we may say right or *left*, observing that not all digits to the left will always be nonzero.

3. In division it is harder to make a completely general statement. Particularizing to the situation of the TYDAC and many others, i.e., twice as many digits in dividend as in divisor or quotient, we may say that the number of places to the right in the quotient is the difference of the number of decimal places to the right in the dividend and the number to the right in the divisor. Note carefully that not all factors are the same size; the location of the point in the dividend is in respect to the accumulator and MQ combined, whereas the quotient is in respect to the MQ alone.

For all of these rules it is not necessary that the point lie *in* the ten-digit number. The "number of places to the right" may be negative, as when the digits 1023456789 in memory actually stand for 1023456789000, or greater than ten as when the same digits stand for 0.000001023456789. All the previous rules apply for these conditions.

For the purpose of stating these rules succinctly and making for a simpler record-keeping job, we may introduce a notation. We shall say that a number which has $m$ places to the left of the decimal point and $n$ to the right is an $(m/n)$ number. Now the rules become quite simple to state:

## ADDITION OR SUBTRACTION

$(m/n) + (p/q) = (m/n)$ or $(p/q)$, i.e., it is necessary that $m = p$, $n = q$, and that the answer have the same point location as the two factors. This is not to imply that we are ignoring the possibility of overflow; it simply says that if the sum or difference *can* be contained in a location the same size as the numbers, its point location numbers must be the same as the original.

## MULTIPLICATION

$(m/n) \cdot (p/q) = (m+p) \cdot (n+q)$. This is a very short way of saying the rule stated earlier. It does not guarantee that all the leading digits will be nonzero, e.g., multiplication of the two $(1/1)$ numbers 1.2 and 3.4 gives a $(2/2)$ number 04.08, but the first digit is zero.  This may appear artificial, but it happens automatically in the computer, since obviously enough space must be provided for the more general case where there are the full number of significant digits as in $(4.9)(6.7) = 32.83$.

## DIVISION

$$\frac{(m/n)}{(p/q)} = (m - p)/(n - q)$$

In this case it is particularly necessary to count the number of places with respect to the accumulator *plus* MQ, since the inverse of the first multiplication example above can be a source of confusion.

In division, it is necessary to know either the minimum size of the divisor or the maximum size of the quotient.  One or the other must be known to be able to avoid divide stop situations.

*Example 1*
Given the problem of evaluating the expression

$$T = \frac{12.67 - (x^2/2) + (x^4/24)}{(p_1/p_2) + 126.94}$$

and knowledge of the following maximum sizes.

| QUANTITY | MEMORY LOCATION | MAXIMUM LESS THAN | POINT LOCATION |
|---|---|---|---|
| $T$ | 400 | 0.1 | $(-1/11)$ |
| $x$ | 401 | 1.0 | $(0/10)$ |
| $p_1$ | 402 | 100 | $(2/8)$ |
| $p_2$ | 403 | 10 | $(1/9)$ |
| $p_1/p_2$ | — | 10 | $(1/9)$ |

The constants are of the following form.

| | | | |
|---|---|---|---|
| 12.67 | 500 | 100 | $(2/8)$ |
| 2 | 501 | 10 | $(1/9)$ |
| 24 | 502 | 100 | $(2/8)$ |
| 126.94 | 503 | 1000 | $(3/7)$ |

As we write the program, it is necessary to keep a running log of the point location of whichever register (accumulator, MQ, or both together) we are interested in.  A zero is stored in 300.

| LOCATION | OPERATION CODE | OPERATION ABBREVIATION | ADDRESS | POINT | COMMENTS |
|---|---|---|---|---|---|
| 1100 | 10 | Clear add | 402 | $(2/8)$ | $p_1$ into acc |
| 1101 | 42 | Load MQ | 300 | $(2/18)$ | Clear MQ |
| 1102 | 18 | Divide | 403 | $(1/9)$ | |

(*Continued on next page*)

| 1103 | 43 | Store MQ | 1500 | (1/9) | Temporary |
|------|----|----------|------|-------|-----------|
| 1104 | 10 | Clear add | 1500 | (1/9) | Prepare to add |
| 1105 | 31 | Acc right | 2 | (3/7) | Line up point for next addition |
| 1106 | 11 | Add | 503 | (3/7) | Denominator |
| 1107 | 40 | Store acc | 1500 | (3/7) | Temporary |
| 1108 | 42 | Load MQ | 401 | (0/10) | |
| 1109 | 16 | Mult | 401 | (0/20) | |
| 1110 | 40 | Store acc | 1501 | (0/10) | For later use in $x^4$ |
| 1111 | 33 | Long right | 3 | (3/17) | Prepare to get correct point for addition |
| 1112 | 18 | Divide | 501 | (2/8) | |
| 1113 | 43 | Store MQ | 1502 | (2/8) | Temporary, $x^2/2$ |
| 1114 | 42 | Load MQ | 1501 | (0/10) | $x^2$ |
| 1115 | 16 | Mult | 1501 | (0/20) | $x^4$ |
| 1116 | 33 | Long right | 4 | (4/16) | Prepare for addition |
| 1117 | 18 | Divide | 502 | (2/8) | |
| 1118 | 43 | Store MQ | 1501 | (2/8) | Temporary |
| 1119 | 10 | Clear add | 500 | (2/8) | 12.67 |
| 1120 | 14 | Sub | 1502 | (2/8) | $-x^2/2$ |
| 1121 | 11 | Add | 1501 | (2/8) | $+x^4/24$ |
| 1122 | 42 | Load MQ | 300 | (2/18) | Clear MQ |
| 1123 | 18 | Divide | 1500 | (−1/11) | |
| 1124 | 43 | Store MQ | 400 | (−1/11) | T |

A few notes are in order. Temporary storages 1500 and 1501 were used in two different places each. This was possible since the first number stored in each case was of no further value once it had been brought back into the arithmetic registers. It is advisable, however, to be extremely careful in the use of temporary storage; it is very easy to forget what is in each location. Careful bookkeeping is necessary, as will be discussed later. In several places numbers were shifted in anticipation of later needs to line up the point, as in steps 1105, 1111, 1116. In a few places it was necessary to change the point location symbol from a ten-digit number to a twenty-digit one, to account for an ensuing division by a ten-digit number.

## 4.3 The Scale Factor Method

The technique to be discussed next is by far the most commonly used of those presented—at least for scientific or engineering work on fixed word length machines. In one sense it is simply an extension of the previous method, as we shall see, but it seems to lend itself better to applications where there is a great deal of fixed decimal work to do. One advantage is that it is easy to do all the planning for point location *before* coding, thus separating two error-prone processes.

The scale factor of a (fractional) number in memory is defined as the power of ten by which the fraction must be multiplied to get the number actually represented. Thus, if $x$ is the actual number and $\bar{x}$ is the fraction in memory, we have the "scale factor" equation:

$$x = 10^q \bar{x}$$

Strictly speaking, the scale factor is $10^q$, but common usage refers simply to $q$ as the scale factor, a practice which will be followed here.

The scale factor may be positive or negative. We may think of the digits 1023456789 in memory as standing for the true numbers:

| | | |
|---|---|---|
| 0.1023456789 | Scale factor 0 | |
| 1023.456789 | Scale factor 4 | |
| 0.0001023456789 | Scale factor $-3$ | etc. |

It happens that the scale factor is the same as the number of places to the left of the point, in the notation of the previous section. Here, however, we do not *think* of the matter the same way, although the machine functioning is of course unchanged. Here, we think of all numbers in memory as having a decimal point fixed at the left end of the word; if a number is shifted in the accumulator, the decimal point does not move, but rather the scale factor changes. This is obviously merely a change in viewpoint, but it turns out to facilitate planning and record keeping.

The application of the scale factor method to programming may be reduced to a five-step rule.

Step 1. Determine, from information about the physical quantities, the maximum sizes of all numbers. (Throughout, "maximum size" will refer to absolute values.) In the case of division, determine also the minimum sizes of divisors or the maximum sizes of quotients. Doing this will ordinarily require knowledge about input, intermediate results, and output; at the very least, the information must be available for the input.

Step 2. Write the relationships between true numbers and scaled numbers by determining the necessary scale factors. These will ordinarily be the power of ten just larger than the maximum size of a quantity. Thus, if $x$ in a certain problem can never be as large as 100, then the scale factor would be 2, and

$$x = 10^2 \bar{x}$$

Step 3.  Substitute the scaled quantities into the equations of the problem.  Cancel exponents wherever possible.

Step 4.  Quantities to be added or subtracted must have the same scale factor.  If this condition is not met in the scaled equation as it stands, some scale factors must be changed by shifting some of the numbers before addition or subtraction.  The number of shifts required will be the same as the difference in scale factors in the scaled equation.

Step 5.  An "uncanceled" scale factor in division specifies a right shift necessary to avoid divide stop.  An "uncanceled" scale factor in multiplication specifies a left shift of the product, which will cause no loss of significant digits at the left.  This retains digits at the right, thus increasing the accuracy of the computation.

*Example* 2.  $x = a + b + c$

Step 1.  $a < 100$
$\quad\quad b < 10$
$\quad\quad c < 1$
$\quad\quad x < 100$

Step 2.  $a = 10^2 \bar{a}$
$\quad\quad b = 10^1 \bar{b}$
$\quad\quad c = 10^0 \bar{c}$
$\quad\quad x = 10^2 \bar{x}$

Step 3.  $10^2 \bar{x} = 10^2 \bar{a} + 10^1 \bar{b} + 10^0 \bar{c}$

Step 4.  The differences in exponents on the right side of the equation specify shifts required before addition.  $\bar{c}$ must be shifted two places right, $\bar{b}$ one place right.  The limit given for $x$ tells us that the numbers $a$, $b$, and $c$ in this problem are such that the maximum value of all three does not occur at the same time, so that there is no danger of overflow.  If this had not been specified, we would have had to assume the worst and used a scale factor of 3 for $x$, which would have required either shifting all the numbers one more place right before addition or shifting the sum one place right.

Step 5.  Not applicable.

If $\bar{a}$ is located in 500, $\bar{b}$ in 501, $\bar{c}$ in 502, and $\bar{x}$ is to be placed in 600, a program to carry out this addition might be:

| LOCATION | OPERATION CODE | OPERATION ABBREVIATION | ADDRESS | PERTINENT SCALE FACTOR |
|---|---|---|---|---|
| 100 | 10 | Clear add | 502 | 0 |
| 101 | 33 | Long right | 1 | 1 |
| 102 | 11 | Add | 501 | 1 |
| 103 | 33 | Long right | 1 | 2 |
| 104 | 11 | Add | 500 | 2 |
| 105 | 35 | Round | | 2 |
| 106 | 40 | Store acc | 600 | 2 |

*Example 3.*   $x = d \cdot e$

Step 1.   $d < 100$
$e < 1000$
$x < 10,000$

The limit on $x$ implies that $d$ and $e$ do not both approach their maximum sizes at the same time; if they did, $x$ could obviously be almost as large as 100,000, not 10,000.

Step 2.   $d = 10^2 \bar{d}$
$e = 10^3 \bar{e}$
$x = 10^4 \bar{x}$

Step 3.   $10^4 \bar{x} = 10^2 \bar{d} \cdot 10^3 \bar{e}$, which is the same as
$\bar{x} = 10^1 \bar{d} \cdot \bar{e}$

Step 4.   Not applicable.

Step 5.   The equation of step 3 states that the product as computed will always have one leading zero, derived from the fact noted above that $x$ does not become as large as the limit on $d$ and $e$ would seem to imply.  In terms of the numbers in the arithmetic unit, this means that the product as formed will always have one leading zero, allowing a left shift of one after the multiplication.

If $\bar{d}$ is in 1200, $\bar{e}$ in 1300, $\bar{x}$ to go into 1307:

| LOCATION | OPERATION CODE | OPERATION ABBREVIATION | ADDRESS | PERTINENT SCALE FACTOR |
|---|---|---|---|---|
| 540 | 42 | Load MQ | 1200 | 2 |
| 541 | 16 | Mult | 1300 | 5 |
| 542 | 32 | Long left | 1 | 4 |
| 543 | 35 | Round | | 4 |
| 544 | 40 | Store acc | 1307 | 4 |

*Example 4.*   $x = f/g$

Step 1.        $f < 1500$
$10 < g < 500$
$x < 100$

Here we are given additional information; it would seem that $x$ could be as large as 150, whereas we see that in fact the maximum is less than 100.

Step 2.   $f = 10^4 \bar{f}$   (Since $10^4$ is larger than 1500, but $10^3$ is not)
$g = 10^3 \bar{g}$
$x = 10^2 \bar{x}$

Step 3.   $10^2 \bar{x} = (10^4 \bar{f})/(10^3 \bar{g})$, or $10^1 \bar{x} = (\bar{f})/(\bar{g})$

Step 4.   Not applicable.

Step 5.   The uncanceled scale factor points out the necessity for shifting the dividend one place right before division.

If $\bar{f}$ is in 1050, $\bar{g}$ is in 1051, $\bar{x}$ to go in 1052, the program could be:

| LOCATION | OPERATION CODE | OPERATION ABBREVIATION | ADDRESS | PERTINENT SCALE FACTOR |
|---|---|---|---|---|
| 1000 | 10 | Clear add | 1050 | 4 |
| 1001 | 33 | Long right | 1 | 5 |
| 1002 | 18 | Divide | 1051 | 2 |
| 1003 | 43 | Store MQ | 1052 | 2 |

Observe in all these examples that it is not absolutely necessary that a size limitation be given for all results. For instance, if the maximum size of $x$ had not been specified in the division example as 100, we would simply have assumed that the quotient could be as large as 150 (1500 ÷ 10). The scaled equation would then have been:

$$10^3\bar{x} = (10^4\bar{f})/(10^3\bar{g})$$

or

$$10^2\bar{x} = (\bar{f})/(\bar{g})$$

The $10^2$ factor would then have specified a right shift of two before division. The maximum size of the result of an arithmetic operation can always be computed in this manner, if more precise information is not available.

This presentation has possibly left the impression that fixed point calculation is a routine matter of applying a few simple rules. This is not exactly the case. The primary difficulty revolves around estimating the maximum and minimum sizes of all quantities in advance. Experience shows that it is quite difficult to foresee all the contingencies, especially in problems where the physical phenomena under study are not well understood. Furthermore, last-minute changes in formulas can require a disproportionate amount of effort in revising decimal point planning.

What happens to the program if a mistake is made in scaling? Suppose the sum of two numbers is assumed to have an upper limit of 999, but turns up in the calculation as 1050. Unless some test is provided which will discover the error before it does any damage, the program will turn out meaningless results. In this case, the effect would probably be to store 050 as the result instead of 1050, since the planning would not have allowed space to store the extra digit. In almost all cases of errors due to an assumed maximum which turns out to be too small, the trouble will be signaled by the presence of some digit other than zero in the overflow position of the accumulator. Since there is such a large chance of error, it seems wise to program periodic tests of the overflow position (using in TYDAC the overflow jump instruction) to determine if any scaling errors have crept in. Divisors which turn out to be smaller than estimated will be signaled by divide stops, which in TYDAC stop the machine. In real computers the signals of trouble may be different, but similar checks can be made. Many machines do not have an overflow position, but simply give a warning if overflow occurs.

## Exercises

(May be coded using any or all of the three methods.)

Exercises 1 through 13 assume the following size and location information. If a size for $y$ is not given, compute the maximum possible.

| QUANTITY | SIZE | LOCATION |
|---|---|---|
| $a$ | $<1000$ | 100 |
| $b$ | $<100$ | 101 |
| $c$ | $>10, <100$ | 102 |
| $d$ | $<125$ | 103 |
| $e$ | $>60, <600$ | 104 |
| $f$ | $>1, <10$ | 105 |
| $y$ | Given, or to be computed | 150 |

1. $y = a + b$

2. $y = a - b$

3. $y = bd$

4. $y = a/c$

5. $y = df$, where $y < 1000$

6. $y = d/f$, where $y < 100$

7. $y = a + (bf)$

8. $y = a/(b + c)$

9. $y = (a + bf)/c$

10. $y = a + 10f + 100bf^2$

11. Same as 10, except $y < 10,000$

12. $y = f/e$

13. $y = a/f + b/f^2 + c/f^3$

14. Write a program to evaluate $y = V_0 t + \frac{1}{2}gt^2$.

| QUANTITY | LOCATION | MAXIMUM SIZE |
|---|---|---|
| $t$ | 150 | 15 sec |
| $g$ | 157 | 32.2 ft/sec$^2$ |
| $V_0$ | 162 | 120 ft/sec |
| $y$ | 200 | To be determined |

15. Write a program to evaluate $y = 1 + x + (x^2/2) + (x^3/6)$. $x$ is in 100, 1 in 200, 2 in 201, 6 in 202. $x$ is always positive and never as large as ten. Assume appropriate point locations for the constants. Place $y$ in 300.

16. Write a program to evaluate $H = \dfrac{A(t_2 - t_1)}{(L_1/K_1) + (L_2/K_2)}$.

| QUANTITY | LOCATION | SIZE RANGE |
|---|---|---|
| $t_1$ | 100 | Between 0–400 |
| $t_2$ | 101 | Between 100–1000 |
| $L_1$ | 110 | $<10$ |
| $L_2$ | 111 | $<10$ |
| $K_1$ | 120 | Between 0.001–0.1 |
| $K_2$ | 121 | Between 0.001–0.1 |
| $A$ | 150 | $<1000$ |
| $H$ | 200 | To be determined |

17. Write a program to evaluate $y = \dfrac{1}{b^2}\left[ -\dfrac{1}{a + bx} + \dfrac{a}{2(a + bx)^2}\right]$.
$a$, in 100, is always positive and less than 50; $b$, in 1200, is between $+1$ and $20$; $x$, in 1800, is between $\pm 5$. Assume locations for needed constants. Determine the maximum and minimum sizes of $y$, avoid divide stop, and store result in 1950. Devise a procedure to handle the possibility that $(a + bx)$ is zero or close to zero.

# 5 ADDRESS COMPUTATION

## 5.0 Introduction

It has been mentioned in earlier chapters that the central feature of a stored program calculator is the ability to perform arithmetic on the instructions which tell the machine what to do. This capability is utilized in several ways. The most important use revolves around the employment of loops, which are discussed in the next chapter. A small section of a program may be used many times with minor changes in some of the instructions. Another application is in the making of "decisions" inside the machine; a jump instruction can have its address modified to go to one of several alternatives depending on some controlling parameter. A further application is in the writing of general-purpose programs. It may be desirable to set up a code to solve a system of simultaneous linear algebraic equations of any size (limited only by memory size). Given only the coefficients and constants in some systematic order, plus the number of equations, the program must be able to do all the various operations a varying number of times. This will involve a very small number of actual arithmetic operations and a much larger number of instructions which compute and place the correct addresses in these instructions and decide when to quit.

These are actually only illustrations of a general method and not distinct techniques. The following sections present three illustrations of this method in some detail because the concept is so important, and because it can sometimes be difficult to grasp. Later chapters will present many examples in connection with discussion of other principles.

## 5.1 Address Modification in Loops

Probably the most frequent use of address computation is in changing instructions in loops. For our purposes here, we may define a loop as a program segment which is repeated, often with some of the instructions altered or *modified* between repetitions. A common modification is to increase the address of certain instructions each time the loop is repeated.

To illustrate how an instruction can be altered by the machine, consider the following. Suppose that a loop is required which will clear to zero all the locations in memory from 200 to 1999. One way to do this is to have zero in the MQ, then successively store the MQ at all the locations specified. An instruction can be written which stores the MQ at 200; then the address of the instruction changed to 201 and the instruction executed again, etc.

All that is required is somehow to get this instruction into the accumulator and add one to the address. Observe that the instruction in memory would appear as 4302000000—simply a number. With this number (instruction) in the accumulator, it is only necessary to add 0000010000, and store the sum, which is the modified instruction, back where the old instruction was. The instruction can then be repeated. Assuming that the MQ has been cleared, and that 90 contains 0000010000, the program might be:

| LOCATION | OPERATION CODE | OPERATION ABBREVIATION | ADDRESS |
|---|---|---|---|
| 100 | 43 | Store MQ | 200 |
| 101 | 10 | Clear add | 100 |
| 102 | 11 | Add | 90 |
| 103 | 40 | Store acc | 100 |
| 104 | 01 | Un jump | 100 |

The instruction at 101 brings the instruction at 100 into the accumulator; 102 adds one to the address; 103 stores the new instruction back in 100; 104 returns control (jumps) to 100. Thus the first step would be repeated over and over, the address being increased by one each time, and eventually all the addresses from 200 to 1999 would be run through. The following listing shows the contents of the accumulator, including overflow position, and of memory location 100, *after* each instruction has been executed:

| INSTRUCTION LOCATION | CONTENTS OF ACCUMULATOR | CONTENTS OF LOCATION 100 |
|---|---|---|
| 100 | Immaterial | 43 0200 0000 |
| 101 | 0 43 0200 0000 | 43 0200 0000 |
| 102 | 0 43 0201 0000 | 43 0200 0000 |
| 103 | 0 43 0201 0000 | 43 0201 0000 |
| 104 | 0 43 0201 0000 | 43 0201 0000 |
| 100 | 0 43 0201 0000 | 43 0201 0000 |

(*Continued on next page*)

| 101 | 0 43 0201 0000 | 43 0201 0000 |
| 102 | 0 43 0202 0000 | 43 0201 0000 |
| 103 | 0 43 0202 0000 | 43 0202 0000 |
| 104 | 0 43 0202 0000 | 43 0202 0000 |
| 100 | 0 43 0202 0000 | 43 0202 0000 |
| 101 | 0 43 0202 0000 | 43 0202 0000 |
| 102 | 0 43 0203 0000 | 43 0202 0000 |
| 103 | 0 43 0203 0000 | 43 0203 0000 |
| 104 | 0 43 0203 0000 | 43 0203 0000 |
| Etc. | | |

Actually, we wish to modify only the *address* of the instruction at 100, whereas the store accumulator instruction at 103 stores all ten digits: operation part and index control as well as address. This is permissible, since the "nonaddress" digits are brought into the accumulator by instruction 101. This is often not allowable, as we shall see in a later example.

(The reader might consider the limitations of this example as a usable program. As a matter of fact, it would clear all the locations from 200 to 1999, but it would be somewhat deficient in other respects. The interesting problems raised here will be discussed in the next chapter.)

The question may be asked how the machine knows the difference between an instruction and a number. The answer is that it does not, and that as far as doing arithmetic is concerned, it makes no difference. Since instructions are simply numbers, the arithmetic unit has no difficulty performing arithmetic on them. It is the responsibility of the programmer to be sure that if arithmetic is done on instructions, the manipulation is really intended; an accidental, unintentional modification of an instruction always leads to trouble. It is also necessary to ensure that the machine does not try to interpret what really are numbers, i.e., data, as instructions. This also leads to trouble, but usually to trouble so drastic that it is easily detected. In some computers, numbers and instructions carry some distinguishing mark which will prevent this particular error.

## 5.2 Computing Jump Addresses

It is fairly common to find computer applications where part of the input to a program is a code number which determines exactly what is to be done on a particular case. For instance, the program may choose between four alternative methods of calculating a quantity, based on whether a code number is 1, 2, 3, or 4.

For an illustration, take the case where a code number in location

500 may be any digit between zero and nine inclusive. If the code is zero, the program should jump to 1400 to handle this case; if the code is one, to 1410; if it is two, to 1420, etc., until if it is nine the jump should be to 1490. At these locations would be stored small subprograms to handle the individual cases. There is a simple pattern here, which can be expressed by the formula:

$$\text{Jump address} = 1400 + 10 \cdot (\text{Code number})$$

The following program will evaluate this formula, store the computed address in a jump instruction, and perform the jump. Note that rather than assign a location to the constant 1400, we have simply written "loc 1400." This is read "location of 1400," and means we realize that in a real problem the constant 1400 would have to be stored somewhere and a numerical address written in place of "loc 1400." For purposes of illustration, the address is immaterial, and we save the trouble of specifying an actual location. As before, the constant and the code number would have to be stored in positions 3–6 of the memory location.

| LOCATION | OPERATION CODE | OPERATION ABBREVIATION | ADDRESS |
|---|---|---|---|
| 400 | 10 | Clear add | 500 |
| 401 | 30 | Acc left | 1 |
| 402 | 11 | Add | Loc 1400 |
| 403 | 41 | Store address | 404 |
| 404 | 01 | Un jump | [0000] |

When the program is written, it is not known what the address of the instruction at 404 should be; as a matter of fact, it is the function of the program to make a decision on this point and compute the appropriate address. When the program is first written, we indicate that the address is to be computed by the program by writing zero for the address and placing brackets around it. The sequence of operations is:

1. The first three steps bring in the controlling code number, multiply it by ten by shifting left one place, and add 1400. This is the address to which the program should now jump, in accordance with the formula developed above. At this point the required address is in the *address part* of the accumulator: positions 3–6. At 404 is the jump instruction with an address of zero; if the address now in the accumulator were placed in the address part of the instruction, the necessary jump could be performed.

2. The *store address* instruction at 403 performs the necessary storing of the address. It stores *only* the address part; if this were not so, the operation part of the instruction at 404 would be wiped out since the accumulator contains zeros in the operation part.

3. The jump at 404—which now has a relevant address—is carried out. As discussed above, whichever subprogram is appropriate to the code number in 500 would be carried out.

The contents of the accumulator and of location 404 during the program execution are shown in the listing below. It is assumed for purposes of this illustration that the code number in 500 is 7.

| INSTRUCTION LOCATION | CONTENTS OF ACCUMULATOR | CONTENTS OF LOCATION 404 |
|---|---|---|
| 400 | 0 00 0007 0000 | 01 0000 0000 |
| 401 | 0 00 0070 0000 | 01 0000 0000 |
| 402 | 0 00 1470 0000 | 01 0000 0000 |
| 403 | 0 00 1470 0000 | 01 1470 0000 |
| 404 | 0 00 1470 0000 | 01 1470 0000 |
| 1470 | | |
| 1471 | | |
| Etc. | | |

## 5.3 Computing Final Address of a Matrix

Suppose we have stored in consecutive locations in memory a rectangular array of numbers as follows, where the numbers written above are locations of the numbers (represented by the letters $a$ to $l$) in storage:

| 1200 | 1201 | 1202 | 1203 |
|---|---|---|---|
| $a$ | $b$ | $c$ | $d$ |

| 1204 | 1205 | 1206 | 1207 |
|---|---|---|---|
| $e$ | $f$ | $g$ | $h$ |

| 1208 | 1209 | 1210 | 1211 |
|---|---|---|---|
| $i$ | $j$ | $k$ | $l$ |

This is a particular case of our more general problem: we know where the first number of a similar array is located, namely 1200, but we do not know how big the array is. We do have stored in memory two numbers which are the number of rows $m$ and columns $n$. Given only this much information, we are required to store the last number in the array (matrix) in location 1000.

The first problem is of course to decide what the relationship is between the first location, $m$ and $n$, and the last location. A little thought shows this to be:

$$\text{Final address} = 1200 + m \cdot n - 1$$
$$= 1199 + m \cdot n$$

Suppose that $m$ and $n$ are stored as integers, i.e., that the decimal point is to the far right of the word in memory. We must also assume that $m$ and $n$ are such that the matrix can fit into the available space. A program for this would be as follows:

| LOCATION | OPERATION CODE | OPERATION ABBREVIATION | ADDRESS |
|---|---|---|---|
| 810 | 42 | Load MQ | Loc $m$ |
| 811 | 16 | Mult | Loc $n$ |
| 812 | 32 | Long left | 14 |
| 813 | 11 | Add | Loc 1199 |
| 814 | 41 | Store address | 815 |
| 815 | 10 | Clear add | [0000] |
| 816 | 40 | Store acc | 1000 |

The first two instructions form the product $m \cdot n$. Again we are quite unconcerned with the *actual* memory locations of some of the data and have merely indicated "location of." A review of decimal point location on multiplication will show that the product is at the extreme right of the MQ. Since addition is not possible in the TYDAC MQ, we must at least shift this into the accumulator and we may as well shift it into the *address* part of the accumulator at the same time. A glance at a diagram of the accumulator and MQ will illustrate the situation:

$$\begin{array}{cccc}
\text{Accumulator} & & \text{MQ} \\
00 \quad 0000 \quad 0000 & \quad 0000000XXX \\
\text{Op.} \quad \text{Addr.} \quad \text{Index} & \quad mn
\end{array}$$

A long (accumulator and MQ) left shift of 14 will evidently bring the product into the address part of the accumulator. The addition of 1199, assumed to be stored as 00 1199 0000 so as to add into the address part, completes the computation of the final address. Instruction 814 places this address in the address part of instruction 815, which instruction brings the last number of the array or matrix into the accumulator. Instruction 816 stores this number in 1000 as required.

This program is a sketchy illustration of what must be done extensively when one program is intended to be able to handle a group of numbers of variable size, given only some such indication of the size as we had here. The technique is quite commonly used, with many of the applications being much more complex than this one.

## Exercises

1. If the number in 507 is zero, jump to 800; if it is one, jump to 802; if it is two, jump to 804, etc.

2. A loop has been written which takes the square roots of a series of numbers located in 50 to 100 and places the roots back in the same locations. The instruction which initially brings in a number is located at 950, and at first reads:

$$950 \qquad 10 \qquad \text{Clear add} \qquad 50$$

The instruction which stores the square root each time is located at 980, and at first reads:

$$980 \qquad 40 \qquad \text{Store acc} \qquad 50$$

Starting at 985, write the instructions necessary to add one to each of these addresses.

3. Location 483 contains one of the digits zero to nine at the far right, i.e., as an integer. If the number in 483 is zero, add one to the number in 490; if it is one, add one to the number in 491; if it is two, add one to the number in 492, etc. This is a frequent application, in which a computed result is used to control which location gets a tally added.

4. $a_{ij}$, the element from the $i$th row and $j$th column of a matrix which has $m$ rows and $n$ columns, is in location 0000. The numbers $i$, $j$, $m$, and $n$ are in memory in 10, 11, 12, and 13 respectively. The first element of the matrix, which is in row order as in the text example, is stored in 1400. Using this information, or as much of it as necessary, store $a_{ij}$ in the correct location in the matrix.

5. Two positive numbers $E_1$ and $E_2$ are stored in memory, as integers. Call the difference $|E_1 - E_2|$, $n$. If $E_1 > E_2$, bring the number in 500 into the accumulator and perform a long right shift of $n$. If $E_1 \leqq E_2$, bring the number in 501 into the accumulator and perform a long right shift of $n$. *Hint:* Note that the numbers $E_1$ and $E_2$ are not in the address part as stored.

6. A code number in 600 is an integer between zero and nine. If it is zero, jump to 805; if it is one, jump to 822; if it is two, jump to 839; if it is three, jump to 856, etc.

7. A number $x$ in 510 is a fraction, i.e., decimal point to the far left. If the number is less than 0.125, add one to the number in 511; if it is in the range $0.125 \leqq x < 0.250$, add one to the number in 512, etc., until if it is in the range $0.875 \leqq x < 1.0$, add one to the number in 518. (This is explained in Chapter 17, but it can be done with techniques available at this point.)

8. A list of one hundred numbers is stored in 100 to 199. The *address* of one of the numbers is in the address part of the accumulator. Store the *number* which is in this address at 850, the number which is in the following address at 851, and the number which is in the next address at 852. For instance, if the number in the accumulator is 162, transfer the numbers in 162, 163, and 164 to 850, 851, and 852. Test whether the number in the accumulator is 197 or smaller and halt if not, since if it is 198 or 199 the complete transfer cannot be made.

# 6 LOOPS IN COMPUTING

## 6.0 Introduction

Several times previously it has been indicated that one of the most powerful features of stored program computers is the ability to repeat, with modification, basic parts of the program at electronic speeds. In earlier machines this is not possible because the instructions are carried out as they are read from the input device, such as cards or paper tape. Or in the case of the external plugboard machines, high-speed repetition is possible but very little modification of the program between repetitions is feasible. The loop ability is probably a good capsule summary of the distinguishing characteristic of the stored program machines. It is certainly typical of the work of programming; it is fairly safe to say that almost never is a program written for a stored program machine which does not involve a loop somehow. This is easy to believe when it is considered that a program which completely filled memory but had no loops would be executed in about one second on modern machines!

We shall accordingly look into the loop idea in some detail and with several examples. Later chapters will also refer to loops.

## 6.1 The Parts of the Loop

The functions of the parts of a loop can best be explained by an example. Suppose we have a list of fifty numbers stored in locations 100 to 149, which must be added and the sum stored in 150. Assume that the numbers all have the same decimal point location and are small enough so that the sum will fit into one word, and that certain constants are available as needed.

The heart of the program will be a series of steps which successively add all the numbers into 150, i.e.:

$$\begin{array}{ll} \text{Clear add} & [\quad] \\ \text{Add} & 150 \\ \text{Store} & 150 \end{array}$$

The variable address of the first instruction will start as 100 and run through all the addresses up to 149. If location 150 contains zero to start, repetition of these three steps fifty times with all the addresses from 100 to 149 will compute the required sum and store it in 150. This portion of the loop does the real work and is called the *computing* part of the loop.

Before we can get to this, however, some preliminaries have to be taken care of. The correct starting address must be given to the Clear add instruction. We cannot usually assume in such a situation that location 150 would already be clear, so we must store a zero there. And for a reason which will become apparent shortly, we will store the number 50 in location 200. These three operations are not repeated; we would obviously not want to clear 150 every time through the loop, because the sum is being accumulated there. The preliminary steps which set up the loop and are not repeated constitute the *initializing* section of the loop.

In the previous chapter, in connection with doing arithmetic on instructions, we discussed the next part of the loop. It is necessary simply to add a one to the address of the Clear add instruction each time through the loop.* In other applications this function can be more complex, as we shall see. It is called *modifying.*

Now obviously some way must be devised to tell the machine when to stop. The parts we have outlined so far would run through all machine addresses and either start over or cause the program to fail, depending on details of how it was written. The part of the loop which determines when it is finished is called *testing.* In this example it amounts to keeping a record of how many times the loop has been executed, and terminating the repetition as soon as it has been done fifty times. This can be accomplished by subtracting one, each time through the loop, from the fifty which we stored in 200.

---

* It is necessary in many computers to observe a precaution in modifying addresses. It is fairly common for instructions to have signs which either specify something about the address or are part of the operation code. When an instruction with a negative sign is brought into the accumulator to be modified, the sign acts just like it always does; it represents a negative number. The fact that the purpose of the sign is something else, or that we are regarding the instruction as an instruction, makes no difference to the accumulator. An instruction with a minus sign attached acts like a negative number.

This must of course be considered in modifying addresses. It is necessary either to take the sign into account and subtract instead of add, or to use the Add absolute value instruction (if the machine has one) to bring the instruction into the accumulator. In the latter case it is essential to use the Store address instruction to replace the address in memory; otherwise the sign of the instruction will be changed incorrectly.

The location where the fifty is stored is called a *counter*. As soon as the number in 200 is down to zero, we are finished. There are simpler ways, as we shall see; this is probably the easiest to understand. We are now in a position to put the parts together.

| | LOCATION | OPERATION CODE | OPERATION ABBREVIATION | ADDRESS |
|---|---|---|---|---|
| Initialize | 450 | 10 | Clear add | Loc 100 |
| | 451 | 41 | Store address | 456 |
| | 452 | 10 | Clear add | Loc 0 |
| | 453 | 40 | Store acc | 150 |
| | 454 | 10 | Clear add | Loc 50 |
| | 455 | 40 | Store acc | 200 |
| Compute | 456 | 10 | Clear add | [0000] |
| | 457 | 11 | Add | 150 |
| | 458 | 40 | Store acc | 150 |
| Modify | 459 | 10 | Clear add | 456 |
| | 460 | 11 | Add | Loc 1 |
| | 461 | 41 | Store address | 456 |
| Test | 462 | 10 | Clear add | 200 |
| | 463 | 14 | Sub | Loc 1 |
| | 464 | 40 | Store acc | 200 |
| | 465 | 04 | Acc zero jump | 467 |
| | 466 | 01 | Un jump | 456 |
| | 467 | | Continuation of main program | |

A few notes should make this program clear. The various constants are assumed to be stored with suitable decimal point locations. Step 461 could be either Store accumulator or Store address; it is probably a good habit to use Store address here always. Using Store address where Store accumulator would have worked cannot hurt, whereas forgetting and using Store accumulator where Store address *should* have been used will ordinarily destroy the program in memory. Notice that step 464 is quite necessary; it does no good to subtract one from the number in 200 if the difference is not stored back in 200. This may seem painfully obvious, but it is, strangely, a fairly common source of error to beginners. Steps 465 and 466 test to see whether the number just stored in 200 is zero. If so, the zero jump takes us to 467 which is the continuation of the main program. If not, the zero jump will not be executed, the loop has not been carried out fifty times, and we go back to 456 to add another term in the summation.*

* In many computers the use of two instructions for this purpose would be unnecessary, either because they have a specific instruction called "nonzero jump" or because on a multiple address machine it is possible to specify the address to which to jump on both alternatives.

It is not at all necessary to carry out the four steps of initialize, compute, modify, test, in that order. Initializing does have to be first, of course, but the other three can be in any order. For reasons peculiar to the loop being written, it may be desirable to test, compute, modify, or modify, test, compute. This brings up a matter which deserves *very* careful attention in writing loops. Suppose in the program above we had tested before computing, so that the step after initializing had looked like this (minor changes being necessary in the initializing part):

| | LOCATION | OPERATION CODE | OPERATION ABBREVIATION | ADDRESS |
|---|---|---|---|---|
| Test | 456 | 10 | Clear add | 200 |
| | 457 | 14 | Sub | Loc 1 |
| | 458 | 40 | Store acc | 200 |
| | 459 | 04 | Acc zero jump | 467 |
| Compute | 460 | 10 | Clear add | [0000] |
| | 461 | 11 | Add | 150 |
| | 462 | 40 | Store acc | 150 |
| Modify | 463 | 10 | Clear add | 460 |
| | 464 | 11 | Add | Loc 1 |
| | 465 | 41 | Store address | 460 |
| | 466 | 01 | Un jump | 456 |
| | 467 | | Continuation | |

This will work, almost. The question is, How many times will the computing part be executed? Suppose, for purposes of this question, that we had been required to go through the loop only once. Then, by the present plan, the counter would have started out at one, one would have been subtracted at step 457, and the zero jump would have been executed. Where we wanted one execution, we got none. We see then that the program as it stands would execute the loop only forty-nine times. This is corrected easily enough by initializing the counter to 51 instead of 50.

Depending on the nature of the loop and of the test, it is possible to make a truly remarkable variety of mistakes in testing. If the loop should be carried out $n$ times, it is quite easy to make mistakes which will result in doing it: (1) not at all; (2) $n - 1$ times; (3) $n + 1$ times; (4) $2n$ times; (5) until the power fails or the machine breaks down. It is fairly safe to say that loops, although one of our most powerful tools, are also a *very* large source of errors. Whatever other prechecking systems may be used, it is always advisable to go back and check the loop-testing parts of the program. As indicated above, one simple way is to analyze what would happen if the loop were to be executed only once.

We should investigate a refinement of the above. It may be apparent to some that the testing method used is a bit wasteful since we already have another counter. The address of instruction 456 is counting the number of executions simultaneously. We could use this as a counter if we had some way of determining by the program what the accumulator contains after step 461. We observe that after step 461, on the first time through, the accumulator contains 10 0101 0000. The 10 is of course the operation code for Clear add; 0101 is the address just modified; 0000 is the index control, which is not used on this instruction. After fifty times through the loop, the accumulator at this point in the program will contain 1001500000; if we subtract the same number, the difference will be zero and we can stop the loop.

What we need, then, is a constant 10 0150 0000 to use as a test number. It is possible to store such a constant simply as a number, but in most cases it is simpler to get it into memory as an instruction. Suppose we have at 201 the instruction Clear add 150. This, with the operation part suitably coded, will be just the constant we need. Observe that the "instruction" at 201 will never be executed *as an instruction;* it is used purely as a test constant. For this reason it is sometimes called an *instructional constant,* or *pseudo instruction.*

The program could now be written:

|  | LOCATION | OPERATION CODE | OPERATION ABBREVIATION | ADDRESS |
|---|---|---|---|---|
| Initialize | 450 | 10 | Clear add | Loc 100 |
|  | 451 | 41 | Store address | 454 |
|  | 452 | 10 | Clear add | Loc 0 |
|  | 453 | 40 | Store acc | 150 |
| Compute | 454 | 10 | Clear add | [0000] |
|  | 455 | 11 | Add | 150 |
|  | 456 | 40 | Store acc | 150 |
| Modify | 457 | 10 | Clear add | 454 |
|  | 458 | 11 | Add | Loc 1 |
|  | 459 | 41 | Store address | 454 |
| Test | 460 | 14 | Sub | 201 |
|  | 461 | 04 | Acc zero jump | 463 |
|  | 462 | 01 | Un jump | 454 |
|  | 463 | Continuation | | |

Observe that we have saved four steps, two because it is no longer necessary to initialize the counter, and two in bringing in and storing the counter.

We have followed a procedure in writing these examples which is to be recommended. The initializing section of each loop has been written to *preset* any address or location which might be uncertain. An alternative procedure would be to write the correct address, etc., originally and then *reset* them after each use of the loop. The whole issue is what happens when a loop is used more than once. If it were used only once, then this discussion would have no point. If it is used the second time, we have the choice of assuming that all variable parts of the loop were reset after the last use, or of presetting them before using the loop again. The presetting procedure is to be preferred, as being more positive. Too much can go on between uses of a loop.

## 6.2 The Square Root Loop

The method commonly used to compute square roots illustrates that a loop need not be repeated a fixed number of times. It also brings in some of the points discussed in previous chapters, and is worth discussing in its own right.

The method most commonly used is the Newton-Raphson iteration. To find the square root $y$ of the number $a$, we repeatedly apply the formula

$$y_{i+1} = y_i + \tfrac{1}{2}\left[\frac{a}{y_i} - y_i\right]$$

which may also be written

$$y_{i+1} - y_i = \tfrac{1}{2}\left[\frac{a}{y_i} - y_i\right]$$

The procedure is to make some guess $y_0$ at the square root of $a$. A corrected second approximation $y_1$ is computed by applying the formula, a third approximation by applying it again, etc. Each time an approximation is computed, it is compared with the previous one. As soon as two approximations agree to as many places as we are concerned with, the process is stopped.

The program to compute this is fairly straightforward. The initialization consists simply of storing the first guess in the location where the answer is to be developed. In the simple versions of this program the first guess is often taken as the largest possible number in the machine, to avoid any possibility of divide stop. The only new concept is testing for the end of the loop by the size of a computed quantity. This amounts simply to computing the formula in the second form above, and testing to see if this (in our case) has ten leading zeros. If so, the last two approximations are as close together as they can get, and we simply jump out. If they are not

$$y_{i+1} - y_i = \frac{1}{2}\left(\frac{a}{y_i} - y_i\right)$$

the same, we add the previous approximation before starting over.

Assume that the number we want the square root of is stored in 93 and has a scale factor of zero, i.e., the decimal point is at the extreme left, and that all calculations are on this basis. The ½ is stored as 5000000000. The answer is to be stored in 94. A program to get the square root is:

| LOCATION | OPERATION CODE | OPERATION ABBREVIATION | ADDRESS | REMARKS |
|---|---|---|---|---|
| 100 | 10 | Clear add | Loc 9999999999 | |
| 101 | 40 | Store acc | 94 | Store first approximation |
| 102 | 10 | Clear add | 93 | $a$ |
| 103 | 18 | Divide | 94 | $a/y_i$ in MQ |
| 104 | 43 | Store MQ | 90 | Temporary |
| 105 | 10 | Clear add | 90 | $a/y_i$ in acc |
| 106 | 14 | Sub | 94 | $a/y_i - y_i$ |
| 107 | 33 | Long right | 10 | Into MQ |
| 108 | 17 | Mult round | Loc $\frac{1}{2}$ | $y_{i+1} - y_i$ in acc |
| 109 | 04 | Acc zero jump | 112 | If all zeros |
| 110 | 19 | Add to mem | 94 | $y_{i+1}$ |
| 111 | 01 | Un jump | 102 | |
| 112 | | Continuation | | |

Many variations are possible. Frequently it is desirable to waste a little space by writing a longer program, in order to save time by requiring fewer iterations. This can be done by starting with a first guess which is closer to the average square root which we will compute. For a number between 1 and 10 the best guess turns out to be 2.3, and it is possible even to compute a first guess by another formula.

On particular machines it may be desirable to carry out the steps in the calculation in a different order, or rewrite the formula as:

$$y_{i+1} = \frac{a + y_i^2}{2y_i}$$

possibly to take advantage of some feature of the instructions available. There may be simpler ways to effect the test for convergence.

These choices illustrate a point which we shall see recurring: there is almost always a choice between memory space, machine time, and programming time. In this case, we could reduce the machine time at the expense of a slightly longer program and more time spent on analyzing and coding. In many cases when a code is being written, savings and refinements become obvious which would require rewriting the code. Quick analysis of the time and space requirements, however, may show that the advantages are overshadowed by the cost of reprogramming, and the code is left as is. In other cases the program being written may be used for hundreds of hours, making it worthwhile to spend much time in reducing the time to a minimum. Or there may be a serious question whether a given program can be made to fit into storage, in which event it would be worth reducing the number of steps to a minimum, probably also at the expense of speed.

This matter is raised here because a similar choice is often available in the writing of loops. Obviously, most of the *time* of computing with a loop is taken up with the instructions that are repeated. Quite often it is possible to write a few extra steps in the initializing part which remove one or two from the computing, modifying, or testing part. The result is a slightly longer program in space, but significantly shorter in time. And finally, we may observe that a loop itself is a sacrifice of speed for space. The problem of the previous section, for example, could be accomplished by writing one Clear add, forty-nine Adds, and one Store. This would be absolutely the shortest possible program in time; the program as written in loop form would take (in most machines) about ten times as long. But of course it is only a third as long in space as well as being more flexible. This is enough of an advantage to justify the extra time.

## 6.3 Linear Interpolation

A very practical example is that of linear interpolation in a functional table stored in memory.

Suppose that $y$ is a function of $x$, and that tables of $y$ and $x$ are in storage as:

| | | | | |
|---|---|---|---|---|
| $x_1$ | 101 | $y_1$ | 201 | |
| $x_2$ | 102 | $y_2$ | 202 | |
| $x_3$ | 103 | $y_3$ | 203 | The $x$'s are stored in ascending |
| $x_4$ | 104 | $y_4$ | 204 | algebraic order |
| . | . | . | . | |
| . | . | . | . | |
| . | . | . | . | |
| $x_{100}$ | 200 | $y_{100}$ | 300 | |

A known value of $x$ is stored in 100; we are to find by linear interpolation the corresponding value of $y$ and store it in 400. It is not certain whether the known $x$ actually lies within the range of the

$x$'s; if it does not, the program obviously cannot interpolate and the machine should be stopped to signal the error.

The two $x$'s which bracket the given $x$ will be designated $x_{n+1}$ and $x_n$; the corresponding $y$'s are $y_{n+1}$ and $y_n$. The desired value of $y$ is then

$$y = y_n + \frac{y_{n+1} - y_n}{x_{n+1} - x_n} (x - x_n)$$

Note that the formula still applies if $x$ equals either $x_n$ or $x_{n+1}$.

The calculation problem may be broken down into these steps:

1. Determine if the given $x$ lies within the range of $x$'s in the table. If it does not, stop the machine; if it does, go on. We must be careful not to give an error indication if the given $x$ is the *same* as either the first or last $x$ in the table.

2. Determine which two $x$'s in the table bracket the given $x$. This is made possible by the fact that the entries are stored in ascending order. It is not necessary that the numbers be positive or that they all have the same sign, as long as they are stored in ascending algebraic order.

This part will of course be a loop.

3. From the addresses of the two $x$'s which bracket the given $x$, compute the addresses of the corresponding $y$'s. Store all addresses where needed for the next step.

4. Evaluate the interpolation formula.

This is a cumbersome way of stating the procedure. In the next chapter we shall see how the block diagram or flow chart helps in this phase of problem solution.

We are ready now to write the code. One or two details will need an explanation, which follows the program.

| LOCATION | OPERATION CODE | OPERATION ABBREVIATION | ADDRESS | REMARKS |
|---|---|---|---|---|
| 500 | 10 | Clear add | 100 |  |
| 501 | 14 | Sub | 101 | $x - x_1$ |
| 502 | 04 | Acc zero jump | 505 | Within range at low end if $x - x_1$ is zero or positive |
| 503 | 03 | Acc plus jump | 505 |  |
| 504 | 00 | Halt-jump | 0 | Stop if out of range |
| 505 | 10 | Clear add | 200 | $x_{100}$ |
| 506 | 14 | Sub | 100 | $x_{100} - x$ |
| 507 | 04 | Acc zero jump | 510 | With range at high end if $x_{100} - x$ is zero or positive |

(*Continued on next page*)

| 508 | 03 | Acc plus jump | 510 | |
| 509 | 00 | Halt and jump | 0 | Stop if out of range |
| 510 | 10 | Clear add | Loc 102 | Initialize address |
| 511 | 41 | Store address | 512 | of bracketing loop |
| 512 | 10 | Clear add | [0000] | $x_i$ |
| 513 | 14 | Sub | 100 | $x_i - x$ |
| 514 | 03 | Acc plus jump | 518 | Jump if table value is larger than given $x$ |
| 515 | 10 | Clear add | Loc 1 | Modify address |
| 516 | 19 | Add to mem | 512 | of testing instruction |
| 517 | 01 | Un jump | 512 | |
| 518 | 10 | Clear add | 512 | Bring in address of $x_{n+1}$ |
| 519 | 41 | Store address | 531 | |
| 520 | 14 | Sub | Loc 1 | Compute address of $x_n$ |
| 521 | 41 | Store address | 532 | |
| 522 | 41 | Store address | 535 | |
| 523 | 11 | Add | Loc 100 | Compute address of $y_n$ |
| 524 | 41 | Store address | 529 | |
| 525 | 41 | Store address | 541 | |
| 526 | 11 | Add | Loc 1 | Compute address of $y_{n+1}$ |
| 527 | 41 | Store address | 528 | |
| 528 | 10 | Clear add | [0000] | $y_{n+1}$ |
| 529 | 14 | Sub | [0000] | $y_{n+1} - y_n$ |
| 530 | 40 | Store acc | 91 | Temporary |
| 531 | 10 | Clear add | [0000] | $x_{n+1}$ |
| 532 | 14 | Sub | [0000] | $x_{n+1} - x_n$ |
| 533 | 40 | Store acc | 92 | Temporary |
| 534 | 10 | Clear add | 100 | $x$ |
| 535 | 14 | Sub | [0000] | $x - x_n$ |
| 536 | 33 | Long right | 10 | Into MQ |
| 537 | 16 | Mult | 91 | $(y_{n+1} - y_n)(x - x_n)$ |
| 538 | 18 | Divide | 92 | $x_{n+1} - x_n$ |
| 539 | 43 | Store MQ | 93 | Temporary |
| 540 | 10 | Clear add | 93 | Into acc |
| 541 | 11 | Add | [0000] | $+y_n = y$ |
| 542 | 40 | Store acc | 400 | |
| 543 | | Continuation | | |

The first ten steps test whether $x$ is within range. If $x - x_1$ is zero, then $x$ and $x_1$ are equal, $x$ is not out of range, and we may jump down to 505 to test the other end. If $x - x_1$ is positive, $x$ is clearly greater than $x_1$ and again the low end of the range is satisfactory. If neither of these conditions is met, the program will continue normally to 504, which is a Halt and jump order. This instruction stops the machine; when the start button is pressed the jump is executed. We are interested here primarily in the "halt" part. If the error were such that it could be corrected, the jump would be to a corrective section of the program, and might be simply an unconditional jump. The assumption here is that the error would be very unlikely, and would be impossible to correct. Therefore, we do not have any particular address to write in the Halt and jump instruction and simply write zeros.*

The loop is fairly simple. It tests each $x$ in the table, starting with the second, to see if it is larger than the given $x$. We safely start with the second one because if the given $x$ should happen to be the same as the first $x$, the formula would still apply. As soon as the difference between some table entry $x_i$ and $x$ is positive, then the $x_i$ is the next larger $x$ than the given $x$, or is equal to it. Either way, we are ready to jump out (step 514) to evaluate the formula.

At this point the instruction at 512 will contain the address of $x_{n+1}$. The address of $x_n$ will be one less. An examination of the addresses of the table of $y$'s shows that the address of $y_{n+1}$ is just 100 more than the address of $x_{n+1}$. The address of $y_n$ is similarly easy to find. These addresses are computed by steps 518–527, and stored as the addresses of six instructions between 528 and 542.

When these latter steps are reached, the instructions contain just the necessary addresses to compute the interpolation formula. It is worthwhile to look into the divide stop situation. Division by zero could occur only if two table entries of $x$ were equal, which should not happen. If $x = x_{n+1}$, we in effect divide $(x_{n+1} - x_n)$ by itself, and as a result we get divide stop.

One way out would be to add one to the last position of the denominator, which would not affect the accuracy of the result significantly and would ensure against divide stop. A better way is to arrange to multiply first. This will take care of the problem, since multiplication of $(x - x_n)$ by any number whatever will give a product which is less than $(x - x_n)$. This blanket statement assumes for the moment, as we may, that all scaling factors are zero. Thus the divide stop problem is sidestepped.

The remark about scaling factors of zero applies only to the analysis of division possibilities. Actually the program will be correct for any scaling factors, as long as all $x$'s have the same scaling factor and all $y$'s have the same—which need not be the same as that of the $x$'s.

* In many computers zero may have either a plus or a minus sign, depending on how it is arrived at. In these machines it would be possible to arrange the calculation so as to combine the zero and plus jumps into one plus jump.

## Exercises

1. Write a loop to clear to zero all of memory from 1000 to 1999 inclusive.

2. The cube root of a number $a$ may be found by repeated application of the formula

$$y_{i+1} = y_i + \tfrac{1}{3}\left[\frac{a}{y_i{}^2} - y_i\right]$$

Write a loop to find the cube root of a number in 500, and place the root in 501. The number has a scaling factor of zero.

3. Locations 100 to 150 contain 51 numbers all of which have the same scaling factor. Write a loop to compute the 50 first differences of this list, and place them in 151–200.

4. A list of numbers is stored in 100–119. Write a loop to multiply each number by the number in 120, and place the individual products in 130–149.

5. Two lists of numbers are stored in 100–119 and 120–139. Write a loop to multiply the number in 100 by the number in 120 and place the product in 140, and similarly for all twenty pairs of numbers.

6. Rewrite Exercise 5 to sum all of the products and store this sum in 140.

7. Six lists of numbers are stored in 100–119, 120–139, 140–159, 160–179, 180–199, 200–219. Multiply the first list by the second and sum the products as in Exercise 6, and store the sum in 220. Multiply the first list by the third and store the sum in 221, etc., to compute five numbers in 220–224.

8. Ten lists of numbers are stored in 100–119, etc., up to 280–299. Multiply the first list by the sixth, seventh, eighth, ninth, and tenth, form the sums as before, and store them in 300–304. Multiply the second list by the sixth through tenth, sum, and store the five numbers in 305–309. Continue until each of the first five lists has been multiplied by the second five to get twenty-five sums of products.

9. A number in 1350 may have leading zeros. Write a loop to "normalize" the number, i.e., shift it left until a nonzero digit appears in the high order (or leftmost) digit in memory. Store in 1351 the number of shifts necessary. The number does have at least one nonzero digit. (Why is the last condition important?)

10. Write a loop to evaluate the summation

$$i = h/3\,(a_0 + 4a_1 + 2a_2 + 4a_3 + 2a_4 + \cdots + 2a_{n-2} + 4a_{n-1} + a_n)$$

$h$ is stored in 100. The $a$'s are stored in 200 to $(200 + n)$; $n$ itself is stored as an integer in 101 (Simpson's rule). *Hint:* There is a choice between evaluating the formula as it stands, or rewriting it as

$$i = h/3\,[(a_0 + 4a_1 + a_2) + (a_2 + 4a_3 + a_4) + \cdots]$$

What are the advantages of each way?

11. A grid of values is composed of values in an array such as:

$$
\begin{array}{llllll}
a_{11} & a_{12} & a_{13} & a_{14} & a_{15} \cdots a_{1n} \\
a_{21} & a_{22} & a_{23} & a_{24} & a_{25} \cdots a_{2n} \\
a_{31} & a_{32} & a_{33} & a_{34} & a_{35} \cdots a_{3n}
\end{array}
$$

The values in the first row are stored from 100 to $(100 + n - 1)$; in the second row, from 200 to $(200 + n - 1)$; in the third row, from 300 to $(300 + n - 1)$. $n$ is stored as an integer in 92. The problem is to calculate a new value of all but the first and last entries in the second row, by the formula

$$ a_{2,i} = \tfrac{1}{4}(a_{1,i} + a_{2,i-1} + a_{2,i+1} + a_{3,i}) $$

where $i = 2, 3, \cdots, n - 1$, i.e., taking the average of the four surrounding points. Each new $a_{2,i}$ is stored back in the same location as soon as it is computed.

12. The formula of Exercise 2 may be generalized to find any integral root:

$$ y_{i+1} = y_i + \frac{1}{n}\left[\frac{a}{y_i^{\,n-1}} - y_i\right] $$

Given $a$ in 100 with a scaling factor of zero, and $n$ in 105 as an integer, write a loop to compute the $n$th root of $a$.

13. Write a loop to evaluate the series

$$ e^x = 1 + x + \frac{x^2}{2!} + \frac{x^3}{3!} + \cdots $$

There are many ways to do this, as discussed in Chapter 17. For this problem, "start from the front" by evaluating the low powers first. Stop the loop as soon as a computed term is less than $10^{-8}$, which number is stored as a constant in 100. $x$, with a scaling factor of zero, is in 101. (What must be the scaling factor of $e^x$?) Assume that all needed reciprocal factorials are stored in 102 and following addresses, starting with one-half. The scaling factors of these are all one.

(Further exercises along the same lines may be found at the end of Chapter 8.)

# 7 FLOW CHARTING

## 7.0 Introduction

Most programs of interest are much too large to visualize at one time. There are too many logical choices and branches throughout the problem to be able to keep them in mind. Another way of saying the same thing is that individual parts of the program must be planned separately; without a way of representing the logic that has been planned so far, it would be forgotten before it could be put into code.

A flow chart is a commonly used solution to this problem. It is a graphical or pictorial representation of a problem, which spells out the result of each choice, the exact sequence of operations on the data, how loops are tested, etc. It seldom itemizes each individual instruction. Long sequences of straightforward algebra are of no concern in a flow chart; the important thing is the logic—how the alternatives fit together.

A completed flow chart allows one to see the over-all picture of a program, or of the part that has been flow-charted so far. This can be a valuable aid in discovering logical errors, which are a common source of trouble during the checkout stage of problem preparation (Chapter 13).

In addition to the important value of picturing the logic and the over-all flow of a problem, the flow chart has a second advantage. If a complex problem must be transferred to another programmer after it is under way, a serious communication problem develops. It is not easy to describe in ten short sentences what has been done to date. The two individuals may have different working habits which complicate the attempt of the second person to understand the first person's work. It is sometimes next to impossible to figure out the logic of a problem given only a listing of the instructions, especially if the coding has logical errors in it! The flow chart helps alleviate all these. It is a good device for establishing continuity between

two workers, and for refreshing the memory of the original programmer when he must return to a problem which has become
"cold."

## 7.1 A Flow Charting Notation

Basically, a flow chart is just a collection of lines and boxes and
arrows and notes about the things to be done. It helps, however, to
have a somewhat standardized system of symbols and ways of writing
the notes. Some of these conventions are simply short cuts which
have developed out of experience; others are somewhat arbitrary,
but are to be recommended as establishing uniformity between
different writers of flow charts in the same organization.

In the following paragraphs we will define a system of flow charting and then give some examples using this system. It is not intended
to represent the "last word" in flow charting, and in some of its
details it will certainly differ from the ideas of some programmers.
However, it is complete, and it will help us to illustrate some of the
fundamentals of flow charting.

At the very least, a system of flow charting must have symbols to
describe the following:

1. The various functions to be performed.

2. Changes in the sequence of calculations as a result of logical
decisions.

3. Changes in the sequence of calculations as a result of modifying
or creating instructions.

For these purposes we define function boxes, choice boxes, and
variable connectors as follows:

### FUNCTION BOX

This rectangle, Figure 1, will contain a description of a function.
It has one entry and one exit, i.e., the function represented by this

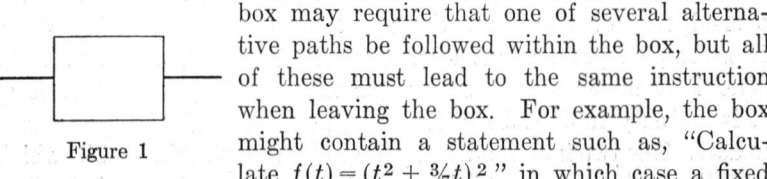

Figure 1

box may require that one of several alternative paths be followed within the box, but all
of these must lead to the same instruction
when leaving the box. For example, the box
might contain a statement such as, "Calcu-
late $f(t) = (t^2 + \frac{3}{7}t)^2$," in which case a fixed
sequence of instructions is always followed; or it might say, "Calculate Social Security withholding," in which case the box represents two
alternative calculations depending upon whether or not the employee
has paid all of his Social Security tax for the year. In either event,

however, the instruction processed following the calculation of the tax is the same.

## CHOICE BOX

This box, Figure 2, indicates which one of two or more paths is to be followed through a program as a result of answering a question; hence, it has a single entry and two or more exits. It often describes a single machine operation such as, "Jump if the contents of the accumulator are zero." This need not be the case, however. For example, if this box is used in a flow chart describing the evaluation of an alternating series, the box might contain the question, "Series converged?" This would imply the performance of half a dozen or so machine instructions.

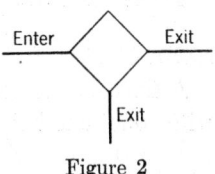

Figure 2

## VARIABLE CONNECTOR

This describes a set of symbols that indicates which one of several paths is to be taken in a program; see Figure 3. Variable connectors differ from choice boxes in that the connectors need not include the instructions which cause the path to vary. In particular, a choice box describes a conditional jump or branch operation and associated calculations; a variable connector describes the modification (or creation as a function of a parameter) of the address portion of a jump.

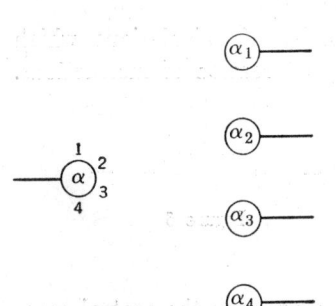

Figure 3

With these three representations we can describe any program. However, limiting ourselves to these three would have some notable disadvantages, such as:

1. Topographical problems would be encountered; i.e., if lines or arrows were the only provision for connecting remote portions of the flow chart with one another, it would soon become a nearly unintelligible maze.

2. No representation except the comparison (choice) box is provided to distinguish red tape operations, i.e., those which operate on instructions and do no work directly concerned with calculating results.

3. No representation is provided to distinguish input-output instructions from others. The distinction is desirable because in-out

boxes usually represent milestones in a program. Hence, representing them in a unique fashion helps the reader of the flow chart
to get a "bird's-eye view" of the program.

4. There is no provision for making parenthetical remarks, elaborations on statements contained in other boxes, or notes to aid the
reader in a clear understanding of the flow chart.

These disadvantages lead us to make five more definitions:

## FIXED  CONNECTOR

A fixed connector is used to connect remote parts of a flow chart
with one another without the use of long or crossing lines, as
illustrated in Figure 4. One or more

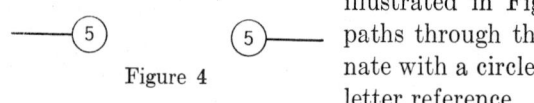

Figure 4

paths through the program will termi-
nate with a circle enclosing a number or
letter reference. All of these paths will
then lead to a single circle (containing the same number or letter
reference) which is the starting point from which to continue through
the program.

Along with this definition usually goes the convention that the flow
chart will be drawn from left to right and top to bottom.

## SUBSTITUTION  BOX

This box, Figure 5, describes any series of calculations which
result in the initialization, modification, or creation of instructions.

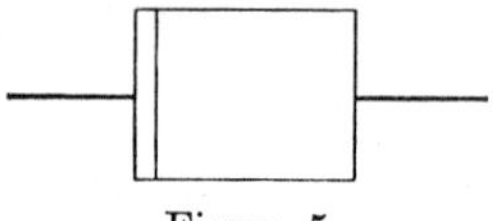

Figure 5                                    Figure 6

## IN-OUT  BOX

The reading or writing of information from or to the central computer via input-output equipment is represented by an in-out box,
as shown in Figure 6.

## HALT  BOX

As its name implies, this circle, Figure 7, indicates a stopping point
in the program. It may or may not have a line
exiting from it, depending upon where it is used.
That is, a particular halt may be inserted to
allow for such things as changing tape reels or
setting switches, in which case the halt box
would be provided with an exit. Or it could be an end-of-job halt

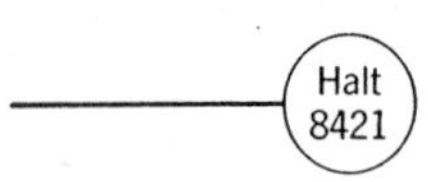

Halt
8421

Figure 7

or error halt, in which case it would not have an exit. In either event, the halt box should contain the address which will appear in the location counter, to distinguish it from other halts.

## ASSERTION BOX

The use of assertion boxes, Figure 8, in sufficient numbers and appropriate places, can enhance the value of a flow chart more than any other single device. If properly used, they will greatly simplify the reading of a "cold" flow chart (one you have not looked at for a month or so) or one written by another person. For example, suppose a certain counter or instruction is loaded in its initialized

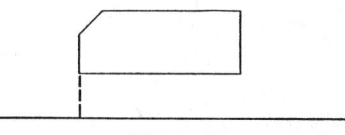

Figure 8

form; this should be stated in an assertion box. Or suppose a coding trick is used in performing some function of the program. Tricks save time and/or storage space, and one usually derives a certain pleasure from writing a clever program. However, a tricky program is difficult to read after the details are forgotten. A note in an assertion box makes the trick clear.

We now have an adequate system, but we may add some further embellishments if we wish:

## LABELING CONNECTOR

This symbolism connects, by means of the circled letters, a function box with modification boxes which affect it; see Figure 9.

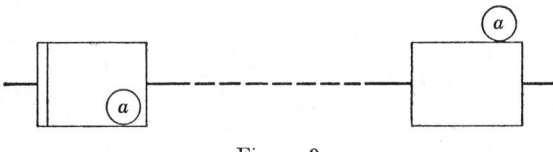

Figure 9

## REFERENCE MARKS

This symbol, Figure 10, is identical in appearance to a fixed connector except for the "not equal" sign. Its function is merely to provide a "landmark" which will also be included in the annotation of the code. This helps to correlate portions of the code with corresponding portions of

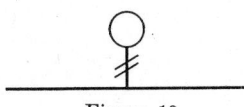

Figure 10

the flow chart from which it is written.

## SWITCHES

This special case of the variable connector is often defined independently, due to its frequent occurrence and because special operations exist on some machines which facilitate simulating the action of a switch; see Figure 11. The switch, however, is in every way analogous to the variable connector illustrated in Figure 12.

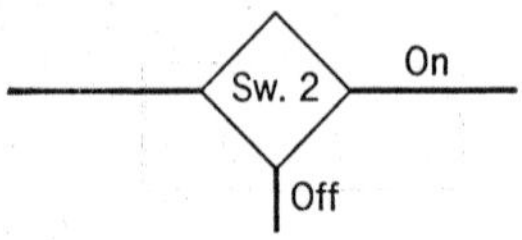

Figure 11 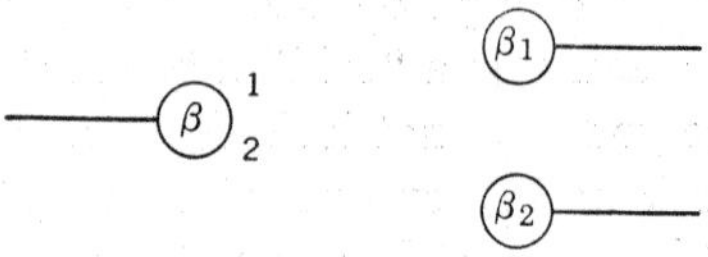                    Figure 12

We now have described a complete flow charting system, but what do we write in the boxes? In general, we can write whatever we wish, but certain things are written sufficiently often to make it helpful to use abbreviations such as these:

1. $I -$     (for initialize)
2. $U -$     (for increment, or "up")
3. $D -$     (for decrement, or "down")
4. $A \rightarrow B$   (for $A$ replaces $B$)
5. $A : B$    (for $A$ compared to $B$)

The fifth abbreviation is used in choice boxes and the possible outcomes $(=$ or $\neq$, $<$ or $\geq$, etc.) are written beside the appropriate lines exiting from the boxes.

Let us now consider some examples.

*Example 1*

$e^x$ is to be approximated by the first five terms of the Taylor series:

$$e^x \cong 1 + x + x^2/2! + x^3/3! + x^4/4!$$

We first factor the polynomial into the form

$$[[[x/4! + \tfrac{1}{3}!]x + \tfrac{1}{2}!]x + 1]x + 1$$

Assume the reciprocal factorials are stored in adjacent memory cells, and let the partial sums of the polynomial be abbreviated P.S. In Figure 13 the "out" reference circle leads to the next phase of the problem.

Notice that the initialization and modification of the addition looks very much as if these operations were being performed on a counter. The fact that the notations are contained in *substitution* boxes reminds us that they refer to instructions. Besides achieving notational conciseness, this method of representation retains the mathematical meaning of $n$ in the series for $e^x$:

$$e^x = \sum_0^\infty \frac{x^n}{n!}$$

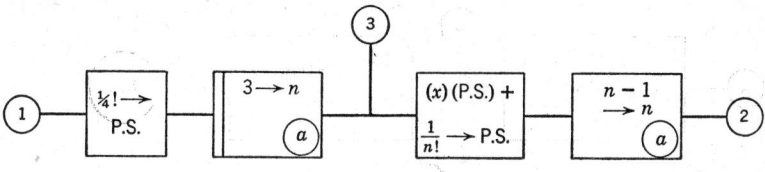

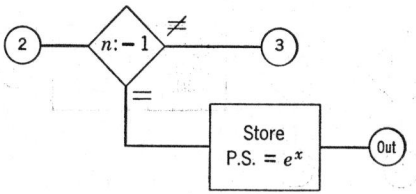

Figure 13

*Example 2*

A questionnaire consisting of fifty yes-no questions is to be distributed to 2000 employees at an industrial plant. The plant has three organizational levels which are numbered as follows:

Departments: Numbered by hundreds
Sections: Numbered by tens
Units: Numbered by units

Thus group 123 means unit 3 of section 2 of department 1; group 120 means section 2 of department 1, etc. Each questionnaire will have on it the group number of the person who fills it out. The responses to the survey are to be tabulated by inverse order of groups (i.e., all departments, then all sections, then all units), with the following items calculated and listed for each question:

$$(1)\ n, \quad (2)\ p, \quad (3)\ N, \quad (4)\ P, \quad (5)\ Z = \frac{P - p}{\sqrt{1 - n/N}}$$

where $n$ is the number of responses by the current organizational entity answering yes to this question; $p$ is the per cent answering yes; and $N$ and $P$ are the corresponding quantities for the entire plant.

It is required that the reports for the three organizational levels be labeled respectively: 1957 Attitude Survey for Department No. XXX, 1957 Attitude Survey for Section No. XXX, 1957 Attitude Survey for Unit No. XXX.

Two things should be noted: First, the $Z$ scores cannot be calculated until the $N$ and $P$ have been obtained for all levels. Hence, these latter quantities will be obtained along with the $n$ and $p$ for each question and organization in a separate preliminary operation. Second, the report format for all organizational levels is the same; hence, the same instructions will be used in each case and the headings will be modified when the organizational level changes.

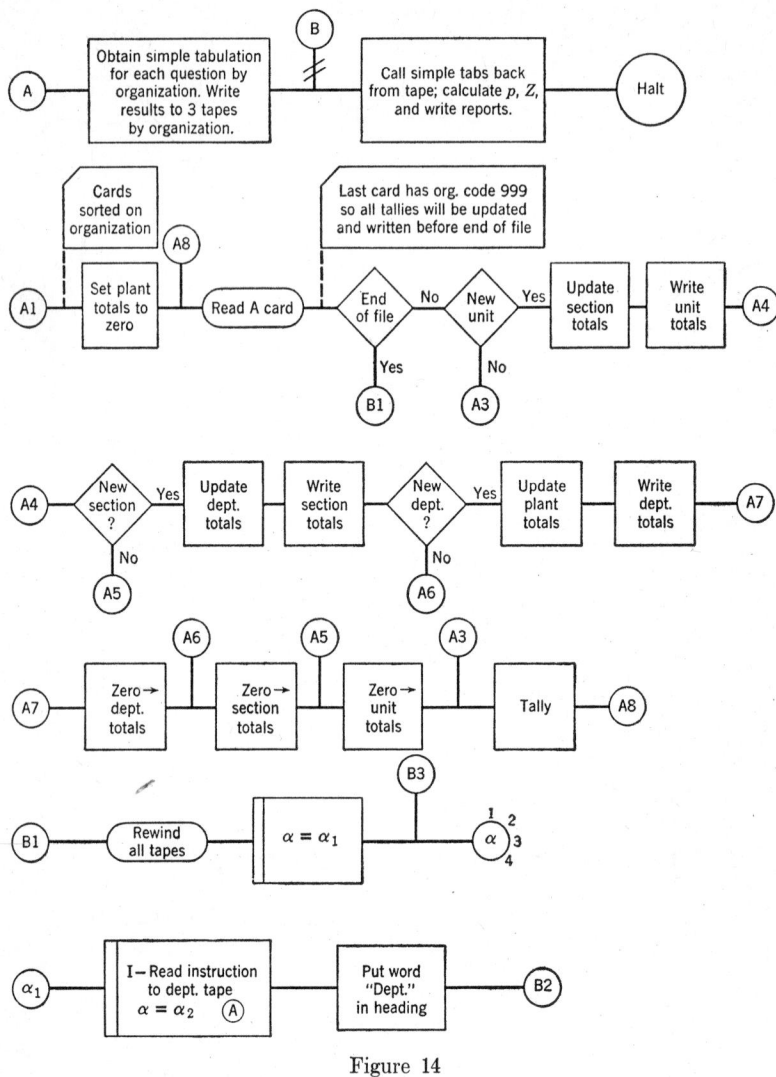

Figure 14

It is assumed that for each questionnaire a card will be keypunched with the organization number sequence at the outset. Assume that there is sufficient memory available in the computer to store the $n$ and $p$ for three levels and the plant at the same time, with enough room left over for all the necessary instructions.

The gross flow chart (sometimes called a diagram) for this example is shown in the first line of Figure 14. The detailed flow chart is given below it, starting at A1.

We have in this example presented two levels of flow chart. They are

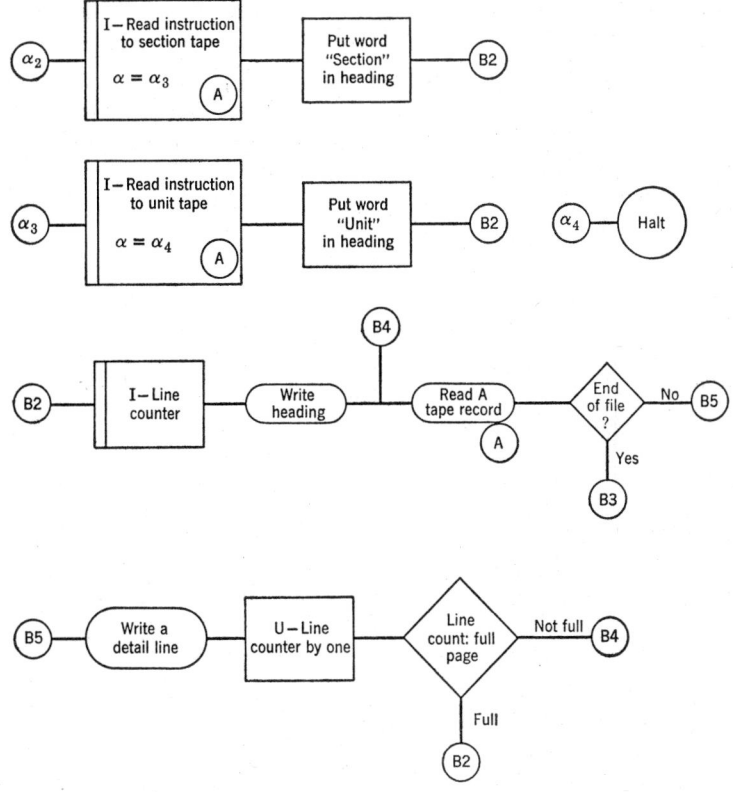

Figure 14 (continued)

similar to the thinking process in their scope; i.e., they go from the general to the particular. If we were to start writing the code for this example at this time, we might find it helpful to get even more particular; this might be done by making more detailed flow charts on scratch paper to elaborate on some of the boxes shown in Figure 14.

In general, it is desirable to define a hierarchy of flow charts. For one thing, this forces the designer of the charts to think in a logical manner—from general to particular. It also gives the various connectors more meaning because it identifies them with the different blocks on the gross flow chart. For example, connector number 57 tells one very little, but connector C7 says that this is in block C and probably gives some idea of what part of the block, since now the numbers do not go so high.

Recall that we have followed the convention that the flow chart be read from left to right and top to bottom. An alternative method

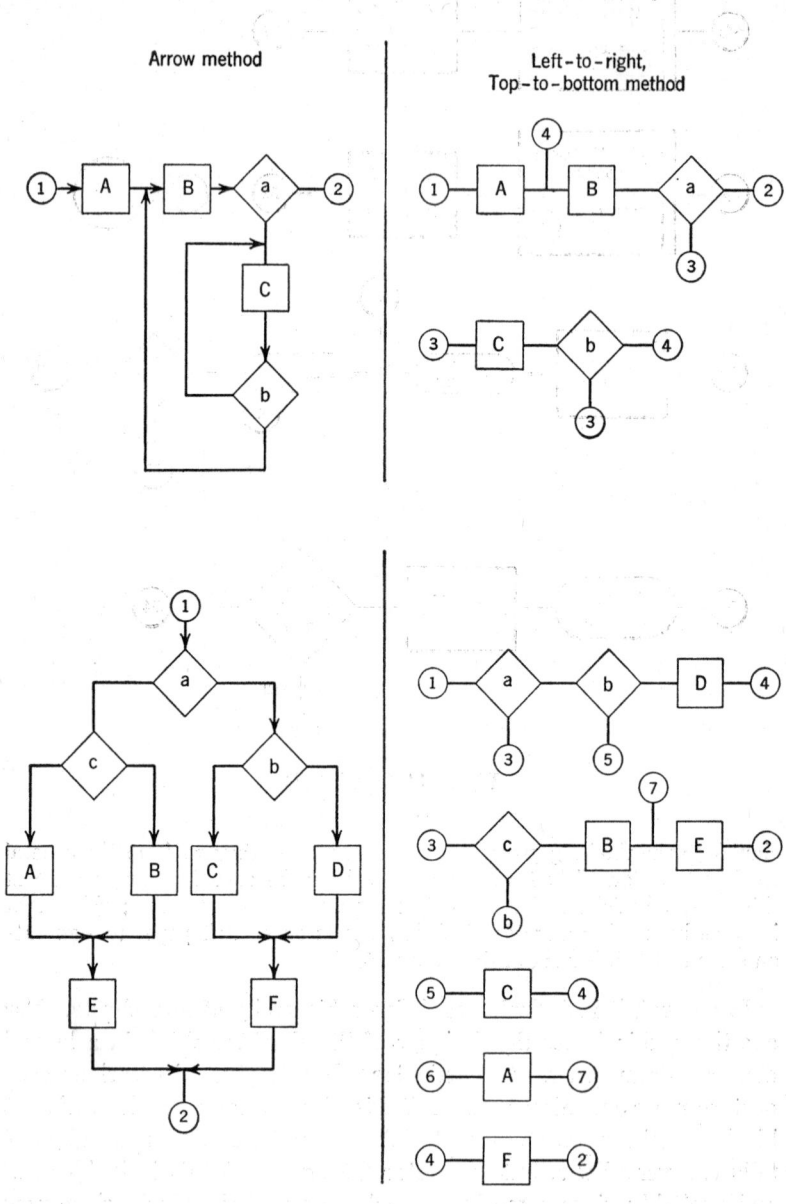

Arrow method

Left-to-right,
Top-to-bottom method

Figure 15

of designating the direction of flow is to connect each box and/or symbol with an arrow. This has the disadvantage that the arrow head must be drawn on each connecting line but it has the advantage that it points up alternate paths, and loops within loops, quite clearly. This is illustrated in Figure 15.

## Exercises

1. Forty numbers in 200–239 are to be added, and the sum placed in 240. Draw a flow chart for this exercise.

2. Draw flow charts for any of the exercises of Chapter 6.

3. Draw a flow chart for the iterative square root procedure described in Chapter 6.

4. Draw a flow chart for the linear interpolation problem of Chapter 6.

5. The average of a group of numbers in 350–370 is to be found. If the contents of any location is zero, the zero should not be used in computing the average. If all twenty-one numbers are zero, a Halt and jump instruction should be executed. Draw a flow chart.

6. A list of positive numbers in 1400–1500 is in random order; the numbers are to be sorted so that the smallest appears in 1400 and the largest in 1500. One possible sorting method is to compare the first number successively with all the others, interchanging the locations of any pair in which the number in 1400 is larger than the number in the other location. Doing this for all pairs will put the smallest number in 1400. Repeating the process with the number in 1401 and all other numbers except that in 1400 will put the second smallest number in 1401. Continuing the scheme through the list will result in sorting the numbers into ascending order. Draw a flow chart for the process.

7. Suppose that in 1200–1212 there are thirteen numbers which represent a bridge hand. Each number is three digits long; the first digit represents the suit, by a scheme such as one for clubs, two for diamonds, three for hearts, and four for spades. The second and third digits represent the denomination within a suit. Draw the flow chart for a program to determine whether the hand is all of one suit. Draw another chart for a program to determine whether the suit which contains the most cards consists of an unbroken sequence, e.g., 2, 3, 4, 5, and 6, or 10, jack, queen, and king. The "hand" in memory may not be assumed to be in any order.

# 8 INDEX REGISTERS

## 8.0 Introduction

We have seen in previous chapters that many instructions in an ordinary program are concerned not with the actual arithmetic operations or logical decisions that are the basis of the application, but with auxiliary operations that are demanded by the nature of the computer. These are often called *red tape* operations: such things as loop testing, shifting to line up decimal points, etc. Index registers, which are frequently also called B-lines, B-boxes, or base registers, help to reduce red tape in a variety of ways.

Their basic function is to allow the "modification" of instructions without ever actually changing them as they appear in memory. This is done by adding the contents of one of the registers, which are in the control section of the computer, to the address of an instruction in memory before the instruction is executed. Thus the *effective* address—the address in memory plus the number in the index register —can be changed simply by changing the index register. Since this can be done more simply and rapidly than modification of instructions in the accumulator, the program is speeded up and red tape reduced. The same characteristic of easy modification of the contents of index registers makes them valuable also for operations involving counting. And finally, an index register can be used to keep a record of the location in memory at which a jump was located, which is the subject of the next chapter.

In Section 8.1, the details of the operation of the index registers in TYDAC will be explained, along with a detailed description of all the operations which affect them. Then examples are presented which compare an indexed loop with the nonindexed form, and show how index registers might be set up in a generalized problem and how they could be used in a counting operation.

## 8.1 Operation of Index Registers

TYDAC contains two index registers, the contents of which may be added to the address part of an instruction in memory before the instruction is executed. If the contents of index 1 are to be added to the address of an instruction, a *one* is written in the tenth digit of instruction. If the contents of index 2 are to be added to the address of an instruction, a *two* is written in the tenth digit of the instruction. Only the last digit is interpreted, so anything may be written in the seventh, eighth, and ninth positions of an instruction; normally zeros are written.

An instruction now looks like:

| SIGN | OPERATION | ADDRESS | INDEX CONTROL |
|---|---|---|---|
| + | XX | XXXX | XXX X |
| Always plus | Any allowable operation | Any allowable address | Normally zero, but immaterial    0, 1, or 2 |

Instructions which call for an index to be added are written with the *one* or *two* following the address:

10    Clear add    1200, 1    or    40    Store acc    0560, 2

If no index is to be used on a particular instruction, we do not write anything, rather than indicating the zero.

Remember the function of the index: the contents of the specified index register are added *after* the instruction is brought into the control section but *before* the instruction is executed. Thus if index 1 contains 23, and we write the instruction

10    Clear add    1200, 1

nothing at all happens to the instruction as it appears in memory, but the *effect* is to Clear add **1223**. This is why we speak of the *effective* address as being the address as written *plus* the contents of the specified index register, if any. If no index is specified or if the specified register contains zero, the actual address and the effective address are of course the same.

There are nine instructions in TYDAC which involve index registers. Four of these move numbers between the index registers and the accumulator or memory. Two modify the contents of the index registers. Three are jump instructions which involve the index registers. Complete descriptions of these appear in the summary of

TYDAC instructions, Appendix 1; we will investigate several of them in detail here.

It is always necessary, before using the registers, to get numbers into them. The basic means of doing this is the Load index from memory instruction:

50          Mem to ind          A, I

I is the index control and is one or two. A is the address at which the number to be placed in the index register I is located. The address part (digit positions 3–6) of the specified word is used. Note carefully that the index control is used in a different sense than on an ordinary instruction which is being modified by the contents of an index register. If we write:

10          Clear add          1200, 2

we mean to add whatever is in index 2 to 1200 before executing the instruction. If we write:

50          Mem to ind          1200, 2

we mean to take the address part of location 1200 and place it in index 2. This does *not* mean to add the contents of index 2 to 1200 before going to memory, then placing the address part of this effective address back in index 2. We express this by saying that these nine instructions are not indexable; in short, the index control cannot be used for two different purposes at once.

The other instruction for setting an index is Load index from accumulator. This is used when the number to be placed in the index has to be computed, as in one of the examples to follow. This instruction makes no use whatever of the address. Any number may be written, but again it is customary to write zeros.

In some cases it is necessary to use the contents of an index register directly, rather than for simply modifying addresses. The instructions Store index in accumulator and Store index in memory take care of this situation. Their operation is straightforward; it should be observed that only the address part of the accumulator or memory location is affected.

The Raise index and Lower index instructions allow us to modify the contents of an index register in one operation, as is frequently necessary in applications. Their operation brings in another function of the address part of an instruction (others discussed so far being an actual memory location for obtaining or storing data, the location of the next instruction, and the number of shifts). In these two operations, the actual address part *itself* is added to or subtracted from the specified register, not the number at a *location* at memory. If we write:

54    Raise ind    0002, 1

we mean to add *two* to index 1, not whatever is stored at location 2 in memory. This may be a little confusing at first, but in practice it represents enough of a saving in computer hardware and execution time to justify its being done this way.

Two of the jump instructions are conditional and the other has a special purpose the point of which will become clear in the next chapter. Zero index jump tests whether the specified register contains a zero; if *not*, the next instruction is taken from A. Equal index jump checks whether the two registers contain the same number; if not, the next instruction is taken from A. In both instructions, if the jump is not executed, the following instruction is taken in normal sequence.

The Set index and jump instruction results in the *location* of the current instruction being placed in the specified index register before the jump is executed. This is quite different from any other instruction in the machine. If we write:

58    Set ind jump    400, 1

the current location, whether it is 0000, 1200, or whatever, is placed in index 1 before jumping. The purpose of this is taken up in the next chapter; it is presented here to gather into one place a discussion of all instructions involving index registers.

It may seem that there is a serious limitation in having index registers which only *add* to the address. This limitation is only an apparent one, however, since we can make an adding index register give the effect of subtracting. We may recall from Chapter 3 that computers subtract by adding complements. Thus the ten's complement of 3, to four digits, is 9997; if we add this to 15, for example, we get $9997 + 0015 = 10012$. Deleting the one at the left we get 12, which is just $15 - 3$. In the arithmetic section of the computer this is done automatically, but we can arrange through programming to do the same thing in the index registers. Take, for example, an application in which it is necessary to bring into the accumulator all the numbers in 100 to 122, *in that order*, and still use Zero index jump to test the loop. We can initialize the index register to 9978, which is the ten's complement of 22, and write Clear add 122, 1 and use Raise index. The first time through we would get

0122 + 9978 = 10100.  The address computing circuits would automatically delete the leftmost one.  The last Raise index instruction, when the register contains 9999, will take it to zero, since here also the fifth (leftmost) digit would be ignored.  Thus we have arrived at the same effect as an index register which subtracts.

The application of these principles and instructions will now be illustrated in three fairly typical problems.

*Example 1.  Linear Interpolation*

As an example of how index registers can be used in loop writing to reduce the number of instructions, we may rewrite the loop discussed in Section 6.3.  For clarity it may be restated here.

**TABLE 1**

| $x_1$ | 101 | $y_1$ | 201 |
|---|---|---|---|
| $x_2$ | 102 | $y_2$ | 202 |
| $x_3$ | 103 | $y_3$ | 203 |
| $x_4$ | 104 | $y_4$ | 204 |
| . | . | . | . |
| . | . | . | . |
| . | . | . | . |
| $x_{100}$ | 200 | $y_{100}$ | 300 |

$y$ is a function of $x$; tables of $x$ and $y$ are in storage as shown in Table 1.  The $x$'s are in ascending algebraic order.  A known value of $x$ is stored in 100; we are to find by linear interpolation the corresponding value of $y$ and store it in 400.  It is not certain whether the known $x$ actually lies within the range of the $x$'s in Table 1; if it does not, the machine should be stopped to signal the error. The two $x$'s which bracket the given $x$ will be designated $x_{n+1}$ and $x_n$; the corresponding $y$'s by $y_{n+1}$ and $y_n$.  The desired value of $y$ is then

$$y = y_n + \frac{y_{n+1} - y_n}{x_{n+1} - x_n}(x - x_n)$$

The index registers will allow three savings.  First, we need not test whether the given $x$ is within the table *at both ends*.  Rather, we can test the low end, then simply count the number of times the loop is repeated; if it exceeds a certain number, the given $x$ must have been outside the range.  Second, a few steps may be saved by the simple modification which will be possible.  Third, getting the four values from the table is greatly facilitated, with a saving here alone of ten instructions.  In this example, the programs will be presented first and then discussed in detail.

| LOCATION | OPERATION CODE | OPERATION ABBREVIATION | ADDRESS | REMARKS |
|---|---|---|---|---|
| 500 | 10 | Clear add | 100 | $x$ |
| 501 | 14 | Sub | 101 | $x - x_1$ |
| 502 | 04 | Acc zero jump | 505 | |
| 503 | 03 | Acc plus jump | 505 | |
| 504 | 00 | Halt-jump | 0 | |
| 505 | 50 | Mem to ind | Loc 0, 1 | Load index 1 with zero |
| 506 | 50 | Mem to ind | Loc 100, 2 | Load index 2 with 100 |
| 507 | 10 | Clear add | 102, 1 | $x_i$ |
| 508 | 14 | Sub | 100 | $x_i - x$ |
| 509 | 03 | Acc plus jump | 513 | Jump to calculation |
| 510 | 54 | Raise ind | 1, 1 | Increase index 1 by 1 |
| 511 | 57 | Eq ind jump | 507 | Jump back unless index 1 contains 100 |
| 512 | 00 | Halt-jump | 0 | Stop if jump is not executed |
| 513 | 10 | Clear add | 202, 1 | $y_{n+1}$ |
| 514 | 14 | Sub | 201, 1 | $y_{n+1} - y_n$ |
| 515 | 40 | Store acc | 91 | Temporary |
| 516 | 10 | Clear add | 102, 1 | $x_{n+1}$ |
| 517 | 14 | Sub | 101, 1 | $x_{n+1} - x_n$ |
| 518 | 40 | Store acc | 92 | Temporary |
| 519 | 10 | Clear add | 100 | $x$ |
| 520 | 14 | Sub | 101, 1 | $x - x_n$ |
| 521 | 33 | Long right | 10 | Into MQ |
| 522 | 16 | Mult | 91 | $(y_{n+1} - y_n)(x - x_n)$ |
| 523 | 18 | Divide | 92 | |
| 524 | 43 | Store MQ | 93 | Temporary |
| 525 | 10 | Clear add | 93 | Into acc |
| 526 | 11 | Add | 201, 1 | $+y_n = y$ |
| 527 | 40 | Store acc | 400 | |
| 528 | | Continuation | | |

This example provides several illustrations of uses of index registers, uses which are not otherwise brought out in the text. For a thorough understanding of the functions of index registers, it is almost essential that the student study this example carefully.

The first five steps are exactly as before: testing whether the given $x$ is smaller than the smallest $x$ in the table and stopping if so. Steps 505 and 506 load the two index registers, the first with zero and the second with 100. On step 507 the "Clear add   102, 1" brings in the contents of 102, since we have just loaded index 1 with zero. If the given $x$ is equal to or less than the second $x$ in the table, the jump in 509 will occur. If the jump is not executed, index 1 is raised by 1 on step 510. Step 511 checks whether the two index registers are equal, which would mean that the loop had been repeated one hundred times. The jump is executed, as specified in the TYDAC instruction list, if the two are *not* equal. The five-step loop, 507–511, is repeated until either the conditional Accumulator plus jump *is* satisfied or the conditional Equal index jump is *not* satisfied.

If the latter occurs, it means that index 1 contained 100 at the time of the test. Since the index was modified before testing, it must have contained 99 when instruction 507 was last executed, which means that the given $x$ must have been larger than the contents of 200, i.e., $x_{100}$. Hence the halt if the Equal index jump does not jump. Thus we have replaced five steps in the previous program by one here: step 506, which loads index 2.

If the accumulator plus jump of step 509 is satisfied, it means that the given $x$ is equal to or less than the $x$ in the table specified by instruction 507. Suppose this happens on the first time around, in which case the given $x$ is between $x_1$ and $x_2$, index 1 contains zero, and the four addresses which concern us are:

$$x_n \quad 101 \qquad y_n \quad 201$$
$$x_{n+1} \quad 102 \qquad y_{n+1} \quad 202$$

Thus if we want $y_{n+1}$ we need merely write "Clear add   202, 1," and similarly for the other locations. If the condtion is met the second time around, the given $x$ is between $x_2$ and $x_3$, index 1 contains one, and the four addresses of interest will be:

$$x_n \quad 102 \qquad y_n \quad 202$$
$$x_{n+1} \quad 103 \qquad y_{n+1} \quad 203$$

To get $y_{n+1}$ we need simply write again "Clear add   202, 1." This (for this problem) is the real beauty of the index registers: once set up, they can be used to modify as many addresses as desired. If this had been a problem in fourth-order interpolation, the ten required table entries could all have been found by tagging the appropriate instructions to add the contents of index 1. In this case, every one of the instructions which set up the addresses of the instructions which evaluate the interpolation formula are unnecessary. Altogether, use of index registers saves fifteen steps: ten as just mentioned, one in the loop proper because modification of the index register takes only one step whereas modification of an address takes two,* and

---

* Three in most single address machines since they do not usually have the add to memory instruction; one in a multiple address machine.

four in the initial testing of the range. This is a 35% reduction of memory space, and about the same saving in time. These figures are roughly representative of the savings to be gained by use of index registers in loop writing.

*Example 2. Polynomial Evaluation*
The next problem is to evaluate the expression

$$y = a_0 + a_1 x + a_2 x^2 + \cdots + a_n x^n$$

given only $x$ and the location of $n$ and of the *address* of $a_0$. That is, we know that $x$ is stored in 1000, that $n$ is stored in 1001, and that the *address* of the first coefficient is in 1002 (the coefficients being stored in consecutive locations after the first). This is a bit different from any example we have seen so far, in that we do not know, when we write the program, exactly where the numbers are stored, or how many terms there are in the polynomial. We only know that this information is available in memory. This is leading into the next chapter, but it is also a good illustration of the use of index registers.

Assume that all the numbers in the problem have scaling factors of zero, i.e., they are all fractions. Observe that a simple way to evaluate this expression is to factor it as follows:

$$y = a_0 + x[a_1 + x[a_2 + x[a_3 \cdots x a_n] \cdots]]$$

This means that the evaluation can be set up as a very simple loop, essentially starting from the back and working forward. This is sometimes called *nesting*. It does mean, however, that we have to start the calculation with the last coefficient and test to see when $a_0$ has been added.

The simplest way to satisfy these requirements is as follows: If we want to add $a_0$, we write an instruction:

Add   Loc $a_0$

If we then had $n$ stored in index register 1, and wrote

Add   Loc $a_0$, 1

we would add $a_n$. This may be seen a little more clearly in Table 2. Recall once again that in this problem we do not know what the initial address and $n$ are, only where they are stored.

The following program will compute $y$ and leave it in the accumulator, since a location was not specified for it:

| LOCATION | OPERATION CODE | OPERATION ABBREVIATION | ADDRESS | REMARKS |
|---|---|---|---|---|
| 1200 | 50 | Mem to ind | 1001, 1 | $n$ into index 1 |
| 1201 | 10 | Clear add | 1002 | Location of $a_0$ |
| 1202 | 41 | Store address | 1205 | |
| 1203 | 42 | Load MQ | Loc 0 | Clear MQ |
| 1204 | 16 | Mult | 1000 | $x$ times sum so far |
| 1205 | 11 | Add | [Loc $a_0$], 1 | Add $a_i$ |
| 1206 | 33 | Long right | 10 | Shift for next multiplication |
| 1207 | 55 | Lower ind | 1, 1 | |
| 1208 | 56 | Zero ind jump | 1204, 1 | |
| 1209 | | Continuation; $y$ in accumulator | | |

This program contains an error which is so typical of the pitfalls of loop writing that the author chooses to admit his initial mistake in the hope that the precautions which must be taken in writing loops will be emphasized.

The intention is as discussed in the paragraph previous to the program. Step 1200 puts $n$ into index 1; steps 1201 and 1202 move the address of the first coefficient from 1002 into the instruction where it is needed. Step 1203 simply clears the MQ so that the loop will get started right. The first time through the loop results in merely placing $a_n$ in the MQ. Step 1207 decreases index 1 by 1; 1208 jumps back to 1204 if index 1 is not zero. The second time through the loop multiplies $a_n$ by $x$ and adds $a_{n-1}$ to get $a_{n-1} + a_n x$.

### TABLE 2

| COEFFICIENT | IS STORED IN: |
|---|---|
| $a_0$ | Initial location (whatever it is) |
| $a_1$ | "    "   $+ 1$ |
| $a_2$ | "    "   $+ 2$ |
| $a_3$ | "    "   $+ 3$ |
| . | |
| . | |
| . | |
| $a_n$ | "    "   $+ n$ |

The trouble is in the last time through. As it is set up now, we need to go through the loop a final time with index 1 containing zero, but we never will: as soon as step 1207 reduces it to zero, the jump at 1208 will not be executed! The solution is to observe that all we really want from the indexing is the *sum* of the index register contents and the indicated address. This can be accomplished as was done above, or by writing one less than the address of the initial coefficient and setting the index register to $n + 1$. Then, when the register goes to zero, we will have just added (Loc $a_0 - 1$) $+ 1$.

The program must be modified to make these changes:

| LOCATION | OPERATION CODE | OPERATION ABBREVIATION | ADDRESS | REMARKS |
|---|---|---|---|---|
| 1200 | 10 | Clear add | 1001 | Bring in $n$ |
| 1201 | 11 | Add | Loc 1 | $n + 1$ |
| 1202 | 51 | Acc to ind | 0, 1 | To index 1 |
| 1203 | 10 | Clear add | 1002 | Loc $a_0$ |
| 1204 | 14 | Sub | Loc 1 | Loc $a_0 - 1$ |
| 1205 | 41 | Store address | 1208 | |
| 1206 | 42 | Load MQ | Loc 0 | Clear MQ |
| 1207 | 16 | Mult | 1000 | |
| 1208 | 11 | Add | [Loc $a_0 - 1$], 1 | |
| 1209 | 33 | Long right | 10 | |
| 1210 | 55 | Lower ind | 1, 1 | |
| 1211 | 56 | Zero ind jump | 1207, 1 | |
| 1212 | | Continuation | | |

The program contains no other changes and we will now evaluate the polynomial as required. The notation of the address of instruction 1208 should be clarified. The brackets indicate that the address which is to appear there when the instruction is executed is computed by the program itself. The "Loc $a_0 - 1$" inside the brackets is a note to ourselves as to what the program will put there. When such an instruction is eventually entered into memory, it appears simply as

$$+11 \ 0000 \ 0001$$

without the reminders.

When the instructions are punched on cards or written on tape, it is possible in most systems to write the reminders off to the side. These would be the "remarks" that have appeared in the coding examples. They are usually printed on a listing, even though they are not entered into the machine as part of the instructions. This is one of the functions of the assembly programs discussed in Chapter 14.

*Example 3. Averaging*

A fairly common problem which arises in the reduction of test data is a special sort of averaging. Frequently, say, in a jet engine test, several or even dozens of readings of the same temperature or pressure will be taken. It is often possible that the measuring or recording equipment can fail to get a particular reading but will record some sort of missing-data symbol.

To be specific, suppose we have, in storage locations 350 to 370, up to twenty-one measurements of a compressor inlet temperature. The average is to be placed in 340. Decimal points are on the "middle-of-the-word" basis described in Chapter 4. There is no guarantee that there actually are twenty-one readings. Any missing data are indicated by a zero in the location. If all data are missing, we want to stop the computer, since the following parts of the program cannot operate without some average value for this temperature.

The method is to bring in each reading separately and test whether it is zero. If not zero, one is added to the index register which is counting the number of good readings, and the reading is added to the summation. The readings are brought in starting from the highest, in order to use the Zero index jump instruction, which means we must be careful of the pitfall of the previous example. Location 340, where the average is placed, must of course be cleared. We will use both index registers: the one to count with must be set to zero, the other to modify addresses must be set to 21. Once all the locations have been examined, the sum must be divided by the count in the first index register, unless this is zero. Decimal point on division must be accounted for. The program is:

| LOCATION | OPERATION CODE | OPERATION ABBREVIATION | ADDRESS | REMARKS |
|---|---|---|---|---|
| 1819 | 10 | Clear add | Loc 0 | |
| 1820 | 40 | Store acc | 340 | Clear sum storage |
| 1821 | 40 | Store acc | 1800 | and temporary storage |
| 1822 | 50 | Mem to ind | Loc 0, 1 | |
| 1823 | 50 | Mem to ind | Loc 21, 2 | |
| 1824 | 10 | Clear add | 349, 2 | |
| 1825 | 04 | Acc zero jump | 1828 | Skip if missing data |
| 1826 | 19 | Add to mem | 340 | Form sum |
| 1827 | 54 | Raise ind | 1, 1 | Count one good point |
| 1828 | 55 | Lower ind | 1, 2 | Decrease address-modifying index |
| 1829 | 56 | Zero ind jump | 1824, 2 | Jump back if not all data examined |
| 1830 | 52 | Ind to mem | 1800, 1 | Store count temporarily |
| 1831 | 10 | Clear add | 340 | Bring in sum |
| 1832 | 04 | Zero jump | 1837 | Jump out to halt if no good data |
| 1833 | 33 | Long right | 6 | |
| 1834 | 18 | Divide | 1800 | |

(*Continued on next page*)

| 1835 | 43 | Store MQ | 340 | Average |
| 1836 | 01 | Un jump | 1838 | Jump over halt |
| 1837 | 00 | Halt-jump | 0 | |
| 1838 | Continuation | | | |

A few points will bear discussion. The first five instructions are clear enough. 1800 must be cleared because the contents of index 1 will be stored there temporarily, and the Index to memory instruction affects only the address part. The first time 1824 is executed it will bring in the contents of 370 since index 2 at this point contains 21. If this reading is zero, the jump simply skips over adding this value to the sum, and also skips over adding one to the count of good points which is being built up in index 1. Step 1828 essentially modifies the address of the next data point to be examined. Observe that in this case we do not want to execute the loop with index 2 containing zero. Instruction 1829 jumps back if we have not examined all points. Instruction 1830 moves the count of good points to a temporary location from which it may be called to divide. 1833 checks whether the sum is zero, which would indicate that no good data were found. 1834 shifts to set up the correct decimal point in the quotient, which is obtained and stored in the next two steps. The jump at 1837 skips around the halt so that we do not get a false error indication.

## Exercises

1. Reprogram Exercises 1, 3 through 11, and 13 of Chapter 6, using indexing.

2. Locations 1200, 1208, 1216, etc., up to 1272 contain ten numbers with scaling factors of zero. Write a program, using indexing, to compute the sum of the squares of these numbers and store it in 1307. The sizes of the numbers are such that overflow will not occur in forming the sum.

3. Forty numbers, each with a scaling factor of 2, are stored in 250–289. Using indexing, compute the mean (average) of the numbers. Overflow is possible, so some shifting will be necessary before accumulating the sum. (*Hint:* What is the maximum number of digits in the sum of forty ten-digit numbers?) Then calculate the deviations from the mean, i.e., each number in the list subtracted from the mean, and store these forty numbers in 290–329. Finally, calculate the squares of these deviations and place them in 330–369. (Is it better to calculate the deviations and squares of deviations in two separate loops or to combine both calculations into one loop?)

4. A table of $y$ as a function of $x$ is stored in memory. The $x$'s, all with the same scaling factor, are stored in 101–200. The corresponding $y$'s, all

with the same scaling factor, are stored in 501–600. A given $x$ in 50 is known to be in the range $x_2 < x < x_{99}$. Thus it is always possible to find four $x$'s such that the given $x$ lies between the middle two. Call these four $x$'s $x_0$, $x_1$, $x_2$, and $x_3$, and the corresponding $y$'s $y_0$, $y_1$, $y_2$, and $y_3$. (Note the change in meaning of the subscripts.) Write a loop, using indexing, to locate the four $x$'s which surround the given $x$; having done so, evaluate the formula:

$$y^* = \frac{(x - x_1)(x - x_2)(x - x_3)}{(x_0 - x_1)(x_0 - x_2)(x_0 - x_3)} \cdot y_0 + \frac{(x - x_0)(x - x_2)(x - x_3)}{(x_1 - x_0)(x_1 - x_2)(x_1 - x_3)} \cdot y_1$$
$$+ \frac{(x - x_0)(x - x_1)(x - x_3)}{(x_2 - x_0)(x_2 - x_1)(x_2 - x_3)} \cdot y_2 + \frac{(x - x_0)(x - x_1)(x - x_2)}{(x_3 - x_0)(x_3 - x_1)(x_3 - x_2)} \cdot y_3$$

(Four-point Lagrangian interpolation.)

5. Generalize Exercise 4 to use as many points in the interpolation formula as may be desired. Suppose that location 51 contains an integer $n$ which is the number of points to be used. Write a completely general program to perform an $n$-point Lagrangian interpolation.

6. Sixty-one values, $y_0$ through $y_{60}$, are stored in 100–160. The sequence of numbers 1, 5, 1, 6, 1, 5, 1 is stored in 90–96. Write an indexed program to form the sum

$$z = 3h/10 \, (y_0 + 5y_1 + y_2 + 6y_3 + y_4 + 5y_5 + 2y_6 + 5y_7 + y_8$$
$$+ \, 6y_9 + y_{10} + 5y_{11} + 2y_{12} + \cdots + y_{60})$$

$h$ is stored in 97. Assume overflow will not occur. A fairly simple loop can be written to do this using two index registers, although testing will be a little more complex. (Numerical integration by Weddle's rule.)

7. A table is stored in memory representing the values of a function at the mesh points of a grid:

| $a_{11}$ | $a_{12}$ | $a_{13}$ | $a_{14}$ | $a_{15}$ | $a_{16}$ | $a_{17}$ | $a_{18}$ | $a_{19}$ |
|---|---|---|---|---|---|---|---|---|
| $a_{21}$ | $a_{22}$ | $a_{23}$ | $a_{24}$ | etc. | | | | |
| $a_{31}$ | etc. | | | | | | | |
| $a_{41}$ | | | | | | | | |
| $a_{51}$ | | | | | | | | |
| $a_{61}$ | $a_{62}$ | | | | | | | $a_{69}$ |

The table is stored in "row order" starting at 200, i.e., the first row is in 200–208, the second in 209–217, etc. Write an indexed program to compute the new value of each interior point by taking the average of the four points surrounding it, and place this new value back in the same location. The loop will thus have to compute new values of twenty-eight interior points. As a second, major loop, repeat the entire process until the new values do not differ significantly from the old. A possible criterion of convergence would be to form the sum of the absolute values of the differences between the old and new values, and stop as soon as this sum is less than some tolerance. (Iteration method of solving Laplace's equation.)

# 9 SUBROUTINES

## 9.0 Introduction

Fairly often in the writing of a large program we need a certain group of steps repeated. For instance, there may be a dozen places throughout the program where a square root must be found, or a cosine evaluated, or a group of numbers sorted, or a system of simultaneous equations solved. It is usually not feasible nor desirable to write out the necessary instructions every time the function is needed, and execute the steps right there. The obvious method is to write out the instructions required once, and then arrange to jump to this *subprogram* or *subroutine* each time.

This is done extensively in most applications of modern stored program computers. In certain machines and certain installations it is used very widely; typical programs may use dozens of subroutines. Our problem at this point is how to tell the subroutine to what point in the program to return when it is finished, and in many cases how to tell it what to work on, i.e., the input data. These are respectively the subjects of linkages and calling sequences, discussed in the next two sections.

## 9.1 Linkage Methods

Suppose for the sake of illustration we have a main program stored between 400 and 1000, and a subprogram from 1207 to 1228 which calculates a square root. The number whose square root is to be taken is placed in the MQ before jumping from the main program over to 1207, and the answer is to be in the MQ on return. Suppose the main program does a few operations, places a number in the MQ, and at 413 jumps to 1207 to calculate the square root of the number. How does the subroutine know where to return? Presumably we could make the last instruction of the subroutine read "Unconditional jump 414." Once the square root was computed and placed in the MQ it would jump back to the instruction in the main program just following the original jump.

So far so good. Suppose, further, that another square root is needed at instruction 449. How do we now instruct the subroutine that this time it should jump back to 450? Remember that what we did before was not to give the subroutine any information with which to discover the "return address." Rather we simply wrote in by hand what we knew the return address to be, which now appears to have been a mistake.

The obvious solution is to have the program itself give the appropriate information to the subroutine, i.e., place the correct address in the last jump instruction. There are many ways of doing this; we shall discuss three.

The first consists of simply storing in memory a table of return jump addresses, and storing the right one each time before leaving the main program. In outline form, the program might look like:

| LOCATION | OPERATION CODE | OPERATION ABBREVIATION | ADDRESS |
|---|---|---|---|
| 413 | 10 | Clear add | Loc 416 |
| 414 | 41 | Store address | 1228 |
| 415 | 01 | Un jump | 1207 |
| . | | | |
| . | | | |
| . | | | |
| 449 | 10 | Clear add | Loc 452 |
| 450 | 41 | Store address | 1228 |
| 451 | 01 | Un jump | 1207 |
| . | | | |
| . | | | |
| 517 | 10 | Clear add | Loc 520 |
| 518 | 41 | Store address | 1228 |
| 519 | 01 | Un jump | 1207 |

The table of return addresses, stored at wherever loc 416, etc., are, would as usual have to be stored with the numbers in the address parts. Of course, we have added two instructions in the main program which would in practice mean that the step previously at 449 would be later, etc.

The second method requires no table, takes one less instruction in the main program, but adds two in the subroutine. Suppose, as before, we are ready at the time of the instruction at 413 to compute the square root. We write:

| 413 | 10 | Clear add | 413 |
| 414 | 01 | Un jump | 1207 |

and as the first two instructions of the subroutine:

| 1207 | 11 | Add | Loc 2 |
| 1208 | 41 | Store address | 1228 |
| . | | | |
| . | | | |
| . | | | |
| 1228 | 01 | Un jump | [ ] |

This is a bit tricky. The instruction at 413 has the effect of bringing *itself* into the accumulator, which then contains:

$$+0\ 10\ 0413\ 0000$$

Observe that, when the jump at 414 is executed, the accumulator contains a number which shows exactly where we came from. Over in the subroutine, the first step adds two to the address part of the accumulator, giving 415, which is stored in the address part of 1228. When the subroutine is finished, it finds its last instruction reading "Unconditional jump 415," which is exactly where it should return. This sort of method makes most sense in a single address machine which does not have a special instruction for the purpose; the Univacs and many others do have such an instruction.

The third method uses an index register. Recall that the Set index and jump instruction places the contents of the location counter in the specified index register before the jump is carried out. This is somewhat similar to the second method, except that it takes two fewer instructions and does not disturb the accumulator. The main program and subprogram now look like:

| 413 | 58 | Set ind jump | 1207, 1 |
| . | | | |
| . | | | |
| . | | | |
| 449 | 58 | Set ind jump | 1207, 1 |
| . | | | |
| . | | | |
| . | | | |
| 1207 | | | |
| . | | | |
| . | | | |
| . | | | |
| 1228 | 01 | Un jump | 1, 1 |

The first time, the number 413 is placed by the control circuits in index 1 and control is transferred to 1207. When the subroutine gets to 1228, it jumps to the effective address. This is: one, plus whatever is in index 1; or, $1 + 413 = 414$. The second time, the same instruction results in a return jump to 450. This method has an additional advantage: in writing the subroutine, it is not necessary to know the address of the last instruction of the subroutine.

This is surely about as simple a linkage as can be conceived. Whether the use of index registers for the purpose will grow is not clear.*

## 9.2 Calling Sequences

Very often in using subroutines there is considerable information which must be conveyed to the subprograms. For instance, in a program for solving a set of simultaneous equations, the subroutine must know where the coefficients are stored, how many equations there are, and where the answers are to be placed. In the previous example we placed all the necessary information in the arithmetic registers; here, we clearly have too much information. How can this be solved, without the clumsiness of storing the needed information in the subroutine before jumping from the main program?

For an illustrative problem, suppose we are coding a problem in which the function $\sqrt{x + y^2 + z^3}$ appears many times. Rather than computing the radicand each time, we wish simply to specify to the subroutine where to find $x$, $y$, and $z$. The square root may be left in the accumulator. This represents a fairly typical extension of the subroutine idea. What the main program has to communicate to the subroutine, in this case, are the addresses at which $x$, $y$, and $z$ can be found. The technique is to store these addresses in dummy instructions just following the linkage, with or without indexing. The linkage plus addresses looks like this, assuming that the routine begins at 800:

| | | | |
|---|---|---|---|
| 450 | 10 | Clear add | 450 |
| 451 | 01 | Un jump | 800 |
| 452 | · 00 | Halt-jump | Loc $x$ |
| 453 | 00 | Halt-jump | Loc $y$ |
| 454 | 00 | Halt-jump | Loc $x$ |

---

* In three-address machines the problem is solved by single instructions which specify:

    a. What number to place at the end of the subroutine.

    b. The jump which needs to have the return specified.

    c. Where the subroutine starts.

Various other methods are possible.

The instructions at 450 and 451 are the ordinary unindexed linkage. The "instruction" at 452 is not an instruction at all. It is never executed as an instruction. The Halt and jump does not mean that the program is to halt at this point. The whole function of "instruction" 452 is simply to carry in its address part the address at which $x$ can be found. The operation part has no real function; we have to write something and 00 is as handy as anything else. If we were forced to regard the thing at 452 as an instruction, we would interpret the operation code as Halt and jump, but it does not really mean anything here. Similarly with 453 and 454.

This group of five instructions is designated a *calling sequence*. It has the usual function of telling the subroutine where to return, and it gives any other information required by the particular program as well. In other situations the information required might include such items as the number of places to retain in a summation, what to do in a situation which the subroutine cannot handle, the number of points to be used in a higher order interpolation, etc.

Of course, the subroutine must get the information in the calling sequence out of the main program and into itself. The important things to remember here are: (1) the subroutine at the start has only the information on where the jump instruction was located, and (2) 452, 453, and 454 are not themselves the addresses of $x$, $y$, and $z$ —they are the *addresses of the addresses* of $x$, $y$, and $z$. The subroutine might start:

| LOCATION | OPERATION CODE | OPERATION ABBREVIATION | ADDRESS | REMARKS |
|---|---|---|---|---|
| 800 | 11 | Add | Loc 2 | 452 in acc |
| 801 | 41 | Store address | 808 | |
| 802 | 11 | Add | Loc 1 | 453 in acc |
| 803 | 41 | Store address | 810 | |
| 804 | 11 | Add | Loc 1 | 454 in acc |
| 805 | 41 | Store address | 813 | |
| 806 | 11 | Add | Loc 1 | 455 in acc |
| 807 | 41 | Store address | 840 | Return address |
| 808 | 10 | Clear add | [452] | Address of $x$ in acc |
| 809 | 41 | Store address | 825 | |
| 810 | 10 | Clear add | [453] | Address of $y$ in acc |
| 811 | 41 | Store address | 817 | |
| 812 | 41 | Store address | 818 | |
| 813 | 10 | Clear add | [454] | Address of $z$ in acc |
| 814 | 41 | Store address | 820 | |
| 815 | 41 | Store address | 821 | |
| 816 | 41 | Store address | 823 | |

*(Continued on next page)*

| 817 | 42 | Load MQ | [Loc $y$] | $y$ |
|-----|----|---------|-----------|-----|
| 818 | 17 | Mult round | [Loc $y$] | $y^2$ |
| 819 | 40 | Store acc | 390 | Store $y^2$ temp |
| 820 | 42 | Load MQ | [Loc $z$] | $z$ |
| 821 | 17 | Mult round | [Loc $z$] | $z^2$ |
| 822 | 33 | Long right | 10 | |
| 823 | 17 | Mult round | [Loc $z$] | $z^3$ |
| 824 | 11 | Add | 390 | $z^3 + y^2$ |
| 825 | 11 | Add | [Loc $x$] | $z^3 + y^2 + x$ |
| 826 | | With $x + y^2 + z^3$ in accumulator, usual square root routine may continue | | |

.
.
.

| 840 | 01 | Un jump | [455] |
|-----|----|---------|-------|

This is a bit involved. Instructions at 800–807 have this function: given that in the address part of the accumulator is the address of the first instruction of a calling sequence, and that the second, third, and fourth instructions following contain respectively the addresses of $x$, $y$, $z$; get the addresses of the following three instructions into the program and store the return address. For instance, in our example 801 stores the address of the address of $x$, in 808, etc.

Down at 808, the dummy instruction at 452 is brought into the accumulator; now we have the address of $x$, not $x$ itself. 809 stores this address at 825 so that when we actually need to add $x$, its address will be in the appropriate instruction. Similarly with the addresses of $y$ and $z$, except that in this example these addresses are needed more than once.

This matter of "the address of the address of $x$" is usually confusing at first contact. It is quite important in the writing of subroutines and elsewhere, and is worth the trouble needed to master it.

Using an index register, this program is shortened somewhat but made no simpler in concept. The calling sequence may now consist of:

| 450 | 58 | Set ind jump | 800, 1 |
|-----|----|--------------|--------|
| 451 | 00 | Halt-jump | Loc $x$ |
| 452 | 00 | Halt-jump | Loc $y$ |
| 453 | 00 | Halt-jump | Loc $z$ |

The first eight steps of the subroutine are now unnecessary, as we may replace the instruction at 808 with

|  | 10 | Clear add | 1, 1 |
|--|----|-----------|------|

To the indicated address, 1, will be added the contents of index 1, before executing the instruction. But index 1 contains 450. The effective instruction is then

$$10 \qquad \text{Clear add} \qquad 451$$

which brings in the address of $x$. The instructions at 810, 813, and 840 are replaced by

| 10 | Clear add | 2, 1 |
|----|-----------|------|
| 10 | Clear add | 3, 1 |
| 01 | Un jump   | 4, 1 |

Perhaps it should be pointed out for emphasis why we go to all this trouble. What we have here may be used at *any* point in the main calculation. At 638, we can call for another evaluation of $\sqrt{x + y^2 + z^3}$ simply by writing the calling sequence:

| 638 | 58 | Set ind jump | 800 |
|-----|----|--------------|-----|
| 639 | 00 | Halt-jump    | Loc $x$ |
| 640 | 00 | Halt-jump    | Loc $y$ |
| 641 | 00 | Halt-jump    | Loc $z$ |

The addresses of $x$, $y$, and $z$ would ordinarily be entirely different now. In summary, we may say that we have gained the following advantages:

1. It is not necessary to evaluate the expression $x + y^2 + z^3$, at every point it is needed, before jumping to the square root routine.

2. It is not necessary to write long complicated routines in the main program for telling the subroutine where to look for its data. Both of these reduce the total size of the main program.

The disadvantages are:

1. Considerable bulk has been added to the subroutine.

2. These added (red tape) instructions must be carried out every time, so that we have a method which is longer in time than if the expression were simply evaluated each time as needed.

What this all boils down to is that we have traded some extra machine time for reduced memory requirements and a simpler main program. Such a trade is quite common.

It is worth pointing out, finally, that we might have used a subroutine within a routine. If the regular square root subroutine were already available when this program was written, the routine we developed might have gone only as far as computing $x + y^2 + z^3$, then calling the square root subroutine itself. This is also done fairly frequently.

## 9.3 Subroutine Libraries

Certain operations and functions are required very frequently in scientific computation. In an operating computing center, it is necessary to have subroutines readily available to carry out these functions. A set of these subroutines, in a form such that they may easily be borrowed by any programmer and incorporated into his program, is called a *subroutine library*. The word "library" implies that the subroutines are very carefully written to take a minimum of time and/or space, are *completely* checked out, are simple to put into another program, and are accompanied by a complete write-up. The write-up includes a general description of the subroutines, defines the calling sequence, outlines accuracy, gives error stops, outlines any mathematics involved, specifies limitations, etc.

Such a library of subroutines is an essential part of any computing center. It includes the ordinary transcendental functions: sine, cosine, inverse tangent, logarithm, exponential, square root, and others, depending on the type of work done. It may include routines for the floating decimal method to be described in the next chapter. It includes subroutines for input and output. The exact list depends, again, on the nature of the work done at the installation. It may amount to fifty or more subroutines.

## Exercises

1. Assume that a subroutine to take a square root is located starting at 1050; the number whose square root is to be taken is placed in the MQ, and the square root is placed there by the subroutine. Write a program to evaluate

$$y = \frac{\sqrt{x + a} + \sqrt{x^2 + a}}{a^{3/2}}$$

$x$ is in 200, $a$ in 201; overflow cannot happen. Scale factors are all the same.

2. Suppose that subroutines similar to those in Exercise 1 are available, i.e., the argument goes in the MQ and the function is returned there. The subroutines and their starting addresses are:

| | |
|---|---|
| Square root | 1050 |
| Sine | 1075 |
| Cosine | 1112 |
| Natural logarithm | 1145 |
| Exponential | 1200 |

Write a program to evaluate the following formula:

$$y = \sqrt{a + bx} + \cos x + \ln (1 + e^x)$$

Assume locations for all the constants; assume scaling factors of zero and ignore divide stop possibilities.

3. Using the assumptions of Exercise 2, write a program to evaluate:

$$y = \frac{\sqrt{a + bx} + \tan (2\pi/x) + a^x}{\ln x^8}$$

4. Incorporate the program of Exercise 3 into a loop to evaluate the formula for all values of $x$ between 1.0 and 2.0 in steps of 0.05.

5. Suppose a list of $x$'s in sequential locations in memory are to be substituted into the formula of Exercise 3. The list starts at location $m$ and runs to location $n$, these being specific but arbitrary locations. The resulting $y$'s are to be placed in memory starting at $p$. Write a subroutine to extract the needed information from this calling sequence:

| | | | |
|---|---|---|---|
| _____ | Clear add | _____ | Linkage |
| _____ | Un jump | _____ | First location of subroutine |
| _____ | Halt-jump | $m$ | |
| _____ | Halt-jump | $n$ | |
| _____ | Halt-jump | $p$ | |

(Write with indexing if desired.)

6. Given the calling sequence:

| | | | |
|---|---|---|---|
| _____ | Clear add | _____ | Linkage |
| _____ | Un jump | 800 | Start of routine |
| _____ | Halt-jump | $n$ | |
| _____ | Halt-jump | Loc $x$ | |
| _____ | Halt-jump | Loc root | |

Loc $x$ is the address of a number whose $n$th root is to be placed in Loc root. Write the required subroutine. (Write with indexing if desired.)

7. A list of $n$ numbers starting at location $m$ is to be averaged. Using the computed average, compute the expression

$$y = \sqrt{\frac{\bar{x}^2}{n - 1}}$$

where $\bar{x}$ is the average of the $n$ numbers. Write a loop to do this (indexed if desired) and set up the program as a subroutine, with a calling sequence.

8. Compare total memory space and time requirements, using the following linkage methods:
a. Storing a table of return addresses.
b. Linkage composed of:

| MAIN PROGRAM | | | | SUBROUTINE | |
|---|---|---|---|---|---|
| $a$ | Clear add | $a$ | | | |
| $a + 1$ | Add | loc 3 | $b$ | Store address | $b + k$ |
| $a + 2$ | Un jump | $b$ | . | | |
| | | | . | | |
| | | | . | | |
| | | | $b + k$ | Un jump $[a + 3]$ | |

*c*. Linkage composed of:

| MAIN PROGRAM | | | SUBROUTINE | | |
|---|---|---|---|---|---|
| $a$ | Clear add | $a$ | $b$ | Add loc 2 | |
| $a+1$ | Un jump | $b$ | $b+1$ | Store address | $b+k$ |
| | | | | . | |
| | | | | . | |
| | | | | . | |
| | | | $b+k$ | Un jump $[a+2]$ | |

*d*. Indexing:

| MAIN PROGRAM | | | SUBROUTINE | | |
|---|---|---|---|---|---|
| $a$ | Set ind jump | $b, 1$ | $b+k$ | Un jump | $1, 1$ |

# 10 FLOATING DECIMAL METHODS

## 10.0 Introduction

In Chapter 4 methods were presented for locating the decimal point during a calculation and for planning number sizes and shifting to obtain correct additions and subtractions. It was noted there that the fundamental problem, in scientific work, is maintaining as much significance as possible while dealing with numbers of widely varying size. It was noted that it must always be possible to predict maximum sizes of quantities calculated, and that to maintain significance and avoid divide stop we often wish to predict minimum sizes as well. It was doubtless observed that the whole process is time-consuming and painstaking work. In certain situations the problem is worse than annoying: it is extremely difficult or even impossible to plan adequately. In preparing a program to solve a general system of simultaneous equations, it is next to impossible to predict the sizes of all numbers in the calculation: input, intermediate factors, and output.

Thus from at least two standpoints we desire an automatic scheme for indicating and keeping records on decimal point location. We need some system which will indicate neatly, *to the machine,* where the decimal point of a number in storage is. We need some way, then, of instructing the machine to take account of this representation in doing almost all operations on numbers. Such a system is called *floating decimal* as distinguished from *fixed decimal.*

This chapter describes how numbers are represented in two alternative methods, the use of floating decimal subroutines, built-in floating point operations, and gives several examples of floating point programs.

## 10.1 Floating Point Representation

The basic idea of floating point numbers is often called scientific representation. It consists of writing all numbers as some number between 0.1 and 1.0, times a power of ten. For instance,

| 123.45678 | is written | $0.12345678 \cdot 10^3$ |
| 0.0045678901 | " " | $0.45678901 \cdot 10^{-2}$ |
| $-12340000$ | " " | $-0.12340000 \cdot 10^8$ |

The range of 1.0 to 10.0 is also sometimes used, with an appropriate modification of the power of ten.

The object of floating decimal methods is to store the power of ten, loosely called the exponent, in memory along with the multiplier, called variously the fractional part, the significant part, or the mantissa, from analogy with logarithms. If the exponent, which effectively "locates" the decimal point, is in memory, we can arrange to take this into account on each operation so that the placement of the point after arithmetic operations is automatic. There are two ways of doing this: build it into the electronics of the computer, or write subroutines to handle it. In TYDAC we assume the availability of built-in floating point operations, but we discuss programming the operations also, since many machines do not have automatic floating point operations.

In either case it is necessary to store the two parts of each number. The easiest way is to assign a memory location for each, usually two consecutively numbered locations. The floating point number might be given the first address, which would contain the fractional part; the control section or the subroutine would then always assume that the exponent was in the next location.

Although simple, the above is quite wasteful, since the exponent cannot possibly require more than two or three digits and we have allowed ten.* A somewhat more common approach, for this reason, is to store the fractional part and the exponent in the same location. The exponent is stored in the first or last two digits and the fractional part in the other eight. For reasons which will appear later, storing the exponent in the first two digits is preferred and is assumed here.

A problem has been created, however: both of the two parts may have minus signs. How to store both in a location which was intended to store only one? This is handled by adding fifty to the actual exponent to get a modified exponent, or exponent-plus-fifty. We are assuming that all numbers represented will lie between $10^{-51}$ and $10^{+49}$ in absolute value, so that the exponent-plus-fifty lies between $+0$ and $+99$; i.e., it is always positive. An original number written with a plus or minus sign and a decimal point anywhere has

---

* This remark would not apply to the IBM 702 or 705, since each *character* is individually addressable.

now been reduced to a number with a well-behaved decimal point times a modified power of ten which is always positive. We do not indicate any decimal points in memory, nor, obviously, do we place the ten in memory. A few examples show the transition.

$$123.45678 \; = \; .12345678 \cdot 10^3 \; = \; .12345678 \cdot 10^{53}* \; = \; 5312345678$$

exponent-     ex-     fractional<br>plus-     ponent- part<br>fifty     plus-<br>fifty

$$.0045678901 \; = \; .45678901 \cdot 10^{-2} \; = \; .45678901 \cdot 10^{48}* \; = \; 4845678901$$

$$-1357.9246 \; = \; -.13579246 \cdot 10^4 \; = \; -.13579246 \cdot 10^{54}* \; = \; -5413579246$$

$$-.000024681357 \; = \; -.24681357 \cdot 10^{-4} \; = \; -.24681357 \cdot 10^{46}*$$
$$= \; -4624681357$$

## 10.2 Operations Necessary in Floating Point Arithmetic

Whether by electronic hardware or by subroutines, a very precise procedure must be followed in working with floating point numbers inside the machine. These are important enough, especially to some readers, to be taken up in detail.

### ADDITION-SUBTRACTION

The fundamental consideration here is that the decimal points must "line up" before the addition or subtraction is carried out. Also to be considered is the possibility that the result has more or less than eight significant digits, in which case an adjustment must be made. In each situation we observe that shifting a number to the right must be compensated for by a larger power of ten, i.e., an increased exponent. Thus

$$.12345678 \cdot 10^0 \; = \; .012345678 \cdot 10^1 \; = \; .0012345678 \cdot 10^2 \cdots$$

as can readily be verified. Similarly, shifting to the left requires decreasing the exponent.

This fact, coupled with another, allows us to carry out all the tests and adjustments necessary. The other fact is that the decimal points of two numbers are "lined up" when and only when they have the same exponent. Thus:

$$5212345678 \; = \; 12.345678$$
$$5223456789 \; = \; 23.456789$$

The following steps outline the procedure in addition and subtraction.

1. The two exponents must be tested to see if they are equal. If so, the two fractional parts may be added immediately.

2. If the exponents are not equal, the fractional part associated with the smaller exponent must be shifted to the right a number of places equal to the difference in the exponents. This is rather long. An example may help clarify it:

$$5212345678 = .12345678 \cdot 10^2 = .12345678 \cdot 10^2$$
$$+ \; 5110203043 = .10203043 \cdot 10^1 = .01020304 \cdot 10^2$$
$$\text{Sum} = .13365982 \cdot 10^2$$
$$= 5213365982$$

The second number has been shifted right one place (52 minus 51) to align the decimal points.

3. The two fractional parts must be added, as shifted if necessary. The exponent of the larger number becomes the exponent of the sum, unless modified below.

4. If the sum is zero, the result must be put into the standard form for floating decimal zero. In most systems this is all zeros, both exponent-plus-fifty and fractional part. That is, zero in memory appears as 0000000000, which facilitates later additions.

5. If the sum is not all zeros but does have some leading zeros, which is called the *underflow* condition, the sum must be shifted left until a nonzero digit appears in the first position, and the exponent of the sum reduced by the number of shifts necessary. This is also called *normalizing;* it is essential since we are trying to retain as many significant digits as possible, and because the numbers are assumed to be in this form for division. Illustration:

$$+ \; 51.12345678 = \quad\;\; .12345678 \cdot 10^1$$
$$- \; 51.12334567 = - \; .12334567 \cdot 10^1$$
$$\text{Sum} = \quad\;\; .00011111 \cdot 10^1 = .11111000 \cdot 10^{-2} = 4811111000$$

6. If the sum contains a digit to the left of the point, which is called *overflow*, it must be shifted right one place and the exponent increased by one:

$$5155555555 = \;\; .55555555 \cdot 10^1$$
$$+ \, 5166666666 = \;\; .66666666 \cdot 10^1$$
$$\text{Sum} = \overline{1.22222221 \cdot 10^1} = .12222222 \cdot 10^2 = 5212222222$$

7. In all cases great care must be exercised in rounding at the right time. As an illustration of what can happen:

$$5099998888 = 0.99998888 \cdot 10^0$$
$$+ 4611116789 = 0.000011116789 \cdot 10^0$$
$$\text{Sum} = 0.999999996789 \cdot 10^0$$

If we now test for the overflow condition we will conclude that it has not happened. However, if we round the sum to eight digits by adding five in the ninth position we get:

$$0.999999996\ 589$$
$$+ 5$$
$$1.000000001\ 789$$

Later operations would not anticipate this condition and would give erroneous results. The solution, in this case, is to round before testing for overflow, but this may not fit in too well with underflow testing. Careful planning is necessary, obviously.

8. Before and after these steps, the exponent and fractional part must be either separated or packed back into one word.

## MULTIPLICATION

Here the procedure is simpler, since there is no necessity to line up decimal points before, overflow is not possible, and only one position of underflow is possible. The exponent of the product is based on the law of exponents that $10^a \cdot 10^b = 10^{(a+b)}$. The only preliminary adjustment is based on the fact that we are dealing with an exponent-plus-fifty. When two such exponents are added, fifty must be subtracted from the sum to correct it. The procedure is:

1. Multiply the two fractional parts. The product will contain either fifteen or sixteen digits, if each factor was normalized.

2. Add the two exponents and subtract fifty. If the product contains sixteen digits, round to eight and store. No change is needed in the exponent as computed.

3. If the product contains fifteen digits, *try rounding before shifting to see if this gives sixteen.* If not, shift left one place, round, and store. Decrease the exponent by one before storing it.

*Example*

$$(5112345678)(5345678901)$$
$$\text{Fractional part} = .0563937003139878$$
$$\text{Exponent} = (51 + 53 - 50) = 54, \text{ uncorrected}$$

Rounding in position nine (from the decimal point) does not cause carry into the first position, so we round in the tenth, shift left one, and decrease the exponent by one to give 5356393700.

## DIVISION

This is about the same as multiplication, except that divide stop must be considered and the exponents are subtracted according to $10^a/10^b = 10^{(a-b)}$.

Since the fractional parts are always assumed to be in normalized form, i.e., with no leading zeros, the divisor and dividend will always have the same number of digits. But the fractional part of the divisor could still be smaller than the fractional part of the dividend, which would give divide stop. The simplest solution is always to shift the dividend one place to the right before dividing, and take account of this in correcting the exponent of the quotient. The division procedure is as follows.

1. The fractional part of the dividend is brought into the accumulator and shifted one place to the right before division by the fractional part of the divisor. The quotient will contain either nine or ten significant digits in the MQ.

2. The uncorrected exponent is the exponent of the dividend, minus the exponent of the divisor, plus fifty.

3. If the quotient contains nine digits, it is rounded to eight and no correction made in the exponent.

4. If the quotient contains ten digits, it is rounded to eight, and one added to the uncorrected exponent.

It is possible on any operation to get a result which lies outside the allowable range, i.e., it may be smaller in absolute value than $10^{-51}$ or larger than $10^{+49}$; e.g., division of $10^{-20}$ by $10^{+40}$, addition of $.99999999 \cdot 10^{49}$ to itself, or multiplication of two very large numbers. Whereas in normal arithmetic operations this will be rare, it may happen occasionally as a result of errors in coding or failure to load data as required. Some provision must be made for these situations.

Usually, floating point machines or subroutines are designed to stop if an exponent exceeds the maximum. This generally means a mistake anyway, but even if the result might be anticipated, which is unlikely, we must stop. There is no way of getting the result into one word, since the exponent would require three digits and we have allowed space for only two. In the case of results which are too small, the problem is that even with fifty added, the exponent would be negative and, of course, we cannot store the minus sign. In some systems the machine is stopped as above. In others it is reasoned that this may normally result fairly often, as in division of zero by any number larger than one, and rather than stopping, the result is put into the form of a floating zero and the program continues.

This is a survey of the operations which must be performed in any floating point arithmetic system. If the machine being used has built-in floating point arithmetic, then all of these operations and contingencies must be provided for in the arithmetic section, which clearly adds considerable complexity. This is a case in point as regards the choice between extra work and cost for the designer or simplicity for the programmer. If the machine under consideration does not have built-in floating point, then these operations must all be coded into subroutines, which are long enough to slow the machine operation down by a factor of perhaps 20 or more over the speed of fixed point operation.

## 10.3 TYDAC Floating Point Operations

Writing the arithmetic sections of codes for a built-in floating point machine is simplicity itself. About the only precaution required is to be sure all the data to be operated on are in floating point form, which is a subject of input-output methods discussed in the next chapter. It is important to note that floating point arithmetic applies only to data. The "logical" operations associated with address modification and most loop-testing and counting must still be done in fixed point. This is because instructions are not in floating point form, and because we do not wish to view address modification from the standpoint of overflow and underflow, etc.; also because we want top speed on red tape instructions.

The following illustration makes use of the four floating point operations described in the summary of TYDAC instructions in Appendix 1.

$$y = e^{-x^2} \sin cx$$

for all $x$ between $-.99$ and $+.99$ in steps of 0.01. The number $-.99$ is in 400, $c$ is in 401, 0.01 is in 402, 1.00 is in 403. The $x$'s should be stored in 500–698; the corresponding $y$'s in 700–898. A subroutine to calculate the exponential of a number in the accumulator and return the result to the accumulator starts in 1600; a similar sine routine starts in 1700. In both cases, the instruction following the linkage is where the subroutine returns if it cannot calculate the function because the argument is too large. Index 1 is used to call both subroutines.

A flow chart for the problem might be as illustrated in Figure 1.

It may be observed that floating point operations add no particular complexity to programming, and completely release the programmer from the decimal point problem. Thus there are fewer steps, and much less possibility of error.

| LOCATION | OPERATION CODE | OPERATION ABBREVIATION | ADDRESS | REMARKS |
|---|---|---|---|---|
| 410 | 10 | Clear add | 400 | $-.99$ |
| 411 | 40 | Store acc | 405 | $x$ storage |
| 412 | 50 | Mem to ind | Loc 0, 2 | |
| 413 | 42 | Load MQ | 405 | |
| 414 | 72 | Fl mult | 405 | $x$ squared |
| 415 | 58 | Set ind jump | 1600, 1 | Take exponential |
| 416 | 00 | Halt-jump | 0 | Error return |
| 417 | 40 | Store acc | 406 | Temporary |
| 418 | 42 | Load MQ | 401 | |
| 419 | 72 | Fl mult | 405 | $cx$ |
| 420 | 58 | Set ind jump | 1700, 1 | Sin $cx$ |
| 421 | 00 | Halt-jump | 0 | |
| 422 | 73 | Fl div | 406 | $1/e^{x^2} = e^{-x^2}$ |
| 423 | 43 | Store MQ | 700, 2 | Store $y$ |
| 424 | 54 | Raise ind | 1, 2 | Up index 2 |
| 425 | 10 | Clear add | 405 | |
| 426 | 40 | Store acc | 499, 2 | Store $x$ |
| 427 | 70 | Fl add | 402 | Add 0.01 to $x$ |
| 428 | 40 | Store acc | 405 | |
| 429 | 14 | Sub | 403 | Loop test |
| 430 | 04 | Acc zero jump | 432 | |
| 431 | 01 | Un jump | 413 | |
| 432 | Continuation | | | |

Note that in some cases (instruction at 429) it is permissible to add or subtract two floating point numbers using ordinary fixed point operations. This happens if all we wish to do in an addition or subtraction is compare the size of two numbers. If the exponent is written as the first two digits of the number in memory, then an ordinary fixed point operation will give a result which has the correct sign of the difference, although the magnitude of the difference will be all wrong. There is point in doing this where built-in floating point is not available, since the fixed operation may be some twenty or thirty times faster than the programmed floating point. And this is, of course, the reason why it is preferable to write the exponent as the first two digits rather than the last two.

## 10.4 Floating Point Subroutines

Floating point subroutines may be used in several ways. The differences resolve around how the subroutines are called. Possibly the most obvious way is to specify two operand locations and a result location in a calling sequence. This requires no conventions with regard to the arithmetic registers, but it does require considerable memory space. Four or five instructions (in a single address machine) are used up getting just one floating point addition or division. It would seem reasonable to assume that at least one of these factors is in the MQ when we jump to the subroutine, and that the result is placed in the accumulator. With such an assumption it is possible to reduce the calling sequence to just one instruction besides the linkage.

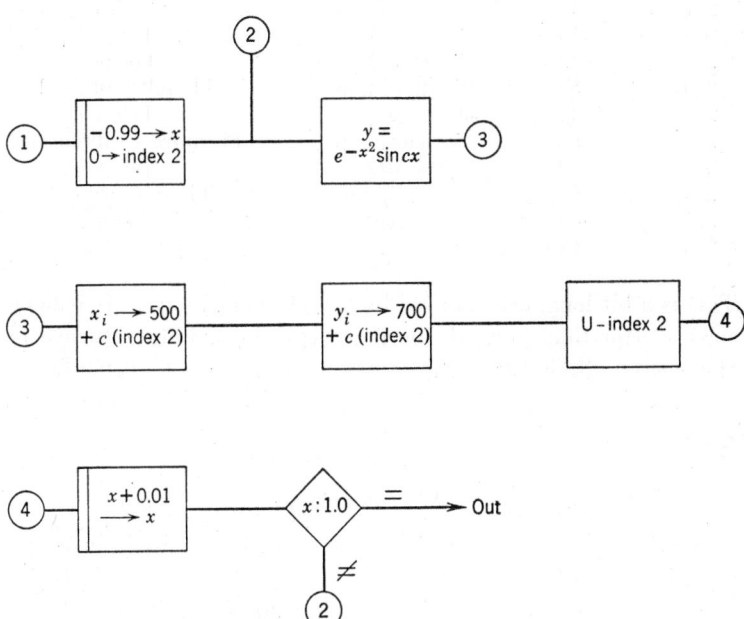

The symbol "$c(\text{index } 2)$" means "the contents of index 2."

Figure 1

In a machine with index registers or the equivalent of the set index jump instruction, an even simpler arrangement is possible. For the operations $a + b$, $a - b$, $a \cdot b$, $a/b$, $a$ is always assumed to be in the accumulator, $b$ is in the MQ, and the result is always placed in the accumulator. It is possible then to write simple sets of calling sequences. Suppose, for instance, we have to evaluate the formula

$$y = \frac{mx - n}{q + x^3}$$

Under these assumptions, the program could read:

| LOCATION | OPERATION CODE | OPERATION ABBREVIATION | ADDRESS |
|---|---|---|---|
| 200 | 10 | Clear add | Loc $x$ |
| 201 | 42 | Load MQ | Loc $x$ |
| 202 | 58 | Set ind jump | Fl mult routine, 1 |
| 203 | 42 | Load MQ | Loc $x$ |
| 204 | 58 | Set ind jump | Fl mult routine, 1 |
| 205 | 42 | Load MQ | Loc $q$ |
| 206 | 58 | Set ind jump | Fl add routine, 1 |
| 207 | 40 | Store acc | Temp |
| 208 | 10 | Clear add | Loc $x$ |
| 209 | 42 | Load MQ | Loc $m$ |
| 210 | 58 | Set ind jump | Fl mult routine, 1 |
| 211 | 42 | Load MQ | Loc $n$ |
| 212 | 58 | Set ind jump | Fl subtract subroutine, 1 |
| 213 | 42 | Load MQ | Temp |
| 214 | 58 | Set ind jump | Fl div routine, 1 |
| 215 | 40 | Store acc | Loc $y$ |
| 216 |  | Continuation |  |

This is a bit long, necessitated by the frequent jumps. It is nevertheless shorter than it would be if a five-word calling sequence had to be written each time. The way which is most economical of main program steps, although not of total time, is an interpretive system as discussed in Chapter 15.

## 10.5 Summary

A floating decimal system is expensive, whether built in or programmed as subroutines. If it is built in, it adds perhaps 10% to the cost of design and construction and adds slightly to the time required to execute a program (since built-in floating operations take slightly longer in most machines than fixed operations). If subroutines are used, they slow the machine down by a factor of 10 to 40 over fixed point speeds. In spite of these costs, floating point methods are used extensively. As we noted before, some problems cannot be done at all otherwise, and most others are greatly simplified.

There is a precaution which should be noted, however. We tend, in presenting the answers to problems run in floating point, to print all eight or ten or thirteen "significant" digits. Sometimes the unwary computer user blithely assumes that all the digits so presented really are significant, without any consideration of either the reliability of the numbers that went into the program or the accuracy of the numerical procedure used in the solution. Suppose, for example, that this calculation occurs:

$$(12345.678 - 12345.567)(9.8765432) = 1.0962963$$

Clearly, this product is not good to eight digits as shown, since the subtraction lost five digits. This is no fault of floating decimal, but with eight digits always printed out, it is easy to overlook the loss of significance. There is less temptation to do this with fixed point answers, possibly because it is usually so simple to throw out non-significant digits in printing. This temptation has led some in the field to advocate using floating point arithmetic only on problems which absolutely cannot be done otherwise, such as some matrix work. This is a healthy reminder, but probably does not represent a trend. Very likely, most future scientific computers will have built-in floating point, at least as an optional feature.

## Exercises

1. Rewrite any of the exercises of Chapters 6 and 8, using built-in floating point and again using subroutines.

2. Write floating point subroutines for all the arithmetic operations. Use the assumptions of Section 10.4.

# 11 INPUT-OUTPUT METHODS

## 11.0 Introduction

The function of getting numbers and instructions in and out of memory has been deferred to this point because it involves techniques which are just now available to the reader. It is perhaps difficult to realize that the part of the machine with which we first have contact on running a problem should require quite this much background to lead to a thorough discussion. This is necessary, however, because input-output programming makes extensive use of address modification, loops, and subroutines—which we have just now covered. Also, some of the discussions relative to planning the storage location and output format would not have made much sense earlier in the book.

In this chapter we will discuss four topics: memory layout, output format, actual machine instructions, and typical subroutines.

## 11.1 Memory Layout

It is important in most problems of any size to plan ahead on several matters. Block diagramming or flow charting as discussed in Chapter 7 represents one form of such planning. Another which can be critical in a problem which is almost too big for memory (and is often very helpful on *any* problem) is planning memory locations. By this is meant: (1) to assign blocks of memory to different functions, such as main program, all subroutines, input, intermediate storage, and output; (2) to keep a very careful record of all data locations. It is necessary to have this done before arranging the input so that we know where to load the data.

Part of this job must be done before a program is written, part during the writing. At this point, not having yet reached Chapter 14 and relative programming methods, we are faced at the very outset of a problem with several questions. Where do we write the first instructions? In the examples in the text so far, we have picked locations at random, mainly to emphasize the point that the data and instructions can be anywhere in memory. But if we anticipate that a program will have about 1200 instructions and 800 data words, and we have a 2000-word memory, it pays not to waste any space by allowing gaps between sections of the program. There is no absolutely certain way to avoid this without relative programming, because there are continual references in any large program to other parts of

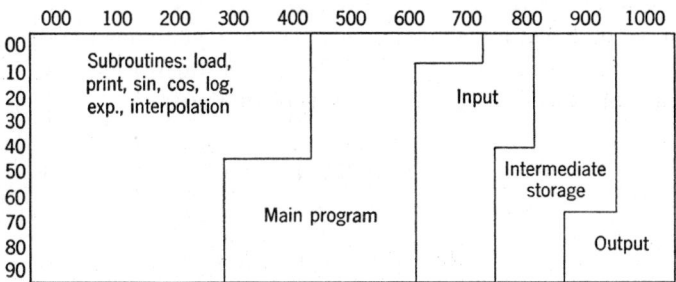

Figure 1. Memory allocation chart.

the same program—parts which are often not yet written. The addresses which define these cross references, however, can be left blank and filled in later.

A possible procedure for deciding what goes where is:

1. Scan the program to decide which of the "library"-type subroutines will be needed. Add up all the memory space required and allocate this much, say at the low-numbered end of memory.

2. Start writing the program at whatever location step 1 indicates will be available.

3. Assign a block of storage to input, of a size which is estimated to be right. If the space allowed turns out to be excessive, the extra space can be assigned elsewhere in storage with about the only loss being the esthetic one of having split up a logical unit of memory into two parts.

4. Similarly, assign blocks of memory to intermediate storage and output.

5. If it turns out in writing the main program that a data storage block is in the way, simply write a jump, at the appropriate point, to a region which is still free.

This is, just as it sounds, a patience-trying procedure. It is *absolutely* necessary only on the type of problem which can just barely be done on the particular computer of interest. On most problems, where there is not much question of feasibility, it is still important, but is much simpler because wasting space between regions does not hurt anything. And finally, to say it for the third time, this is precisely one of the major reasons for relative programming.

The chart of memory locations might look something like Figure 1. Assuming for a moment that we use only 1000 words of storage, this chart says that locations 000 to about 450 are taken up with library programs, 450 to 710 with the main program, etc. (The relative sizes are not intended to be representative.)

The second feature of planning memory layout mentioned above is to keep a careful record of where all the quantities used in the program are located. Table 1 is a typical chart.

### TABLE 1

#### INPUT

| Location | Quantity |
|----------|----------|
| 708 | 0 |
| 709 | 1 |
| 710 | 2 |
| 711 | $\pi$ |
| 712 | $\pi/2$ |
| 713 | 12 |
| 714 | 3600 |
| 715 | 0.048 |
| 716 | 0.5 |
| 717 | 60 |
| 718 | 53.33 |
| 719 | $Mp$ |
| 720 | $T_2$ |
| 721 | $P_2$ |
| 722 | $\%N$ |
| 723 | $x_1$ |
| 724 | $x_2$ |
| 725 | $x_3$ |
| 726 | $x_4$ |
| 727 | $x_5$ |
| 728 | $x_6$ |
| 729 | $y_1$ |
| 730 | $y_2$ |
| 731 | $y_3$ |
| 732 | $y_4$ |
| 733 | $y_5$ |
| 734 | $y_6$ |
| Etc. | |

This is merely an offhand illustration of what might be the input for some particular problem; every problem would be different. Decimal points have been ignored so far; this is a function of the intended use for the input and the particular loading program used. This question is taken up in Section 11.4.

Possibly a word of caution is needed about the use of tables of input like Table 1. These are often made out during the course of programming, the programmer writing down a constant and its location as each number is needed. (The loading program and the cards or tape necessary to get the numbers actually into storage are figured out later.) Sometimes there is a strong temptation to use a number in two different ways. Suppose, for instance, that in a loop iterative procedure, a new guess is calculated each time through the loop by adding one-half of the difference between two guesses to the latest guess. The 0.5 at 716 was originally intended for this purpose. Suppose that later in the program the constant 0.5 is needed for other purposes, and since a convenient 0.5 is already at 716, it is used. Now the plot thickens. At some time during checkout of the program it is discovered that the iteration procedure does not work when the new guess is calculated as described, so we try taking one-twentieth of the difference instead of one-half. The simplest way to make the change is obviously to change the 0.5 at 716, which perhaps can be done by changing just one punched card. Of course, all the other places that 0.5 was used are now in error.

This example leads us to suggest labeling each constant, on the planning sheet, to indicate its purpose if that is not obvious. Table 1 then might appear as in Table 2.

The notes are references to the assumed program. In practice, the different types of input would be separated. For instance, there might be a region for the universal constants 0, 1, 2, 3, in floating point, another for the same in fixed point as address modifiers, another for constants which are peculiar to the particular program, such as the 3600, 0.048, 53.33, etc., in Table 2, and another for such numbers as the ones called flight conditions, which specify the particular case being calculated and normally change from case to case.

## 11.2 Output Format Planning

When cards or tape are being read into memory, the only requirement is that the rules governing the input medium and the subroutine in question be met. It makes no great difference what the cards *look* like, as long as the information gets into memory in convenient form. With output, however, we are concerned with the ultimate reader, who may be an engineer or physicist or auditor. The output scheme must not only satisfy the peculiarities of the machine and the subroutine being used but must also produce an easily readable report.

### TABLE 2

INPUT

| Location | Quantity | |
|---|---|---|
| 708 | 0 | ⎫ |
| 709 | 1 | ⎪ |
| 710 | 2 | ⎬ Constants used in all parts of program |
| 711 | $\pi$ | ⎪ |
| 712 | $\pi/2$ | ⎪ |
| 713 | 12 | ⎭ |
| 714 | 3600 | Seconds per hour |
| 715 | 0.048 | Equation 1.8 |
| 716 | 0.5 | Iteration constant, equation 1.10 |
| 717 | 60 | Seconds per minute |
| 718 | 53.33 | Gas constant |
| 719 | $Mp$ | ⎫ |
| 720 | $T_2$ | ⎬ Flight conditions |
| 721 | $P_2$ | ⎪ |
| 722 | $\%N$ | ⎭ |
| 723 | $x_1$ | ⎫ |
| 724 | $x_2$ | ⎪ |
| 725 | $x_3$ | ⎪ |
| 726 | $x_4$ | ⎪ |
| 727 | $x_5$ | ⎪ |
| 728 | $x_6$ | ⎬ Curve fit, gamma vs. temperature |
| 729 | $y_1$ | ⎪ |
| 730 | $y_2$ | ⎪ |
| 731 | $y_3$ | ⎪ |
| 732 | $y_4$ | ⎪ |
| 733 | $y_5$ | ⎪ |
| 734 | $y_6$ | ⎭ |
| 735 | 0.5 | Universal constant, all places |
| 736 | 0.5 | Program constant, equation 3.17 |

The usual device is called a *layout chart*. It has a space for each digit or character position which can be printed, punched, or typed. On this chart we can lay out the alphabetical headings, if any, the number of digits in each number, the line identification, if there is one, and the location of all decimal points, plus and minus and dollar signs, etc. This may be done for each line if the lines are different, or once for the entire output if a standard format is used, as, for instance, in a floating point system which may be the standard for all results. Samples of this are shown in reduced form in Figure 2.

The charts are used in planning either printer board wiring or the

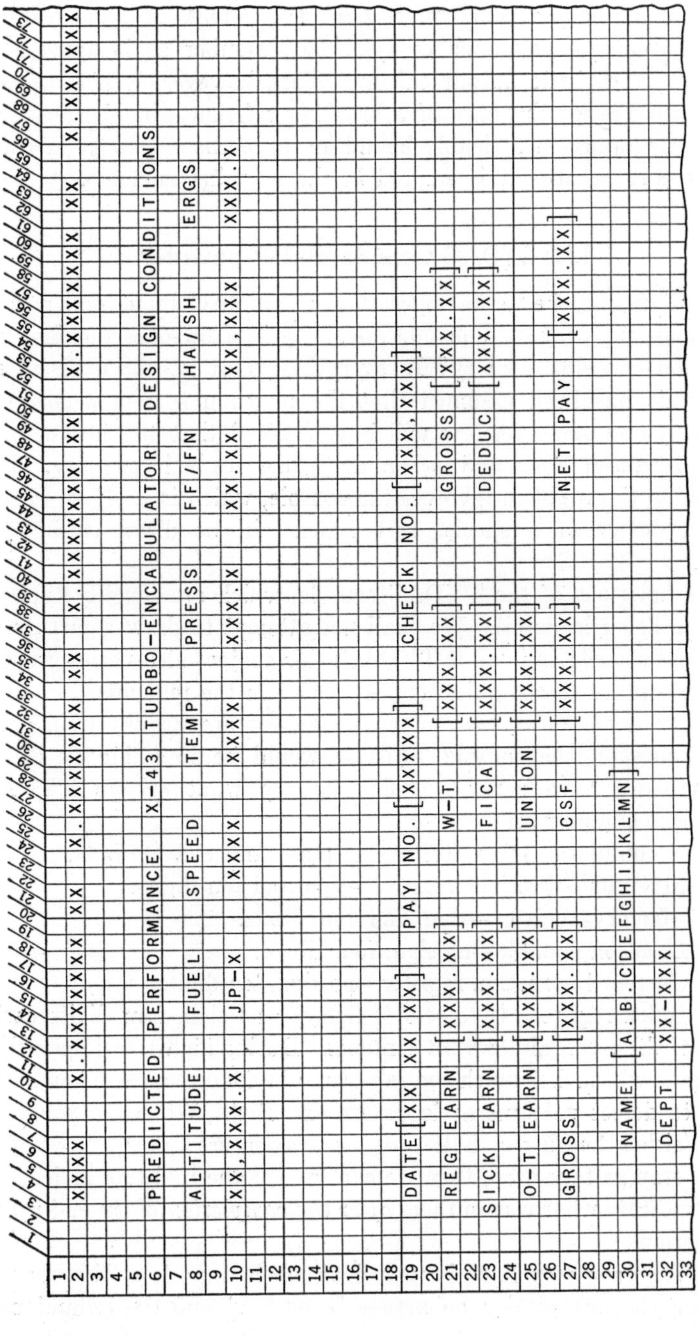

Figure 2. Sample of output planning chart. (Form courtesy Remington Rand Univac Division, Sperry Rand Corporation.)

programming of the output. This is given considerable attention in the manuals on individual machines. In TYDAC and the text we shall be content to punch or type each number as it appears in memory, with little output editing. This, however, is not because the subject is worthy only of a brushing reference, but because the subject is almost inextricably bound up in details of particular computers, and because it is treated in the machine manuals.

## 11.3 TYDAC Console and Typewriter

In discussing the actual operation of TYDAC input and output functions, the primary question obviously is, How does the first instruction get into memory? In everything that has been discussed so far, it has been assumed that the program somehow got into memory, and some readers will have noticed that the instructions which read and punch and type must themselves be in memory. The answer to the problem involves the console, which is itself an input-output device of a special sort which will be discussed at this point.

The functions of the TYDAC console, which are roughly typical, may be listed in detail. We shall not attempt to draw a picture of a typical console and call it TYDAC; this subject also varies greatly from computer to computer and is treated in the manuals.

The contents of several internal registers are displayed in neon glow tubes on the console. (These would be in a binary coded decimal—we have never specified exactly what system TYDAC uses. See Chapter 3.)

1. Accumulator—sign (off means plus) and eleven digits.
2. Multiplier-Quotient register—sign and ten digits.
3. Memory register—sign and ten digits.
4. Location counter—no sign, four digits.
5. Current instruction register—no sign, ten digits.
6. Index registers (two sets of lights)—no sign, four digits each.

All of these contain *current* contents. During high-speed operation the lights will flicker much too rapidly to be followed, except in some cases to detect patterns as loops are executed. When the program stops, either because a halt order is encountered or because of a divide stop or tape stop, then we can inspect the registers at leisure. They indicate what was in them *after the completion* of the indicated instruction.

7. The *tape stop* light is turned on when there is a discrepancy between the information on a tape being read and the redundancy

check on the tape. See Chapter 12. It is turned off by the reset button.

8. The *program stop* light is turned on when the control circuits execute a Halt and jump instruction.

9. The *divide stop* light is turned on when a division is attempted with a divisor which is not larger than the dividend. It is turned off by the reset button.

10. The *automatic* light is on when the machine is in its automatic mode of operation and is actually executing the instructions in the program. It goes off if the automatic-manual switch is placed on manual, the machine stops because of the program, the stop key is pressed, or the reset button has been pushed and nothing yet loaded.

11. When the *automatic-manual switch* is on automatic, pressing the *start* button will cause the machine to execute the next instruction. Placing the automatic-manual switch on manual stops the program, if it has been running, after the current instruction, unless an input or output operation is in process in which case the machine stops after completion of the input-output function.

12. The *single step* key allows the programmer to observe the operation of his program one step at a time. If the automatic-manual switch is on manual, pressing the single step key causes execution of one instruction. If the switch is on automatic, the single step key has no effect.

13. Ten switches are available which may in effect be interrogated by the program through the Switch-jump instruction. The switches are on if down. Any number of switches may be down at once.

14. The *break point switch* is rotary, with ten positions numbered 0 through 9. It can, of course, be set to only one position at a time. Its function is described in the summary of TYDAC instructions.

15. The eleven *input switches*—one sign switch and ten rotary digit switches—may be used to enter a number or instruction into the MQ, or to carry out an instruction. Any number or instruction may be set into the switches. If the *enter MQ* key is then pressed, the number on the switches replaces the contents of the MQ. If the *execute console instruction key* is pressed, the instruction in the switches will be executed just as though it were in memory. A number can be entered into memory by: (1) entering it into the MQ, then (2) executing from the switches the instruction Store MQ ———, with the appropriate address.

16. Pressing the *load card* button causes a card to be read, if one is in the card reader, into locations 0–7. The first ten digits are read into 0, the next ten into 1, etc. After the card is in memory, a

jump to 0 is automatically executed. The program on the first card ordinarily is a program to load the following cards. See page 145.

17. Pressing the *load typewriter* button causes eight words to be entered from the typewriter into locations 0–7, and a jump to 0 to be executed. If the *tape* button on the typewriter is depressed, these will be read from the attached paper tape; if not, the computer will wait for the operator to type them in manually. If fewer than eight words are to be typed in, the *carriage return* key may be pressed after typing in a word. Remember that this operation applies only after pressing the *load typewriter* button; it would probably be fairly unusual to manually type in the first words of a program this way. As described later in this chapter, it is possible to call for words from the typewriter by an instruction in the stored program.

18. Pressing the *load tape* button causes eight words to be loaded from magnetic tape 1 into locations 0–7, and a jump to 0 to be executed. This can be used, as with load card and load typewriter, to enter a self-loading program into memory which in turn loads further records.

19. The *reset* button clears all the registers to zero and turns off the divide stop, tape stop, and program stop lights, if they have been on.

20. The *reset and clear* button performs the above function, as well as setting all memory locations to +0.

21. Pressing the *display* button causes the word located at the address set into the address part of the input switches to be displayed in the memory register light.

22. Pressing the *stop* key causes the program to stop after completion of the current instruction.

The typewriters used on different computers vary considerably. In general, it is possible to type one word at a time into a memory location which may be specified at the typewriter keyboard. Typewriters are ordinarily used with computers which are able to store alphabetic information in memory, either one character in each digit position or using two digit positions to represent each character. Computers intended primarily for scientific work are usually not directly alphabetic and do not have typewriters, but they may be made to store alphabetic information for printing headings or as codes to control the program. This is done by some storage technique which depends strongly on the particular machine and the form of representation of alphabetic characters. The largest computers have specially built typewriters. Several machines use the Flexowriter, built by the Commercial Controls Corporation.

## 11.4 TYDAC Input and Output Instructions

Input and output in TYDAC move basically in blocks of eight words.* The basic scheme is that an input or output unit is specified by a Select instruction. The Select instruction does not transfer any information; it simply establishes the circuits and causes the mechanical parts to begin to move. The eight-word block is actually moved by a Read or Write instruction which ordinarily immediately follows the Select. A new Select instruction must be given for each block, but if a Select follows within a specified time interval after the preceding Select, the time that is necessary to start the mechanical parts moving will be saved.

The address of a Select instruction performs a special function, unlike anything we have seen so far. The address specifies *which* input or output device is to be used. The table of addresses is:

| ADDRESS | DEVICE |
|---------|-------------|
| 1 | Reader |
| 2 | Punch |
| 3 | Typewriter |
| 11 | Tape unit 1 |
| 12 | Tape unit 2 |
| 13 | Tape unit 3 |
| 14 | Tape unit 4 |

The address of a Read or Write instruction specifies the *first* of the eight words, the others being in sequence after that. Thus all we need to do to read a card into 1100–1107, for instance, is to write:

$$60 \quad \text{Select} \quad 1$$
$$61 \quad \text{Read} \quad 1100$$

We should discuss the format of the information on the card, which is assumed to be a standard eighty-column IBM card, as shown in Figure 3. The eight numbers on the card would be punched in columns 1–10, 11–20, 21–30, etc., up to 71–80. The punching of plus and minus signs varies in practice; a typical scheme might be to punch an "X" (first row above zero) to signify minus, and a "Y" (second row above zero, on top row of card) to signify plus. One or the other would be punched over the first or last digit of the

---

* In Univac I and II, a tape block is sixty words. In the ELECOM 120, fifty. In the IBM 701 and 704, the basic unit is one binary number, and all other transfers have to be built up, which is complicated library programming. The IBM 702 and 705 are variable word and variable record length machines.

number. For purposes of discussion we shall assume that in TYDAC the sign is punched over the last or low-order digit of each number. In circuits in the card reader, this is detected and stored in the sign position of the words in memory.

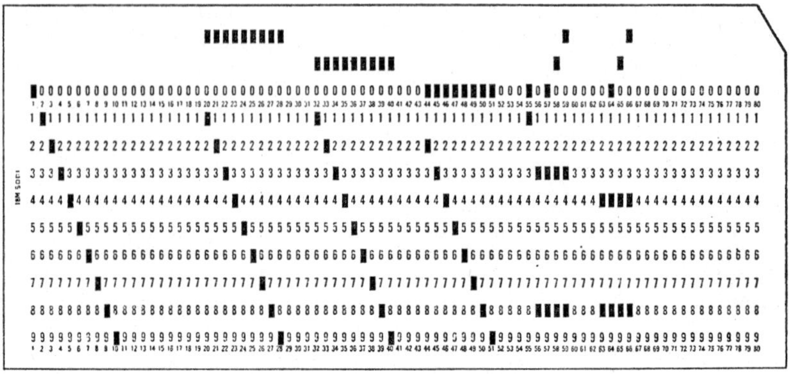

Figure 3. Sample of eighty-column card. (Courtesy International Business Machines Corporation.)

Note that there is a testing scheme built into the Read instruction. The description states that normally the first instruction following a Read instruction is skipped. It will *not* be skipped if:

1. There are no more cards in the card reader, or
2. Blank tape is found in the typewriter tape reader, or
3. A tape mark is found on a magnetic tape (see Chapter 12).

This means that we can set up an otherwise untested loop to read cards indefinitely; when the last card has been read, giving another Select and Read will cause the following instruction *not* to be skipped. We can, of course, arrange to have an Unconditional jump just following the Read.

For an illustration of the type of program which may be written, take the following situation. Suppose we have a deck of cards to be loaded into memory. The eight words on the first card will be loaded into 0–7 by pushing the load card button. The second card is to be loaded into 8–15, the third into 16–23, etc. After the last card is read, a jump to 8 should be executed.

At this point we are looking at the problem "from the outside," so to speak, where up until now we have always assumed that a program had somehow gotten into memory by the time it was to be executed. In our situation here, we are walking up to a machine which is completely blank. We must somehow get the first card in, which must have on it a program which will load the remaining cards. It should be pointed out that the proposed problem is not typical of how cards are loaded. This will be taken up in Section 11.5 on typical input-output subroutines.

The program on the first card could be:

| LOCATION | OPERATION CODE | OPERATION ABBREVIATION | ADDRESS | REMARKS |
|---|---|---|---|---|
| 0 | 60 | Select | 1 | Prepare to read a card |
| 1 | 61 | Read | 8 | |
| 2 | 01 | Un jump | 8 | |
| 3 | 10 | Clear add | 6 | 8 in address part |
| 4 | 19 | Add to mem | 1 | Modify address |
| 5 | 01 | Un jump | 0 | |
| 6 | 00 | Halt-jump | 8 | Instructional constant |

The word at 2 is the one following read, and will be skipped as long as there are cards in the reader when the instruction is called for. When all the cards have been read, the jump to 8 will be executed as required. The instruction at 3 brings an 8 into the address part of the accumulator; the "instruction" at 6 is there simply to provide the constant 8. Note that the program would still fit into eight words if TYDAC did not have the Add to memory instruction. With indexing, the program would be:

| LOCATION | OPERATION CODE | OPERATION ABBREVIATION | ADDRESS | REMARKS |
|---|---|---|---|---|
| 0 | 50 | Mem to ind | 0, 1 | Loads index 1 with 0 |
| 1 | 60 | Select | 1 | |
| 2 | 61 | Read | 8, 1 | |
| 3 | 01 | Un jump | 8 | |
| 4 | 54 | Raise ind | 8, 1 | |
| 5 | 01 | Un jump | 1 | |
| 6 | | | | |
| 7 | | | | |

In this case, indexing saves only the instructional constant. Even this depends on using the instruction at 0 as the source of a 0 to load into the index register.

This possibility gives an idea of the general techniques. We shall look into some subroutines which might actually be used in Section 11.5.

Punching information from memory is simplicity itself. A Select

Punch, followed by a Write instruction, punches eight words onto a card. Loops may be written to punch *blocks* of memory.

Programming input and output for the typewriter is not much harder. A block of eight words may be brought in by giving a Select Typewriter, followed by a Read. If the key on the typewriter is set to tape, the eight words will be read from the punched paper tape attached to the typewriter. If not, eight words or fewer may be typed in manually; if fewer, the carriage return button may be pushed after the last word desired. Typewriter input may be used to enter standard programs at high speed. Another common use is to program the machine to call for one word of input at critical points through the calculation or to call for a code word to be typed in if the program fails. This is more commonly done, however, on the smaller computers, since machine time is so expensive on the large-scale machines. It is more common to have the computer type out a few words of comment during or after the solution of a problem. Under program control, the typewriters used operate in the neighborhood of 600 characters per minute.

The details of tape programming are taken up in Chapter 12.

## 11.5 Typical Input-Output Subroutines

In this section we shall indicate some typical input-output routines, and analyze a few in detail. This will give an idea of what is commonly done in this area, besides providing some review of coding.

A typical routine loads an indefinite number of cards at addresses specified on each card, and recognizes a signal to stop reading and jump into some part of the stored program. Suppose we impose the following requirements.

1. The loading program must first get itself into memory, i.e., be a self-loading program based on the load card key described above.

2. If a particular card contains data to be loaded into memory, the first word on the card will be negative. The address part of the first word will be the address at which the second word should be loaded, with the other six going in sequence after that. The first word itself is not stored anywhere, except temporarily. The index control part of the first word will be the number of words which are on this card, which may be from one to seven. This is called the *word count.*

3. If a particular card is a "transition card," i.e., it specifies to the load program that we now wish to jump into memory and stop loading, there will only be one word on the card and it will be positive.

The address to which to jump will be punched into the address part of the first word.

In short, the load program must be able to sense the sign of the first number to determine whether a given card holds data or is a transition card. The program to do this without indexing might be:

| LOCATION | OPERATION CODE | OPERATION ABBREVIATION | ADDRESS | REMARKS |
|---|---|---|---|---|
| 0 | 60 | Select | 1 | Bring in |
| 1 | 61 | Read | 8 | second |
| 2 | 00 | Halt-jump | 0 | card |
| 3 | 60 | Select | 1 | Bring in |
| 4 | 61 | Read | 16 | third |
| 5 | 00 | Halt-jump | 0 | card |
| 6 | 60 | Select | 1 | Bring in |
| 7 | 61 | Read | 24 | fourth card |
| 8 | 00 | Halt-jump | 0 | |
| 9 | 60 | Select | 1 | Bring in data |
| 10 | 61 | Read | 0 | or transition card |
| 11 | 00 | Halt-jump | 9 | |
| 12 | 10 | Clear add | 0 | Bring in first address |
| 13 | 41 | Store address | 14 | from card. Jump to |
| 14 | 03 | Acc plus jump | [ ] | transition address if positive. |
| 15 | 41 | Store address | 21 | If not, store initial address. |
| 16 | 30 | Acc left | 4 | Store word count |
| 17 | 41 | Store address | 8 | |
| 18 | 10 | Clear add | 31 | Initialize loop |
| 19 | 41 | Store address | 20 | |
| 20 | 10 | Clear add | [1] | Move word from temp. |
| 21 | 40 | Store acc | [0000] | to perm. storage |
| 22 | 10 | Clear add | 31 | Modify address |
| 23 | 19 | Add to mem | 20 | |
| 24 | 10 | Clear add | 31 | |
| 25 | 19 | Add to mem | 21 | |
| 26 | 10 | Clear add | 8 | Modify word count |
| 27 | 14 | Sub | 31 | counter |
| 28 | 40 | Store acc | 8 | |
| 29 | 04 | Acc zero jump | 9 | Read new card if zero |
| 30 | 01 | Un jump | 20 | New word if not zero |
| 31 | 00 | Halt-jump | 1 | Instructional constant |

The load program consists of four cards, which are not in the same format as the cards they load. The first card is loaded into 0–7 when the load card button is pushed. The first nine instructions are necessary to bring in the other three cards of the load program and store them consecutively. They are needed only once, and since we will need eight words of consecutive temporary storage anyway, we allow for it in the first eight words by starting the main body of the program at 9. The reason for the temporary storage is that until the card full of information is somewhere in memory, we do not know where to put it since the loading address is right on the card with the data. The instructions at 9 and 10 bring in a card into 0–7. 12–14 check whether this is a transition card and, if so, jump out to the specified address. If not, step 15 places what must therefore be the initial address in instruction 21. Instructions 16 and 17 store the word count in 8, which space is also no longer needed. 18 and 19 initialize the address of the instruction with which numbers are brought in from temporary storage. 20 and 21 store one word from temporary storage. 22–25 modify addresses. 26–28 modify the word counter. If the counter is down to zero, the zero jump goes back to 9 to bring in the next card. If not, the unconditional jump goes back to 20 to store another word out of temporary storage. 31 is the constant 1. Data or instructions may be loaded into any location above 31.

The program is considerably shorter with indexing.

| LOCATION | OPERATION CODE | OPERATION ABBREVIATION | ADDRESS | REMARKS |
|---|---|---|---|---|
| 0 | 60 | Select | 1 | Bring in |
| 1 | 61 | Read | 8 | second |
| 2 | 00 | Halt–jump | 0 | card |
| 3 | 60 | Select | 1 | Bring in |
| 4 | 61 | Read | 16 | third |
| 5 | 00 | Halt–jump | 0 | card |
| 6 | 01 | Un jump | 8 | |
| 7 | 00 | Halt–jump | 0 | |
| 8 | 60 | Select | 1 | Bring in data |
| 9 | 61 | Read | 0 | or transition card |
| 10 | 00 | Halt–jump | 8 | Back to eight if reader |
| 11 | 10 | Clear add | 0 | is out of cards |
| 12 | 41 | Store address | 13 | Check whether transi- |
| 13 | 03 | Acc plus jump | [0000] | tion card |
| 14 | 41 | Store address | 19 | Store initial address |
| 15 | 30 | Acc left | 4 | Store word count |
| 16 | 51 | Acc to ind | 0, 1 | in index 1 |
| 17 | 50 | Mem to ind | 16, 2 | Store 0 in index 2 |
| 18 | 10 | Clear add | 1, 2 | Move one word from |
| 19 | 40 | Store acc | [0000], 2 | temp. to perm. storage |
| 20 | 54 | Raise ind | 1, 2 | Modify |
| 21 | 57 | Eq ind jump | 18 | Test |
| 22 | 01 | Un jump | 8 | |

In the light of the previous discussion and the discussion of indexing, almost everything here should be clear. The address of the instruction at 17 is the location of another instruction because this is a simple way to get a zero into the index register without otherwise storing one. Any location above 22 may be used for instructions or data, a saving by indexing of nine instructions.

The advantages of such a load program are several. If the individual data or instruction cards get out of order, nothing is lost; the load program can still handle each card separately. The load program need not know in advance how many cards are to be loaded, by virtue of the transition card scheme. Individual cards may be replaced or inserted at will. Corrections may be made in a deck by punching the correct word on a card and loading it after the card containing the error. The correction will simply load on top of the error word and wipe it out.

Most computers have internal electronic speeds much greater than their input speed. A program like the above could easily be executed in the time available between reading cards; in other words, the above program could be executed without slowing down most machines.

Other load programs may have special purposes. In TYDAC we have assumed that each number going into memory from a card has exactly ten digits, and, if floating, the number appears punched in the exponent-plus-fifty form in which it must be stored in memory. In many computers much more flexibility is possible. About as much flexibility as we have assumed for TYDAC is the possibility of loading two five-digit positive numbers per word, and then splitting them into separate storage locations during the move from temporary storage to permanent storage. In some large computers it is possible to read literal decimal points into memory from a card, along with commas or asterisks to separate successive words, and slashes (diagonals or virgules) to separate the fractional part from the true (not plus-fifty) exponent. This allows for almost complete flexibility in input. A particular card might look like:

$$1000, \quad 12.6, \quad -.0047, \quad 22, \quad -1.234567/05, \quad 2.302/-12$$

The 1000 might be the initial address, at which to load the first number. The five numbers are loaded into

| | |
|---|---|
| 1000 | 12.6 |
| 1001 | $-.0047$ |
| 1002 | 22.0 |
| 1003 | $-1.234567 \cdot 10^5$ |
| 1004 | $2.302 \cdot 10^{-12}$ |

all in correct internal floating point form.

Binary computers use separate load programs to read binary, octal, or decimal cards; some programs will interpret the numbers on a card as either octal or decimal, depending on a code number somewhere on the card.*

Many computers can store alphabetic information in memory. In some machines this is very simply done; in others it is a matter of a little extra effort because the machine is only incidentally alphabetic. For instance, in TYDAC it would be possible to use two digit positions to store a letter, thus allowing for five letters per computer word. Load programs may be built, either way, to accept the alphabetic information from cards.

It is not infrequent for a load program to be written for a special application. The assembly programs discussed in Chapter 14 always have their own built-in load program, since the card format is usually specialized. Some problems may be of such a nature as to require a special-purpose load program for efficient or feasible operation.

Certain input programs can be called from memory only by a calling sequence. These would tend not to require a transition card, since if the programmer wishes he can specify the number of cards to be read.

Almost all output programs are called by a main program through a calling sequence. There tends to be a greater variety and/or more flexibility of output routines, for the reason mentioned previously that we are more concerned with what the final printed report looks like to an ultimate reader. In TYDAC we have not assumed a direct connected printer. Flexibility is available in the machines which are used to list the cards. Many computers have either a printer which can print information from memory directly, or the ability to write output onto magnetic tape and print this tape on a separate machine. In such computers there is a demand for the wide variety of output programs.

A fairly typical example of the simplest type of output program and its calling sequence is as follows. It is desired in TYDAC to call for a certain block of numbers in consecutive locations to be punched on cards, in exactly the same format as the cards in the input example discussed previously. It is intended to punch cards

---

* The programming of binary computers to load decimal information is somewhat complex, since it involves knowing in intimate detail the characteristics of the particular computer. Many of the programmers of binary computers never have occasion to learn the details of loading programs, since these are usually prepared by one or two programmers for the use of all others. Such work is interesting and necessary, but it is definitely "graduate level" coding.

which may be loaded back into the machine for later processing. The block is identified by its initial and final addresses. The number of words to punch per card is specified in the calling sequence. If the last card has less than this number of words, the correct word count must be put on this card.

The calling sequence might be of the form:

Set index jump or Clear add

$n$, initial address, final address

That is, the number of words to be punched per card is written as the operation part, the initial address of the block as the address part, and the final address of the block as the index control part, of the instruction immediately following the Set index jump or the linkage.

The program to carry out this function would be slightly more complex than the loading program detailed above, but there would not be any radically new principles.

## Exercises

1. Complete the planning for any of the medium-sized problems of the previous chapters. None of these are large enough to involve any problems of memory space, but the questions remain of memory layout, input cards, input and output calling sequences, output format, etc. Write out the input in floating point, as it would appear on the cards of Section 11.5.

2. A special card format has been set up for a problem. It is quite similar to that of Section 11.5, except that each ten-digit field contains two positive numbers. The number of five-digit words on the cards is always even. Write a program to split each ten-digit field into two numbers which are loaded as integers into successive locations, and recognize a transition card.

3. Write the output program outlined at the end of Section 11.5.

# 12 MAGNETIC TAPE PROGRAMMING

## 12.0 Introduction

It frequently happens in preparing problems for computer solution that we run out of memory space. The 2000 words of TYDAC would not be nearly enough for many problems—both scientific and commercial. It could certainly not hold all of the master payroll file for any medium-sized plant. It could not hold at one time all the coefficients of a system of fifty simultaneous linear algebraic equations. And there are many problems that run into more than 2000 instructions, even without consideration of the data.

In each of these situations there is a need for an auxiliary storage device which can hold many more numbers than the main memory, but may be considerably slower and must be much cheaper. At present there are two main devices which fall into this category. On computers which do not use it as *main* memory, the magnetic drum is such a device. A magnetic tape may be used on almost any computer as auxiliary storage. Other devices are being developed which promise to give much larger capacities at much lower costs.

## 12.1 Physical Characteristics of Magnetic Tapes

Magnetic tape for computer use is made either of a plastic base coated with a magnetic oxide or a bronze steel base plated with an iron alloy. Binary information is recorded or written on tape by passing it at high speed over the cores of small windings which magnetize small areas of the tape. Information is read from the tape by passing the tape over the same coils and sensing the voltage induced in them by the magnetized coating. The information recorded on tape must always be binary, no matter what the representation elsewhere in the computer, since in order to gain speed and reliability only *pulses* are recorded on tape. In many systems, a zero is recorded simply as *no change* in the magnetization at a point; a one is recorded as a *reversal* of the magnetization.

In a decimal, nonalphabetic machine like TYDAC, a possible representation would be to record each decimal digit, in its binary form, in a row across the tape. In addition, a *parity bit* would be recorded along with each group of four bits, as a check on the reliability of tape operation. The parity bit is automatically computed by the tape control circuits; in TYDAC it is either zero or one, whichever is required to make an *odd* number of binary one's in each row across the tape. The parity bit is recomputed during tape reading; if this parity bit is not the same as the one recorded on tape, the machine stops in the *tape stop* condition. Thus the TYDAC tape would have five *channels* across it; each decimal digit recorded on tape would be represented by four binary digits and one parity bit, one in each channel. Figure 1 shows the TYDAC representation of the number 0123456789.

Since in most computers it is possible to record alphabetic information on tape, it may be of interest to note a typical form of representation. A common system is to assign six bits to each character, where a character may be a number, a letter, or any of the punctuation or other marks available on the particular machine. The six bits and the parity bit are then recorded in a row, which requires a seven-channel tape. A possible representation for the characters might be:

| CHARACTER | BINARY CODED REPRESENTATION | CHARACTER | BINARY CODED REPRESENTATION |
|---|---|---|---|
| 0 | 1 00 0000 | K | 1 10 0010 |
| 1 | 0 00 0001 | L | 0 10 0011 |
| 2 | 0 00 0010 | M | 1 10 0100 |
| 3 | 1 00 0011 | N | 0 10 0101 |
| 4 | 0 00 0100 | O | 0 10 0110 |
| 5 | 1 00 0101 | P | 1 10 0111 |
| 6 | 1 00 0110 | Q | 1 10 1000 |
| 7 | 0 00 0111 | R | 0 10 1001 |
| 8 | 0 00 1000 | S | 0 11 0001 |
| 9 | 1 00 1001 | T | 0 11 0010 |
| A | 1 01 0001 | U | 1 11 0011 |
| B | 1 01 0010 | V | 0 11 0100 |
| C | 0 01 0011 | W | 1 11 0101 |
| D | 1 01 0100 | X | 1 11 0110 |
| E | 0 01 0101 | Y | 0 11 0111 |
| F | 0 01 0110 | Z | 0 11 1000 |
| G | 1 01 0111 | + | 0 01 0000 |
| H | 1 01 1000 | . | 0 10 0000 |
| I | 0 01 1001 | $ | 1 11 0000 |
| J | 1 10 0001 | Etc. | |

Actual machines have systems along these lines. In some machines the parity bit is such as to make the number of pulses in a row even instead of odd.

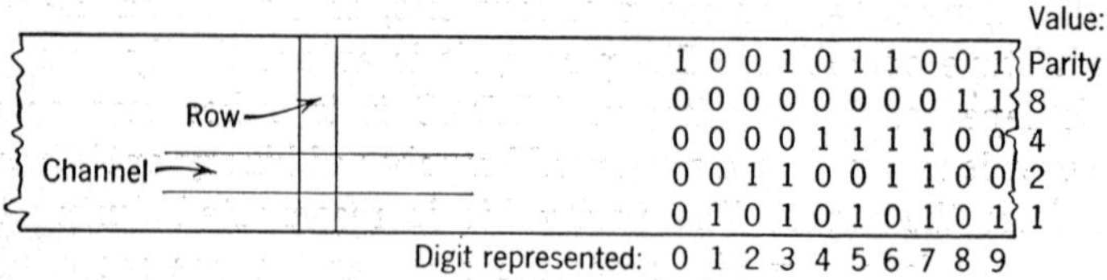

|  |  |  | Value: |
|---|---|---|---|
|  |  | 1 0 0 1 0 1 1 0 0 1 | Parity |
| Row | | 0 0 0 0 0 0 0 0 1 1 | 8 |
| | | 0 0 0 0 1 1 1 1 0 0 | 4 |
| Channel | | 0 0 1 1 0 0 1 1 0 0 | 2 |
| | | 0 1 0 1 0 1 0 1 0 1 | 1 |

Digit represented:   0 1 2 3 4 5 6 7 8 9

Figure 1. One possible representation of numbers on magnetic tape.

A typical pulse recording density is one hundred or more per inch in each channel. Tape typically moves past the heads at 100 inches/sec, in order to obtain sufficiently large pulses when reading. With such densities and speeds, small defects in the magnetic surfacing or small errors in tape position can easily lead to faulty recording or reading of information. It is in order to detect such faults that the parity bit is used. Permanent flaws in the tape are handled in existing machines in at least three ways. In one group of computers, the bad section must simply be discarded, which means that if the flaw is near the end of the tape it is shortened or if in the middle it is cut into two smaller sections. A bad spot on a Univac tape is signaled by a hole punched in the tape, near the flaw. The hole is sensed photoelectrically and writing or reading is suspended momentarily. Another small group of machines records on the tape what amounts, for this purpose, to a signal that the tape in the vicinity is good. Absence of the signal suspends reading or writing.

It is clear that with only $\frac{1}{100}$ inch between adjacent bits on the tape, it would be impossible to position the tape accurately enough to stop between pulses. For this reason, information is always recorded on tape in *records*, which are groups of words of some fixed or variable length. With TYDAC, we assume that a record is made up of eight words, which, under the assumptions above, would require less than 1 inch of tape. The *interrecord gap*, which allows for the tape to start and stop, would be about the same length as a record.

For some applications it is necessary to record on the tape a signal that there is no more information on the tape, or at least not on the particular section of the tape. This signal is called a *tape mark;* it is sensed by the tape unit as part of the read instruction discussed below.

Magnetic tape is not addressable in the sense that a specific position on the tape corresponds to a specific address, as is true of most other forms of memory. Basically, it is necessary to know where each word is located on tape *with respect to other words and records on the same tape.* It is not enough to know that the quantities $a, b, c, d, e, f, g$, and $h$ are present in a TYDAC record; it is necessary to know also which quantity is first, which second, etc. It is similarly necessary to know the relationship between records on a tape.

This statement should be qualified, however. Suppose it is known that the eight quantities above are always present in every record on a certain tape, and it is necessary to find the one record in which $a$ is equal to 167. It would not be difficult to read each record from tape into memory, then immediately examine the first word of the record to determine whether this is the record in which $a$ is equal to 167. If not, the next record would be read. Such a procedure can be programmed for any tape unit; in certain machines there are special instructions which make the search process nearly automatic. And in some equipment the search can proceed while the central part of the computer does something else. In such machines it is not necessary that the *key* for which the search is made ($a$ in the example here) should be the first word of the record.

## 12.2 Programming Techniques and Subroutines

A block of eight words is written on a TYDAC tape by the two instructions:

Select   A
Write    B

where A is 11, 12, 13, or 14 to specify one of the four tapes, and B is the start of any eight-word sequence in memory. If a block close to the top of memory is called for, the effect is that the address after 1999 is zero. For instance, if B were 1995, the eight words written on tape would be 1995, 1996, 1997, 1998, 1999, 0, 1, 2.

Eight words are read from a tape by the three instructions:

Select   A
Read     B
Unjump   C

where A and B are as before, and C is the address to which it is desired to jump if a tape mark appears on the tape at this point. If there is no tape mark at the point, then the instruction following the Read is skipped. It is not essential that the third instruction be Unconditional jump; if the application is such that the tape mark never *should* be sensed, it might be a Halt and jump.

The tape mark is written on a tape by the sequence:

$$\text{Select} \qquad \text{A}$$
$$\text{Write mark}$$

No address is required for the Write mark instruction.  Observe that the tape mark is "discovered" and the instruction following the Read is skipped, only by trying to read a record which is not there. The instruction following the read *is* skipped on the last record before the tape mark, but *is not* skipped when an attempt is made to read the next record.

The last instruction which applies specifically to tapes is Rewind. Once a tape has been written, it is necessary to return to the beginning to read the information.  Most real computers either provide for reading the tape records while the tape is moving backwards, or have the ability to skip over records in one direction or the other without reading them.  In TYDAC we assume only the Rewind operation, which moves the tape completely back to the beginning of the reel.  This is accomplished by the single instruction Rewind A, where A is the desired tape number; no Select is necessary.

The subroutines used in connection with tapes are fairly simple. A few typical ones are listed; they are not different enough from the input-output routines discussed in Chapter 11 to warrant detailed discussion of the codes.

1. *Tape write and check sum.*  A block of memory from an initial address to a final address is written on a specified tape.  As an additional check on tape reliability, all the words going onto the tape are "summed" and the sum written as an additional record at the end of tape.  The "sum" need not be a meaningful arithmetic sum at all, but simply some pattern formed from the words going on tape which characterizes the words.  It might be formed in TYDAC by adding all the words into the accumulator without any consideration for overflow.

The calling sequence might be:

$$\text{Set ind jump} \qquad \text{A, 2}$$
$$\text{N} \qquad \text{IA, FA}$$

where A is the start of the subroutine, N is in the operation part and is the desired tape number, IA is the initial address of the block, and FA is the final address of the block.  The subroutine breaks the memory block up into eight-word blocks and gives the appropriate Selects.  If the last record does not require eight words, zeros are added to fill out the block. An extra tape block contains the check sum and seven zeros.

No checking system can give *complete* assurance that no errors have gone undetected. There is no guarantee that an error in writing a record will not be compensated for by an error in recomputing the check sum. The parity check will not detect an error caused by a failure to read *two* one's in one row. The usual point of view on these matters is that it is impossible to get an *absolute* check on anything; the types of errors which would get by the checks imposed are so extremely unlikely, we hope, that we have virtual assurance of the accuracy.

2. *Tape read and check sum.* This could be just the complement of the above, with a calling sequence exactly the same except the address of the Set index jump. It would be feasible to write a combined subroutine to read or write. Which to do would be indicated by jumping to a different location in the same subroutine.

3. Another subroutine might read records into consecutive locations after a specified initial address until a tape mark was sensed. It could not very well include check summing.

4. A simulated search program could be devised which would make TYDAC tapes act like addressable tapes. The calling sequence might be:

$$\text{Set ind jump} \quad A, 2$$
$$N \qquad B, C$$

The first word in each record on tape N is compared with the word in the accumulator. If a match is found, the record is read into memory starting at B. If no match is found anywhere on tape, the subroutine jumps to C to indicate that fact.

5. It is possible to write a self-loading tape read program. The first record on tape is almost exactly the same as that discussed in Chapter 11. Since tapes load so much faster than cards, this is an approach which is used fairly often in computers where it is possible. And of course in many machines, this is the *only* way to get information into memory.

## 12.3 Typical Tape Applications

There are four main uses of tapes: (1) storage of intermediate results; (2) self-loading programs; (3) data input and output, on machines where this is possible; (4) permanent storage of voluminous data. Some illustrations of these four applications:

1. The multiplication of two 50 by 50 matrices obviously cannot

be carried out entirely in the high-speed memory of a machine with less than about 8000 words of storage. To do the job in a smaller machine, the elements of the two matrices are stored in the correct order on two tapes, and the elements of the product matrix stored on a third as they are computed. If sizes allow, it is much faster to store one or two of the matrices in high-speed memory.

This application can be considered intermediate storage in the sense that the elements are read in from cards before computation is begun, or in the frequent case that the elements are computed by the program before multiplication.

2. As another illustration of the intermediate storage application, it is not too unusual to find situations where averages must be compiled from many individual calculations. Suppose, for instance, that some identical calculation is to be made on fifty different sets of input, and that there are twenty numbers as output for each case. From the answers, 1000 in all, certain statistical measures must be computed. The obvious way is simply to dump onto a tape each set of answers as it is computed. When the last case has been read in and calculated and stored (the program need not know at this point how many cases there are), a tape mark is written and the tape rewound. The statistics, including the total number of cases, can then be compiled from the answers on tape.

These are illustrations of situations where problems could not be done without the use of tapes, in the usual sizes of high-speed memories. Of course, it would be possible to build machines with much larger high-speed memories, but the cost would be prohibitive. The question as usual is the economic one: it is preferable to accept the considerably lower speed and additional complexity of tapes than to pay for the additional cost of larger high-speed memories. This sort of decision recurs frequently in the design of computers, and is the reason why design specifications are set by a team which includes some persons very familiar with applications and programming.

3. Another economic consideration arises in the use of self-loading tape programs. It is usual to find tape speeds which are in the neighborhood of twenty-five times as fast as card loading speeds. If a voluminous program has to be loaded from cards frequently, there is a considerable saving in loading the program instead from tape. A program has to be set up for tapes, similar to the self-loading card loader described in the previous chapter; then the program deck on cards has to be converted to tape. The economic choice, then, is between the time saved by the faster loading from

tape and the time consumed in writing the necessary programs and in converting the program to tape.

4. In some machines, primarily the largest, it is possible to use auxiliary equipment to prepare tapes. Cards may be read by a separate card reader and the information written on tape, at the usual slow card reading speeds, while the computer works at high speed on something else. The reel of tape may then be removed from the auxiliary ("off-line") tape unit, placed on a tape unit which is connected to the computer ("on-line"), and read in at high speeds. Output may be handled in reverse fashion. Here the economic choice is between the cost of on-line reading of cards and printing or punching answers and the additional cost of the auxiliary equipment. On large machines this comes out very clearly in favor of the auxiliary tape equipment.

5. In many applications, particularly in the business or commercial area, there are voluminous records to be consulted during the course of the problem. All the information on the policy holders of an insurance company requires dozens or even hundreds of reels of tape. All the master payroll data for a plant personnel accounting application require several reels of tape. These tapes may be prepared by auxiliary equipment or by the computer itself, depending on the application.

## 12.4 Conclusion

For a machine with electrostatic or magnetic core memory, a magnetic drum is an auxiliary storage device with many of the same economic considerations as tapes. There is no question of a waiting period of up to 2 or 3 minutes while the correct record is found if a tape happens to be positioned unfavorably. On many computers, of course, the magnetic drum is the primary storage device.

Several other types of intermediate speed storage are being investigated. Some of these promise to hold a great many words, and still not have excessive *access time*, i.e., the wait required to get a particular word located anywhere in the medium. The IBM Random Access Memory is such a device.

## Exercises

1. On tape 1 are 1000 values of $x$ (125 blocks). On tape 2 are 1000 values of $y$. For each pair of $x$ and $y$, calculate $x^2$, $xy$, and $y^2$. For each pair, write a record on tape 3 which consists of:

$$x$$
$$y$$
$$x^2$$
$$xy$$
$$y^2$$
$$0$$
$$0$$
$$0$$

Thus, tapes 1 and 2 will be read 125 times to calculate 1000 records which will be written on tape 3.

2. Suppose that in paragraph 2 of Section 12.3 there are just eight results (one block) per case, and a variable number of cases with a tape mark at the end. The eight numbers are

$$a_i$$
$$b_i$$
$$c_i$$
$$R_i$$
$$S_i$$
$$T_i$$
$$x_i$$
$$y_i$$

where the subscript indicates the case numbers. Write the program to bring in this information from tape 1 and calculate

$$\sum_{i=1}^{n} (R_i + S_i + T_i), \qquad \sum_{i=1}^{n} x_i y_i, \qquad \frac{1}{n} \sum_{i=1}^{n} a_i, \qquad \frac{1}{n} \sum_{i=1}^{n} b_i, \qquad \frac{1}{n} \sum_{i=1}^{n} c_i$$

where $n$ is the number of cases, and must be calculated.

3. Write a self-loading tape program which then loads tape blocks which are exactly the same as the card format of Section 11.5. This would be approximately the situation if auxiliary tape equipment were available.

4. Write the program of subroutine 1 of Section 12.2.

5. Write the program of subroutine 3 of Section 12.2.

6. Write the program of subroutine 4 of Section 12.2.

# 13 PROGRAM CHECKOUT

## 13.0 Introduction

Once a program has been written, it must be verified or *checked out* to determine if it actually does the job it is designed for. The steps of analysis and programming can lead to many *logical* errors, i.e., errors in conception or in flow through the problem. The testing of a loop may be set up improperly or the alternatives to be taken in certain situations may not have been thoroughly thought out. Possibly a mathematical procedure will not work in a certain case.

A large source of errors is the actual coding. This part of the task involves such a great mass of detail that simple mistakes can easily be made. An operation code may be copied incorrectly or remembered wrongly. Errors can be made which are simply blunders: the index control may be omitted, or a two written where there should be a three, or a tape address indicated which does not exist. There are so many possibilities of making mistakes that a perfect program is practically never written.

All these errors must be corrected before right answers can be obtained. There are several general approaches which may be taken, and several ways of making the machine help track down the errors. We shall discuss these in some detail, since checkout is a rather sizable part of the total cost of preparing a problem for computer solution.

## 13.1 Approaches to Checkout

The first attack on the checkout problem may be made before coding is begun. In order to fully ascertain the accuracy of the answers, it is necessary to have a hand-calculated check case with which to compare the answers which will later be calculated by the machine. This means that stored program machines are never used for a true one-shot problem. There must always be an element of iteration to make it pay. The hand calculation may be done at any

point during programming.  Frequently, however, computers are
operated by computing experts who prepare the problems as a service
for engineers or scientists.  In these cases it is highly desirable that
the "customer" prepare the check case, largely because logical errors
and misunderstandings between the programmer and customer may
be pointed up by such a procedure.  If the customer is to prepare the
test solution, it is best for him to start well in advance of actual
checkout, since for any sizable problem it will take several days or
weeks to hand-calculate the test.

In view of the time required, it is reasonable to ask why we
bother with a check case.  Is it not possible to check the computer's
answers some easier way?

There are three answers to this.  The first is the point mentioned
above, which revolves around the serious communication problem in
a service-bureau or "closed shop" type of computer operation.  It
is surprising how frequently misunderstandings can arise about
details.  These all have to be ironed out sooner or later, and a detailed
check case is a good way to discover them fairly early.

The second reason revolves around a disastrous type of error
which can be very difficult to catch, namely, the small error that
results in a fairly reasonable answer.  Suppose that a constant is
entered incorrectly as 1.01 instead of 1.001.  This is only about a
1% error, which from a standpoint of reasonableness of final answers
may not be detected by anyone.  Often the problem originator
knows within 5% or 10% what the answers ought to be, from general
knowledge of the physical situation—but not within 1%.  Yet the
data and numerical methods may be good to 0.1% and be used with
this accuracy assumption.  This sort of error is next to impossible to
catch without a detailed, accurate test case.  It is worth pointing out
also that errors in input may result in much larger or much smaller
errors in the final answers.  If the number above appeared in a
formula such as

$$F_n = \frac{14,576}{C_f - 1.001}$$

the error in the final answer would be quite large if $C_f$ were close
to 1.001, but undetectable (and probably harmless) if $C_f$ were 10 or so.

This emphasizes that as far as possible the test case should pick
the situations most likely to point up errors.  If possible $C_f$ should
be chosen close to 1.  A particularly important consideration is not to
pick values which could cover up other errors.  For instance, take

the formula

$$y = (a - 1)e^{(x+2)/2} + be^{-x^2}$$

If a value of 1.0 is used for $a$, the final answer is of course independent of the first exponential. The answer could come out correctly even with major errors in the exponential term. Similarly, a $b$ value of 0 should not be used. Again, if $x$ is chosen larger than 2 or so, the second exponential term will be nearly 0 and will have little effect on the result. A major error in the value of $b$ might then go undetected.

The third reason for a detailed check case revolves around the importance of many computer applications. Some large problems may use literally hundreds of hours of computer time, which in itself is expensive. More important, the results may be the design of equipment or tests involving in some cases millions of dollars. This perhaps emphasizes that it is very worthwhile to expend considerable effort to be positive the answers are right.

The next general approach will become clearer when we discuss various machine methods: writing the code so it will be easy to check. This implies keeping intermediate storage in tidy blocks, if, as usual, memory print is to be the primary checkout tool. It also sometimes implies writing a less fancy code which will be easier to follow. This is a bit hard to illustrate; we may simply say that occasionally it is possible to use tricks in coding which save a few steps (and give a glow of inner satisfaction) but cause grief when the problem is put on the machine, particularly if anyone else has to assist in the checkout.

The third general approach is to make a detailed check of the code as written, before trying it on the machine. This is aimed at all types of errors: conceptual, logical, and stupid. Perhaps its primary mission, however, is to catch the stupid mistakes like wrong operation codes and addresses.

There are various ways of going about a detailed code check. The obvious way is for the person who wrote the code to go back over it, preferably after a few days' delay between writing and checking. The coder may simply read the instructions carefully, checking addresses, constants, loop testing, making sure operations are correct, ascertaining that the tape was rewound before reading after writing, etc. Some coders like to draw a second flow chart, working backward from the code, and compare it with the original flow chart.

A well-recommended technique is to have someone else do the checking, with or without drawing a new flow chart. The reason for this is the well-known fact that we tend to become somewhat entranced with our own mistakes. Reading stale code is uninteresting at best, and errors do not always exactly stand out from the page. This is true no matter who reads the code, but it seems to be a lot harder to check one's own work. The code is familiar, and there seems to be a strong tendency to skim over the instructions without really being critical of each little mark on the page. This corresponds exactly to the difficulty of proofreading one's own writing. A second person does not know what to expect, and is not partially blinded by what he knows *ought* to be written in a given instruction. He is more in a position of trying to read the code and understand *from it* what was done; this requires a much more careful reading than for the original writer to force himself to look it over, trying to find blunders.

It sometimes works out very satisfactorily for two people to work on a problem. If one is much more experienced, he will do most of the original work with the second doing mostly checking (which, incidentally, is a fine training method for the second person). If the two are equally qualified, both can write code and check each other's work.

This may seem like a large effort for the gain. As may become more obvious from the discussion in the next section, finding errors once a problem is on the machine is very expensive. It has been estimated that on a large machine of the IBM 704 or Univac Scientific class, each coding error costs between twenty and fifty dollars to find, including machine time and programmer time. The plan of using another person to check over codes before attempting the problem on the computer answers this high cost in two ways. First, the prechecking cost required to find an error, on the average, is not as great as the total cost of finding it later. This is because in most cases the computer costs much more per minute than a programmer does. The second economic consideration is that the checker is frequently not as highly paid as the original writer, nor as highly skilled.

Tests of accuracy can often be programmed, to be carried out along with the solution. One technique is to compute each important quantity twice, using different memory locations and different sequences of instructions, and compare the answers. If done consistently, this of course requires twice the computer time to get a solution. It is usually not done on machines which have extensive self-checking, such as Univac, or on machines which are felt for other reasons to be sufficiently reliable. Neither is it often done if there are other ways of accomplishing the same result with less effort. For instance, after solving a system of linear equations it is not very time-consuming to substitute the answers back into the original equations to test whether they actually satisfy the system. It would be more precise to say, satisfy the system *within satisfactory limits*. Because of round-off and other errors inherent in digital solutions, the unknowns will almost never satisfy the system exactly, and some allowance must be made for this in programming the back substitution. The same comment applies to other examples of checking which are not so lengthy as computing the answers twice. After computing a long chain of tabulated values of some function, it may be possible to apply an asymptotic formula to check the last value. If the sine and cosine of an angle are computed in the course of a problem, the identity $\sin^2 x + \cos^2 x = 1$ can be programmed. The list could be extended.

The last general approach to the checkout problem which we will discuss is that of testing all possibilities in a program. Some applications involve many branches and forks all the way through; *any* problem has some alternatives built into it. An engineering calculation may specify that a certain parameter has a limit of one; if it is calculated as greater, *one* should be substituted. An accuracy check might be built into a problem to find the sum of the sine squared and cosine squared; if the sum is more than $10^{-7}$ away from one, the program should stop. Examples could be multiplied. The point is, of course, that a program is not necessarily free of all errors simply because it gets correct answers to one set of input. As far as feasible, all possibilities in the program must be checked. Sometimes the nature of the problem is such that this is almost impossible, particularly if contingencies can occur in pairs or triples.

This again points up a kind of error that may go undetected for months. A parameter is supposed to have a programmed limit of one, but the code is wrong so that nothing happens if it is actually greater than one. For the first 6 months the program is run, this situation never arises; then a particular set of input results in the parameter going to 1.04. It may take days to track the trouble down.

Checkout is perhaps a fourth or a third of the total cost of problem preparation prior to first production running. It is costly and time-consuming enough to be worthy of more careful planning than it often receives.

## 13.2 Machine Checkout Methods

There are several ways to make the computer itself assist in the checkout procedures. Two of these are simple adaptations of machine features; the others make use of a special-purpose program which must be in memory along with the program being checked.

The most elementary machine checkout technique is the use of the single step key. It will perhaps be remembered that with the automatic-manual switch set to manual, pressing the single step key causes one instruction to be executed. This will be in normal sequence or a jump, depending on the instruction in the current instruction register. It is possible also to make a manual jump to any location via the enter instruction key. Single-stepping consists of getting the first instruction of interest into the current instruction register, then repeatedly pressing the single step key and watching what happens. In many cases it is necessary to copy down certain information from the registers, such as the actual addresses and contents of index registers. In some cases the arithmetic may be verified against a hand-calculated case.

This is unfortunately an extremely expensive method and is seldom used except on very small sections of programs in order to find errors which resist more conventional attacks. Besides the high cost of machine time, the method has the disadvantage that there is no permanent record of what is happening. Frequently in such cases, the programmer takes his scratch paper back to his desk to analyze, only to discover that there was one critical piece of information which was not copied down.

This is obviated by a tracing program, the next level of sophistication in checkout. As the name implies, this is a program which must be in memory along with the program being checked. Its purpose is to record on tape or printer or punch all the information which a person using single step might record. A fairly typical tracing program for TYDAC might punch out on a card the following information:

Location of instruction.

Operation-address-index control, i.e., current instruction register.

Contents of accumulator.

Contents of MQ.

Contents of memory location specified by address part of instruction.

Contents of index registers.

All of the arithmetic information is punched or printed as it appears after the execution of the instruction specified by the location counter and the current instruction register. All of the information can be obtained in much less time than it takes to punch it, so that tracing can proceed at full punching or printing speed. However, this is still vastly slower than the high-speed operation of the arithmetic section. The IBM 650, for instance, can punch only 100 cards per minute, whereas arithmetic can be carried out at an average of perhaps 25,000 operations per minute. Another way of illustrating this is to point out that the single loop used as the first example in Chapter 6, which simply added fifty numbers, would take almost 10 minutes to trace at 100 cards per minute.

We need not be concerned as yet with the details of how the tracing program operates; it is an interpretive method, as discussed in Chapter 15. It is controlled by jump instructions just as the program is; in other words, it gives a record or *trace* of what went on at each point through the program. It is subject to the rather obvious limitation that no sequences of instructions may be traced which depend on timing of mechanical parts. For instance, a Select instruction must be followed within a certain time limit by a read or write, so there would be no time to trace these.

Since tracing is so slow, it is often desirable to make it a selective process, where only some of the instructions are traced. It is not too difficult to design the trace program so that it automatically skips over input-output instructions where there would be timing problems. The program can be designed to accept information as to where to start tracing, such as the location of the first instruction to be traced. The information can be more complete, consisting of a table of regions of instructions to be traced. In some machines, instructions may have either a plus or a minus sign. This choice can often be used to control tracing; instructions might be written with plus signs if they are to be traced, minus if not. This demands foresight in the code writing, since what will be selectively traced must be established in advance. A usual procedure would be to plan to trace the instructions which compute significant intermediate answers. It is possible to change the signs of the affected instructions during checkout, but this is not too convenient.

The procedure allowed by some trace programs, of specifying regions to be traced, gives more flexibility. The regions to be traced are usually signaled by punching initial and final addresses on control cards. These can quite simply be inserted in the deck, or removed, as the checkout progresses and different sections of the program become of primary interest.

Tracing is not only expensive but it very often does not give all the information needed. A trace may show that a certain loop contains wrong addresses. The programmer sitting at his desk with no more information than the trace may wish to know what happened

in an early section of the program which set up the initialization.
Since it is almost never possible to trace an entire program—which
might literally require hours of computer time—he probably has no
printed record at all of what happened in that initialization. With
the clue of where the error is, he may be able to go back to the
instructions in question and figure out the trouble without the printed
record, but often he cannot.  What is really needed is a listing of
what the instructions in question looked like after the trouble arose.

A listing of a consecutive section of memory, either numbers or
instructions, is called a *memory print*, or often, a *memory dump*.
It has the characteristic of some tracing programs of being highly
selective: as little or as much of memory may be dumped as may
be pertinent.  At any one point it gives a great deal more information than tracing does.  A significant point here is that the memory
dump does give information *at one point*.  In this sense it is funda-
mentally different from tracing.  We may say that tracing gives a
dynamic record of what happened at each instruction as the program
was executed.  It is a sort of *vertical* record: a little information at
many points.  The dump is a sort of *horizontal* record: it gives a
complete cross section consisting of much information at a few points.
This often requires a partial memory dump at several points through
the program.

The break point switch is frequently a help in such situations.  To
review, this is a rotary switch on the console which may be set to one
of ten positions, 0 through 9.  A test instruction is used to "interro-
gate" this switch.  If the switch is set to 3, say, and the instruction

Break jump   a, 3

is given, the machine will stop.  When the start button is pressed,
the next instruction is taken from *a*.  If the switch is set to any other
position, the next instruction in normal sequence is taken, and there
is no stop.

This instruction may be used to control a memory dump by
inserting Break jump instructions at points in the program where
information is needed.  The switch can be set to different positions
as checkout proceeds.

To understand this more fully, we must discuss how memory dump
programs operate.  One fairly common technique requires the initial
and final addresses of a region to be entered manually into the MQ.
Under this plan, when a Break jump stops the machine, the operator
specifies the region(s) to be printed or punched and makes a manual
jump to the start of the dump program.  The dump program stops

after completion, at which point the operator makes a manual jump back to the instruction following the Break jump. Depending on the circumstances, he may change the setting of the break point switch before starting the program again, to prepare to get another dump when and if the program arrives at another critical juncture. In this case the important feature of the Break jump is not the jump, but the stop.

Another way of using the instruction requires more foresight as to what information may be needed during checkout, but saves considerable console fiddling. It is possible to print or punch sections of memory by using a program called from memory. The plan is to have in memory several calling sequences to dump sections of storage; the addresses in the Break jump are the addresses of the appropriate calling sequence. At the end of each group of calling sequences is an Unconditional jump back to the instruction following the appropriate Break jump. All the operator has to do now is push the start button when the stops occur, and possibly change the setting of the break point switch before doing so.

These break points, at which memory is dumped or other information is obtained, are simply critical spots in the program, at which a little information may tell a great deal about the process.

A memory dump may be used in two ways. We have discussed how to use it to get information during the execution of a program. It is also employed to get information after completion of a program, or when it unexpectedly "dies" during a checkout run. In either situation it is desirable to have a complete listing of all numbers and instructions to use as reference in tracking down troubles. It is also very desirable to have the contents of all registers at the time of the breakdown so that the immediate fault can be pinpointed.

As a final indication of the time comparison between tracing and dumping, we may observe that the entire 2000 words of TYDAC could be punched in the format discussed in Chapter 11 in 3 minutes at 100 cards per minute. In the same time, only 300 instructions could be traced, which in a program with extensive looping would be a very small part of the total number of instructions to be executed. And even in the same time, the memory dump would give much more pertinent information. We may safely say that memory dumping is a much more sophisticated approach to the checkout problem. A common tendency is for new programmers to learn tracing first, and to misuse it very badly. The experienced programmer uses tracing occasionally, for small parts of a program, but only after other methods have failed to locate the trouble.

Special-purpose diagnostic programs can be designed which combine the best features of all these techniques, and at the same time allow quite flexible control. Some of these depend on special features of machines;* one will be described which could be used on any machine, and the TYDAC in particular.

A reasonable name for the program might be "dynamic diagnostic." It has the following characteristics:

1. Small regions to be traced may be specified by an initial and final address entered on a card.

2. At any point in the program which is not limited by timing requirements, a memory dump of several sections of memory may be called for.

3. At any memory dump a simple code, punched on the card which calls for the dump, will call for punching out the contents of all registers.

4. Items 2 and 3 may be done only a limited number of times through a loop, or not until a specified number of times through, according to a code punched in the same card.

5. Provision may be made to get certain information if the program breaks down—which we might call "post-mortem" information. By entering a "post-mortem control" card, we may ask for the contents of the arithmetic and control registers, a dump of specified sections of memory, and a count of the number of times certain instructions were executed.

All of the above except the last are carried out automatically during execution of the program. There are no stops as when the branch switch is used, but the execution of the program is slowed down by any tracing or dumping and by internal red tape operations associated with counting the number of executions, etc. The fact that much of the operation of the diagnostic work is carried on simultaneously with the operation of the program being checked is the basis of the word "dynamic."

The post-mortem information is wanted only after the program breaks down, and since this cannot be predicted, a manual jump is required to start the post-mortem punching. The dynamic diagnostic program itself would occupy several hundred storage locations. This space could not be used unless there was information to go into the program which would not be needed during checkout and which could be entered later. This would not usually happen, so we must admit that we have given up a significant fraction of memory to the checkout problem.

* Such as the trap jump on the IBM 704.

To be more specific about how such a program would work, the details of input and output will be discussed.

The deck for dynamic diagnostic checkout would consist of:

1. The card loading program discussed in Chapter 11.

2. The deck being checked out, including all data.

3. The diagnostic program, which would load on normal cards. The last card would be a transition to the dynamic diagnostic program.

4. The program transition card.

5. The various control cards for dynamic traces or dumps, plus any post-mortem controls.

All these would load at full speed before any diagnostic procedure began. The program transition card and the control cards would be loaded by the diagnostic program; the program transition card would not immediately be executed, but the information on it would be stored for use after the controls were loaded. It is important to note that these control cards are taken to *be* control cards only because of their position in the deck, and because they are loaded by a special input program in the dynamic diagnostic.

The output of the program is fairly straightforward. In TYDAC it would be a deck of cards which would be listed on a tabulator. Any sections of tracing would be obvious enough. Dumps would be in standard memory output form with initial addresses and seven numbers per line. Contents of registers would be punched out in much the same format as a line of tracing. Counts of the number of times an instruction was executed would punch with the instruction location in the address part and the count in the index control part.

## 13.3 Conclusion

There are many programs available for actual machines to assist in checkout. Properly used, they can save much personnel time and practically eliminate aimless console fiddling. These programs will become more and more sophisticated as experience is gained in their use.

# 14 RELATIVE PROGRAMMING METHODS

## 14.0 Introduction

In writing programs up to this point, we have written addresses exactly as they appear when the instructions are later executed by the control circuits. This is called *absolute* coding. It has been mentioned in earlier chapters that we usually do not wish to write absolute addresses, but prefer to defer the decision as to where instructions and data actually fit in memory by writing *relative* addresses.

To illustrate the point, suppose we are starting a program which is anticipated to take 1500 steps including library subroutines. We begin writing instructions at 400 to avoid an assumed diagnostic program. About the tenth step requires that a square root be calculated, but of course the square root program has not been written yet, and even if a library routine is to be used we do not yet know where a convenient location for it will be. We are faced with two choices: (1) leave the jump address blank and fill it in later, or (2) make an estimate of where the routine would fit and write that address. The first solution involves making fairly thorough notes, because there will be many blank addresses and a correspondingly large possibility of error. The second solution is no solution at all, because the guesses would ordinarily be so bad that many gaps and overlaps would occur.

This last suggests the problem of making changes in an absolute-language program, which is a second motivation toward relative coding. If a missing instruction is discovered halfway through a long program, we are faced with the unhappy choice of either renumbering all the following instructions while being careful to change any addresses which might be affected, or jumping out to a clear section of memory, adding the instruction, and jumping back. Neither is particularly satisfactory.

A third incentive for avoiding absolute coding is the problem of relocation. This may be illustrated with a simple loop. Suppose we merely need a loop to clear to zero all of memory between 1000 and

1999. The following would do the job quite simply:

| LOCATION | OPERATION CODE | OPERATION ABBREVIATION | ADDRESS |
|---|---|---|---|
| 0 | 42 | Load MQ | 50 |
| 1 | 43 | Store MQ | 1000 |
| 2 | 10 | Clear add | 51 |
| 3 | 19 | Add to mem | 1 |
| 4 | 14 | Sub | 52 |
| 5 | 04 | Acc zero jump | 7 |
| 6 | 01 | Un jump | 1 |
| 7 | | Continuation | |

50 contains 0
51 contains 1
52 contains Store MQ 2000

This loop was written in locations 0 through 6. Suppose now someone wished to borrow the program, but had other things in 0–400 and needed to *relocate* the program with the constants in 401–403 and the program in 404–410. He might wish to save himself the trouble of figuring out the logic, and try instead to set up a semimechanical procedure for changing the addresses. He would rapidly discover, however, that there are three kinds of addresses in this program:

1. Those affected by the change in location of the program: instructions 3, 6, and 7.

2. Those affected by the change in location of the data: 0, 2, and 4.

3. Those affected by neither: 1.

In most programs there would be a fourth category of addresses:

4. Those which could not be affected by any relocation process, since they do not refer to memory: shift and input-output instructions.

All of these categories would have to be handled differently in moving a section of a program from one location to another.

Thus we see three reasons for preferring relative over absolute addresses: (1) many addresses are not known (absolutely) at the time they are needed; (2) it is quite difficult to make a change in a long absolute program after it is written; (3) relocation of an absolute program is not easy. A relative programming system helps to alleviate all these problems, as we shall see.

## 14.1 TYDAC Relative Programming System

The fundamental idea of the relative programming system to be presented here is as follows. In writing locations and addresses, we set up a number of *regions*, each of which is identified by a two-digit code number. Each region may be thought of as a block of memory. The absolute address of the first word of the block is called the *origin*, and all other locations in the region are *relative* to that origin. The point of the method is that the origin can be assigned by the programmer, but it need not be done until *after* the program is completed and all the needed information is available. The whole program is first written in terms of regions, with addresses relative to the origins of the regions. Then the origins of the different regions are assigned, often by the machine, and the relative locations and addresses converted to absolute.

For instance, region 10 might be used for the locations of the instructions of a subroutine. The first relative location in the region would be 0000, and we would write the combined location as 10.0000 with the decimal point added for clarity. The following locations would be 10.0001, 10.0002, etc. Regions would also be set up for all temporary and permanent storage, and a dummy region assigned for addresses which never change, such as shifts. When the program was completely written in this form, origins would be assigned in such a manner as to allow just enough space for each region with no gaps or overlap. If region 10 were to start just after a diagnostic routine which used 0–399, the origin of region 10 would be 400. Then the locations which were previously written as 10.0000, 10.0001, etc., would become 400, 401, etc. Origins would be assigned for all other regions, and relative locations and addresses converted to absolute. This conversion, which is almost always done by the machine, is called *assembly*.

In many relative coding systems, great flexibility is allowed in the form of the region symbols. Here we are using a simple system of two digit numbers. A few of the regions are assigned conventions; these are of course completely arbitrary, since the instructions are never executed in relative form by the machine.

1. Region 00 is reserved for addresses which are invariant, such as shift and input-output addresses.

2. Region 01 is reserved for temporary storage which may be used in any part of the program.

3. Region 02 is used for all permanent storage required by the program. The very commonly required address modifying constants zero and one are ordinarily stored in the first two locations, namely 02.0000 and 02.0001.

4. Region 03 is reserved for instructional constants, i.e., numerical constants which are entered as instructions. For instance, *pi* to nine

decimals could be entered as the instruction Acc right    (31) 4159,2654.
Even though it went in as an instruction it would behave perfectly
well as a number.   This particular usage would be less common than
entering an instruction which is used for loop testing, etc.

5. Regions 04 through 09 are not used.

6. Regions 10 through 99 may be used for instructions or data as
needed.   Each subroutine would ordinarily be a separate region.

As an elementary example, the loop mentioned earlier could be
written:

| LOCATION | OPERATION CODE | OPERATION ABBREVIATION | ADDRESS |
|---|---|---|---|
| 10.0000 | 42 | Load MQ | 02.0000 |
| 10.0001 | 43 | Store MQ | 00.1000 |
| 10.0002 | 10 | Clear add | 02.0001 |
| 10.0003 | 19 | Add to mem | 10.0001 |
| 10.0004 | 14 | Sub | 03.0000 |
| 10.0005 | 04 | Acc zero jump | 10.0007 |
| 10.0006 | 01 | Un jump | 10.0001 |
| 10.0007 | | Continuation | |

02.0000 contains 0
02.0001 contains 1
03.0000 contains Store MQ 00.2000

The address of instruction 10.0001 is written 00.1000, i.e., as an
absolute address, because this is a special-purpose program.   No relocation would be likely which would change that address, since the
purpose of the program is simply to clear the upper half of memory.

Writing programs in this form helps to avoid the three problems
mentioned earlier.   The problem of not knowing the necessary absolute addresses at the time of writing is obviously eliminated.   The
question of making changes is not completely eliminated, but greatly
reduced, by the fact that ordinarily we break up the regions in small
enough pieces so that even if renumbering is necessary, it is not so
bad because there is less to renumber.   In many relative coding
systems, it is not necessary to write location symbols for every instruction location, but only for those to which reference is made
elsewhere in the program; making changes then requires no renumbering.   The relocation problem is reduced to the much simpler one of
merely assigning new origins.

The mechanics of the assembly procedure are:

1. The instructions in relative form are punched on cards according
to a format such as:

Columns 1–6:      Relative location
Columns 7–8:      Operation code
Columns 9–14:     Relative address
Columns 15–21:    Index control
Columns 22–80:    Comments

On many computers these comments could be alphabetic; they are the "remarks" written off to the side as a reminder of what happens at each step. In the example below, the remarks are very detailed; often they are much more sketchy.

2. The origins, as needed, are determined and punched on cards in a format similar to that of the instruction cards.

3. A deck is loaded which is made up of:

A. The assembly program
B. Origin cards
C. Instruction cards

4. The program is assembled, i.e., converted to absolute locations and addresses, inside high-speed memory. This process includes breaking up the relative information as it appears on the cards and operating appropriately on the region numbers, etc.

5. A deck containing seven absolute instructions per card is punched.

The problem has not been solved at this point; we merely have an absolute program on cards which may be put into a deck with data to actually do a calculation. This may well seem like a great deal more trouble than it is worth. Actually, however, the mechanical parts of the procedure become quite automatic and the programmer is left with the appreciable gains in convenience that have been discussed. Some of the operating details of the method will perhaps be clarified by consideration of an example.

## 14.2 Relative Programming Illustration

Suppose we have a simple table preparation problem:

$$y = e^x \sqrt{1 + x^2}$$

for $x$ between 0.0 and 1.0 in steps of 0.1. A subroutine to take the exponential of a floating point number in the accumulator starts at 40.0000; a square root routine starts at 45.0000. In both cases the instruction following the linkage is an error return, for an $x$ too large or less than 0 respectively. The answers will be punched by the routine mentioned in Chapter 11.

A floating point program could be as follows.

| LOCA-TION | OPERA-TION CODE | OPERATION ABBREVIATION | ADDRESS | REMARKS |
|---|---|---|---|---|
| 10.0000 | 10 | Clear add | 02.0002 | Initialize $x$ to 1.0 |
| 10.0001 | 40 | Store acc | 01.0000 | Location of $x$ |
| 10.0002 | 50 | Mem to ind | 03.0000, 00.0002 | Load index 2 with 11 |
| 10.0003 | 10 | Clear add | 01.0000 | Bring in $x$ |
| 10.0004 | 58 | Set ind jump | 40.0000, 00.0001 | Jump to exp routine |
| 10.0005 | 00 | Halt-jump | 00.0000 | Error return |
| 10.0006 | 40 | Store acc | 01.0001 | Store exp $x$ temp. |
| 10.0007 | 42 | Load MQ | 01.0000 | Compute |
| 10.0008 | 72 | Fl mult | 01.0000 | $x$ squared |
| 10.0009 | 70 | Fl add | 02.0002 | Add 1.0 |
| 10.0010 | 58 | Set ind jump | 45.0000, 00.0001 | Compute square root |
| 10.0011 | 00 | Halt-jump | 00.0000 | Error return |
| 10.0012 | 33 | Long right | 00.0010 | Into MQ |
| 10.0013 | 72 | Fl mult | 01.0001 | |
| 10.0014 | 40 | Store acc | 20.0000, 00.0002 | Store result |
| 10.0015 | 10 | Clear add | 01.0000 | Subtract |
| 10.0016 | 71 | Fl sub | 02.0003 | 0.1 |
| 10.0017 | 40 | Store acc | 01.0000 | From $x$ |
| 10.0018 | 55 | Lower ind | 00.0001, 00.0002 | Test whether last |
| 10.0019 | 56 | Zero ind jump | 10.0003, 00.0002 | $y$ computed |
| 10.0020 | 58 | Set ind jump | 50.0000, 00.0001 | Punch routine |
| 10.0021 | 07 | | 20.0001, 20.0011 | 7 numbers per line |
| 10.0022 | 00 | Halt-jump | 00.0000 | Program end |
| 02.0000 | 00 | | 00.0000 | Zero |
| 02.0001 | 00 | | 00.0001 | Address-modifying one |
| 02.0002 | 51 | | 00.1000 | Floating one |
| 02.0003 | 50 | | 00.1000 | Floating one-tenth |
| 03.0000 | 00 | | 00.0011 | Instructional constant 11 |

(*Note:* If the data to be entered were voluminous, they would probably be entered with a special-purpose loading program, rather than assembling the data as in this example.)

This is the program as it would be written. In order to assemble it, the programmer would need only to assign some origins, punch this information in a suitable form, and put the cards into a deck with the assembly program and cards for the subroutines. The origins are assigned primarily according to the rule that regions must not overlap. Suppose that in order to avoid a diagnostic program we start the program at 400. Since the program proper takes twenty-three locations, region 02 could start at 423; 03 could start at 427; 20 could start at 428; and since region 20 has eleven locations, the subroutine 40 could start at 439. The origins of 45 and 50 would depend on the number of instructions in these subroutines. Suppose we assign the origins 480 and 527. We must put 01 somewhere, say 600. The complete table of origins is then

| Region | Origin |
|---|---|
| 10 | 400 |
| 02 | 423 |
| 03 | 427 |
| 20 | 428 |
| 40 | 439 |
| 45 | 480 |
| 50 | 527 |
| 01 | 600 |

It will be observed that the assignment of these origins is quite arbitrary; we could have put the whole program starting at 1450; the order of the regions could have been entirely different.

When these origins are punched on cards and combined with the instruction cards and the cards of the assembly program, the program is ready to be assembled. The output of assembly would be the complete listing of everything on the original cards plus the absolute location and instruction, plus a deck of absolute cards ready to be loaded into the computer.

In most computers it is possible, with more or less difficulty, to enter alphabetic information and at least get it back out; in many machines extensive manipulation with alphabetic information is possible. In most cases, we would get the alphabetic comments back on the assembly listing.

If such an ability were assumed for TYDAC, the assembly listing for the problem above (with the origins assumed), would be as follows. The columns on the extreme right are, from left to right, the absolute location, operation code, absolute address, absolute index control. The subroutines are not shown.

| | | | | | |
|---|---|---|---|---|---|
| 10.0000 | 10 | Clear add | 02.0002 | Initialize $x$ to 1.0 | 0400 10 0425 0000 |
| 10.0001 | 40 | Store acc | 01.0000 | Location of $x$ | 0401 40 0600 0000 |
| 10.0002 | 50 | Mem to ind | 03.0000, 00.0002 | Load index 2 with 11 | 0402 50 0427 0002 |
| 10.0003 | 10 | Clear add | 01.0000 | Bring in $x$ | 0403 10 0600 0000 |
| 10.0004 | 58 | Set ind jump | 40.0000, 00.0001 | Jump to exp routine | 0404 58 0439 0001 |
| 10.0005 | 00 | Halt-jump | 00.0000 | Error return | 0405 00 0000 0000 |
| 10.0006 | 40 | Store acc | 01.0001 | Store exp $x$ temp. | 0406 40 0601 0000 |
| 10.0007 | 42 | Load MQ | 01.0000 | Compute | 0407 42 0600 0000 |
| 10.0008 | 72 | Fl mult | 01.0000 | $x$ squared | 0408 72 0600 0000 |
| 10.0009 | 70 | Fl add | 02.0002 | Add 1.0 | 0409 70 0425 0000 |

*(Continued on next page)*

| | | | | | | | | | |
|---|---|---|---|---|---|---|---|---|---|
| 10.0010 | 58 | Set ind jump | 45.0000, 00.0001 | Compute square root | 0410 | 58 | 0480 | 0001 |
| 10.0011 | 00 | Halt-jump | 00.0000 | Error return | 0411 | 00 | 0000 | 0000 |
| 10.0012 | 33 | Long right | 00.0010 | Into MQ | 0412 | 33 | 0010 | 0000 |
| 10.0013 | 72 | Fl mult | 01.0001 | | 0413 | 72 | 0601 | 0000 |
| 10.0014 | 40 | Store acc | 20.0000, 00.0002 | Store result | 0414 | 40 | 0428 | 0002 |
| 10.0015 | 10 | Clear add | 01.0000 | Subtract | 0415 | 10 | 0600 | 0000 |
| 10.0016 | 71 | Fl sub | 02.0003 | 0.1 | 0416 | 71 | 0426 | 0000 |
| 10.0017 | 40 | Store acc | 01.0000 | From $x$ | 0417 | 40 | 0600 | 0000 |
| 10.0018 | 55 | Lower ind | 00.0001, 00.0002 | Test whether last | 0418 | 55 | 0001 | 0002 |
| 10.0019 | 56 | Zero ind jump | 10.0003, 00.0002 | $y$ computed | 0419 | 56 | 0403 | 0002 |
| 10.0020 | 58 | Set ind jump | 50.0000, 00.0001 | Punch routine | 0420 | 58 | 0527 | 0001 |
| 10.0021 | 07 | | 20.0001, 20.0011 | 7 numbers per line | 0421 | 07 | 0429 | 0439 |
| 10.0022 | 00 | Halt-jump | 00.0000 | Program end | 0422 | 00 | 0000 | 0000 |
| 02.0000 | 00 | Halt-jump | 00.0000 | Zero | 0423 | 00 | 0000 | 0000 |
| 02.0001 | 00 | Halt-jump | 00.0001 | Address-modifying *one* | 0424 | 00 | 0001 | 0000 |
| 02.0002 | 51 | | 00.1000 | Floating one | 0425 | 51 | 1000 | 0000 |
| 02.0003 | 50 | | 00.1000 | Floating one-tenth | 0426 | 50 | 1000 | 0000 |
| 03.0000 | 00 | Halt-jump | 00.0011 | Instructional constant 11 | 0427 | 00 | 0011 | 0000 |

In other relative programming systems, it is not always necessary to locate all regions by giving origins if the instructions may be assigned locations *in sequence* as they are read. This greatly reduces the difficulty of inserting additional instructions. Quite often, alphabetic information is used, either as part of the regional identification or in a fairly flexible system which allows limited use of symbols which amount to ordinary English. It is not too uncommon to find some error-checking built in. For instance, almost all indexing instructions require an index control; the assembly program might make a note if one were not written. Many other variations are possible. Some further discussion of the subject may be found in Chapter 18 on automatic coding.

## Exercises

1. Rewrite any of the medium-sized problems of the previous chapters in relative form. On at least one program, assign origins and "assemble" the program by hand, i.e., convert to absolute locations as in the text example.

2. There is a small error in the program of Section 14.2. Probably the program should be rewritten when such a mistake is discovered; for practice, however, find a "fix" for the mistake which requires only changing one digit somewhere in the program or in the origins. How would this error have manifested itself during checkout?

# 15 INTERPRETIVE PROGRAMMING METHODS

## 15.0 Introduction

Often problems must be done which basically require a different type of operation than is available in the computer at hand. For instance, a problem in electric transients may require extensive use of complex arithmetic. In writing such a program there are several choices.

The complex arithmetic may be done by writing out the required arithmetic on the real and imaginary parts, each time a complex operation is needed, according to the usual formulas:

$$(A + Bi) \pm (C + Di) = (A \pm C) + (B \pm D)i$$

$$(A + Bi) \cdot (C + Di) = (AC - BD) + (BC + AD)i$$

$$\frac{A + Bi}{C + Di} = \frac{(AC + BD)}{(C^2 + D^2)} + \frac{(BC - AD)}{(C^2 + D^2)} \cdot i$$

The real and imaginary parts would be stored in separate locations. Writing out the required operations would get to be burdensome, and we would be inclined to turn very quickly to subroutines.

For each complex operation, there are four input numbers and two output, counting all real and imaginary parts. We could assume that one of the two complex numbers has its real part in the accumulator and its imaginary part in the MQ; the result could be returned to the same registers. Thus there is only one complex number to be specified in the calling sequence. A program is shown which evaluates

$$X + Yi = \frac{[(A + Bi) + (C + Di)][E + Fi]}{[G + Hi]}$$

by means of subroutines starting at:

| | |
|---|---|
| Complex addition: | 20.0000 |
| Complex multiplication: | 21.0000 |
| Complex division: | 22.0000 |

The calling sequence in each case is

> Set ind jump   $n$, 1
> Halt-jump, loc real, loc imaginary

where $n$ is the first instruction in the appropriate subroutine. The eight constants are stored in order in 40.0000 through 40.0007. $x$ goes into 41.0000, $y$ into 41.0001.

| LOCA-TION | OPERA-TION CODE | OPERATION ABBREVIA-TION | ADDRESS | INDEX CONTROL | REMARKS |
|---|---|---|---|---|---|
| 10.0000 | 10 | Clear add | 40.0000 | | $A$ |
| 10.0001 | 42 | Load MQ | 40.0001 | | $B$ |
| 10.0002 | 58 | Set ind jump | 20.0000 | 00.0001 | To add routine |
| 10.0003 | 00 | Halt-jump | 40.0002 | 40.0003 | Add $C + Di$ |
| 10.0004 | 58 | Set ind jump | 21.0000 | 00.0001 | To multiply routine |
| 10.0005 | 00 | Halt-jump | 40.0004 | 40.0005 | Multiply by $E + Fi$ |
| 10.0006 | 58 | Set ind jump | 22.0000 | 00.0001 | To divide routine |
| 10.0007 | 00 | Halt-jump | 40.0006 | 40.0007 | Divide by $G + Hi$ |
| 10.0008 | 40 | Store acc | 41.0000 | | |
| 10.0009 | 43 | Store MQ | 41.0001 | | |

This is a considerable saving in space and trouble over writing out the steps each time, as is always true with subroutines. Nevertheless, there is still considerable red tape to the program. At best it is necessary to write a calling sequence to do each complex operation. Bringing any number into the arithmetic registers, or storing the registers, takes two operations per complex number. If there is a great deal of complex arithmetic, we begin to wish there were some way to cut down the number of instructions to be written—even at the expense of a slower program.

## 15.1 A TYDAC Interpretive System

Interpretive programming is actually an extension of the calling sequence idea. It may be recalled from earlier chapters that we characterized a linkage as a way of telling a subroutine where we came from, and a calling sequence as a way of telling a subroutine not only where we came from but what to work on. "Instructions" 10.0003, 10.0005, and 10.0007 in the example have this function. In a calling sequence there must be an understanding between the writer of the subroutine and the writer of the main program as to the exact form and length of the calling sequence.  In an interpretive program, there is an understanding as to format, but not length. Once the jump has been made to the interpretive program, the "instructions" following the linkage are interpreted one by one until a special instruction is encountered which tells the interpretive program to break out of the sequence.  The "instructions" following the linkage are no more than the code words they are in a calling sequence; the interpretive program has to come back to find out what it is supposed to do.  However, the "instructions" (or *pseudo instructions*) also tell the interpretive program *what* to do with the numbers, so that the instructions written following the linkage give the appearance of instructions in a new type of computer with altogether different characteristics.

We will describe a TYDAC complex arithmetic program in order to illustrate these ideas.

The interpretive program is located at 90.0000.  The linkage

$$\text{Set ind jump}\quad 90.0000, 1$$

gets one into the interpretive mode.  The "instructions" following the linkage should be of the form:

| $+$XX | XXXX | XXXX |
|---|---|---|
| Operation | Real part location | Imaginary part location |

The "operation" is totally unrelated to the TYDAC operation code, since it is interpreted just as are the address and index control.  The operation list is:

| | | |
|---|---|---|
| 00 | Take next instruction as real language | No addresses needed |
| 01 | Clear complex accumulator | No address |
| 02 | Add | |
| 03 | Subtract | |
| 04 | Multiply | |
| 05 | Divide | |
| 06 | Exponential | No address |
| 07 | Sine | No address |
| 08 | Unconditional jump | 1 address |
| 09 | Real part zero jump | 1 address |
| 10 | Imag. part zero jump | 1 address |
| 11 | Store | |

Instruction 00 is the signal to the interpretive program that the interpretive section is finished and that the next instruction is an ordinary TYDAC instruction.  01 calls for clearing of the "complex accumulator" which has nothing to do with the "real" TYDAC accumulator, but is rather two locations in memory. The real accumulator is used extensively during the interpretation and the arithmetic of the complex operations, but locations in memory must be assigned to carry the result of each complex operation during the bookkeeping of interpretation. 02 through 05 call for the arithmetic operations. 06 and 07 take the stated function of the number in the complex accumulator and place the result back there; thus no data address is required. 08, 09, and 10 are jumps; only one address is required, but it must be the location of an interpretive instruction since the program will still be in the interpretive mode after the jump. 11 stores the complex accumulator.

The example above may now be written simply:

| LOCATION | OPERATION CODE | OPERATION ABBREVIATION | ADDRESS | INDEX CONTROL |
|---|---|---|---|---|
| 10.0000 | 58 | Set ind jump | 90.0000 | 00.0001 |
| 10.0001 | 01 | Clear acc | | |
| 10.0002 | 02 | Add | 40.0000 | 40.0001 |
| 10.0003 | 02 | Add | 40.0002 | 40.0003 |
| 10.0004 | 04 | Mult | 40.0004 | 40.0005 |
| 10.0005 | 05 | Divide | 40.0006 | 40.0007 |
| 10.0006 | 12 | Store | 41.0000 | 41.0001 |
| 10.0007 | 00 | Out | | |
| 10.0008 | | Real language continuation | | |

This is a saving of only two steps, but it is evident that the comparison is poor mostly because there are few operations in this example.

A fairly large number of types of interpretive programs have been written. Among them are floating decimal routines, matrix algebra, tracing as mentioned in Chapter 13, double precision discussed in Chapter 16, indexing, and multiple addressing. A tracing routine is an interpretive system since it goes to the program being traced only to pick up each instruction in turn and interpret it. A pseudo accumulator, pseudo MQ, pseudo control registers, even a programmed operation decoder, all have to be provided. The interpretive program in this case has a built-in output program as an integral part.

## 15.2 Internal Operation of an Interpretive Routine

It may be of interest to some readers to know how an interpretive system works "on the inside." Therefore, a possible program for TYDAC complex arithmetic routine is presented below. It is somewhat long; it may be omitted without loss of continuity.

The first task is to define memory locations for the various registers. These are:

| | |
|---|---|
| Real part of accumulator: | 30.0000 |
| Imaginary part of accumulator: | 30.0001 |
| Real part of word specified by address: | 30.0002 |
| Imaginary part of word specified by address: | 30.0003 |
| Location counter: | Index 1 |
| Current instruction register: | 30.0004 |

The pseudo accumulator is the only arithmetic register; the result of each operation is returned there, including multiplication *and* division. No pseudo MQ is therefore provided. The real and imaginary parts of the word specified by the address of the pseudo instruction are obtained and stored as shown. The current (pseudo) instruction and its location must be stored in order to keep track of where the interpretive program should look for its next instruction at each point.

The very first order of business on jumping into the interpretive routine is to increase index 1 by 1 so that it contains the location of the first pseudo instruction. Then the instruction is obtained and the words specified by the two addresses are obtained and stored —even though it may turn out that not both are really addresses. It is simpler to get these words in all cases and then decide whether to use them than to have to obtain them in ten different places *if needed*. Next, the operation code must be interpreted to decide what is to be done on this operation. This is accomplished by use of a *jump table*, a very useful technique in such a situation. It was mentioned in passing in Chapter 5 on address computation. The table looks like:

| | | | |
|---|---|---|---|
| 11.0000 | 01 | Un jump | First instruction of jump out routine |
| 11.0001 | 01 | Un jump | First instruction of clear routine |
| 11.0002 | 01 | Un jump | First instruction of add routine |
| 11.0003 | 01 | Un jump | First instruction of subtract routine |
| 11.0004 | 01 | Un jump | First instruction of multiply routine |
| 11.0005 | 01 | Un jump | First instruction of divide routine |
| 11.0006 | 01 | Un jump | First instruction of exponential routine |
| Etc. | | | |

These correspond to the pseudo operation codes defined on page 180. All that the interpretive routines have to do is use the operation part of the pseudo instruction to decide where to jump to in the above jump table, which in turn jumps to the appropriate part of the interpretive routine for this particular instruction. The final part consists of the individual routines to do the various operations.

The program follows. A few details of some of the individual routines are given after the programs. All numbers are assumed to be in floating point.

### Jump Table

| | | | | | |
|---|---|---|---|---|---|
| 11.0000 | 01 | Un jump | 70.0000 | Jump out |
| 11.0001 | 01 | "      " | 71.0000 | Clear |
| 11.0002 | 01 | "      " | 72.0000 | Add |
| 11.0003 | 01 | "      " | 73.0000 | Subtract |
| 11.0004 | 01 | "      " | 74.0000 | Multiply |
| 11.0005 | 01 | "      " | 75.0000 | Divide |
| 11.0006 | 01 | "      " | 76.0000 | Exponential |
| 11.0007 | 01 | "      " | 77.0000 | Sine |
| 11.0008 | 01 | "      " | 78.0000 | Un jump |
| 11.0009 | 01 | "      " | 79.0000 | Real zero jump |
| 11.0010 | 01 | "      " | 80.0000 | Imag. zero jump |
| 11.0011 | 01 | "      " | 81.0000 | Store |

| LOCA-TION | OPERA-TION CODE | OPERATION ABBREVIATION | ADDRESS | REMARKS |
|---|---|---|---|---|
| 90.0000 | 54 | Raise index | 00.0001, 00.0001 | |
| 90.0001 | 10 | Clear add | 00.0000, 00.0001 | Bring in current pseudo instruction |
| 90.0002 | 40 | Store acc | 30.0004 | |
| 90.0003 | 41 | Store address | 90.0009 | Prepare to get real part |
| 90.0004 | 33 | Long right | 00.0004 | |
| 90.0005 | 11 | Add | 03.0000 | Loc 11.0000 |
| 90.0006 | 41 | Store address | 90.0013 | Prepare to get operation code |
| 90.0007 | 32 | Long left | 00.0008 | |
| 90.0008 | 41 | Store address | 90.0011 | Prepare to get imag. part |
| 90.0009 | 10 | Clear add | [00.0000] | Get real part |
| 90.0010 | 40 | Store acc | 30.0002 | |
| 90.0011 | 10 | Clear add | [00.0000] | Get imag. part |
| 90.0012 | 40 | Store acc | 30.0003 | |
| 90.0013 | 01 | Un jump | [00.0000] | To jump table |

### Jump Out Routine

| | | | | |
|---|---|---|---|---|
| 70.0000 | 01 | Un jump | 00.0001, 00.0001 | |

### Clear Routine

| | | | | |
|---|---|---|---|---|
| 71.0000 | 10 | Clear add | 02.0000 | Loc 0 |
| 71.0001 | 40 | Store acc | 30.0000 | |
| 71.0002 | 40 | Store acc | 30.0001 | |
| 71.0003 | 01 | Un jump | 90.0000 | |

(Continued on next page)

### Add Routine

| | | | | |
|---|---|---|---|---|
| 72.0000 | 10 | Clear add | 30.0000 | $A$ |
| 72.0001 | 70 | Fl add | 30.0002 | $A + C$ |
| 72.0002 | 40 | Store acc | 30.0000 | |
| 72.0003 | 10 | Clear add | 30.0001 | $B$ |
| 72.0004 | 70 | Fl add | 30.0003 | $B + D$ |
| 72.0005 | 40 | Store acc | 30.0001 | |
| 72.0006 | 01 | Un jump | 90.0000 | |

### Subtract Routine

| | | | | |
|---|---|---|---|---|
| 73.0000 | 10 | Clear add | 30.0000 | $A$ |
| 73.0001 | 71 | Fl sub | 30.0002 | $A - C$ |
| 73.0002 | 40 | Store acc | 30.0000 | |
| 73.0003 | 10 | Clear add | 30.0001 | $B$ |
| 73.0004 | 71 | Fl sub | 30.0003 | $B - D$ |
| 73.0005 | 40 | Store acc | 30.0001 | |
| 73.0006 | 01 | Un jump | 90.0000 | |

### Multiply Routine

| | | | | |
|---|---|---|---|---|
| 74.0000 | 42 | Load MQ | 30.0001 | $B$ |
| 74.0001 | 72 | Fl mult | 30.0003 | $BD$ |
| 74.0002 | 40 | Store acc | 01.0000 | Temporary |
| 74.0003 | 42 | Load MQ | 30.0000 | $A$ |
| 74.0004 | 72 | Fl mult | 30.0002 | $AC$ |
| 74.0005 | 71 | Fl sub | 01.0000 | $AC - BD$ |
| 74.0006 | 40 | Store acc | 01.0001 | Real part temporary |
| 74.0007 | 42 | Load MQ | 30.0001 | $B$ |
| 74.0008 | 72 | Fl mult | 30.0002 | $BC$ |
| 74.0009 | 40 | Store acc | 01.0000 | Temporary |
| 74.0010 | 42 | Load MQ | 30.0000 | $A$ |
| 74.0011 | 72 | Fl mult | 30.0003 | $AD$ |
| 74.0012 | 70 | Fl add | 01.0000 | $BC + AD$ |
| 74.0013 | 40 | Store acc | 30.0001 | |
| 74.0014 | 10 | Clear add | 01.0001 | |
| 74.0015 | 40 | Store acc | 30.0000 | |
| 74.0016 | 01 | Un jump | 90.0000 | |

### Divide Routine

| | | | | |
|---|---|---|---|---|
| 75.0000 | 42 | Load MQ | 30.0002 | $C$ |
| 75.0001 | 72 | Fl mult | 30.0002 | $C^2$ |
| 75.0002 | 40 | Store acc | 01.0000 | Temporary |
| 75.0003 | 42 | Load MQ | 30.0003 | $D$ |
| 75.0004 | 72 | Fl mult | 30.0003 | $D^2$ |
| 75.0005 | 70 | Fl add | 01.0000 | $C^2 + D^2$ |
| 75.0006 | 40 | Store acc | 01.0000 | Temporary |
| 75.0007 | 42 | Load MQ | 30.0000 | $A$ |

(*Continued on next page*)

| 75.0008 | 72 | Fl mult | 30.0002 | $AC$ |
| 75.0009 | 40 | Store acc | 01.0001 | Temporary |
| 75.0010 | 42 | Load MQ | 30.0001 | $B$ |
| 75.0011 | 72 | Fl mult | 30.0003 | $BD$ |
| 75.0012 | 70 | Fl add | 01.0001 | $AC + BD$ |
| 75.0013 | 73 | Fl div | 01.0000 | Real part |
| 75.0014 | 43 | Store MQ | 01.0001 | Temporary |
| 75.0015 | 42 | Load MQ | 30.0000 | $A$ |
| 75.0016 | 72 | Fl mult | 30.0003 | $AD$ |
| 75.0017 | 40 | Store acc | 01.0002 | Temporary |
| 75.0018 | 42 | Load MQ | 30.0001 | $B$ |
| 75.0019 | 72 | Fl mult | 30.0002 | $BC$ |
| 75.0020 | 71 | Fl sub | 01.0002 | $BC - AD$ |
| 75.0021 | 73 | Fl div | 01.0000 | Imag. part |
| 75.0022 | 43 | Store MQ | 30.0001 | |
| 75.0023 | 10 | Clear add | 01.0001 | |
| 75.0024 | 40 | Store acc | 30.0000 | |
| 75.0025 | 01 | Un jump | 90.0000 | |

Since both the exponential and sine functions of a complex variable require the evaluation of sines, cosines, and exponentials, subroutines for the sine and exponential are written separately. The cosine is obtained from:

$$\cos x = \sin (x + \pi/2)$$

The exponential is calculated from:

$$e^x = 1 + \frac{x}{1!} + \frac{x^2}{2!} + \frac{x^3}{3!} + \cdots$$

by the recursion formula:

$$\text{term } 0 = 1$$

$$\text{term } n = \frac{x}{n} (\text{term } n - 1)$$

The process is continued until a term is less than $10^{-7}$. The sine series is:

$$\sin x = x - \frac{x^3}{3!} + \frac{x^5}{5!} - \frac{x^7}{7!} + \cdots$$

The recursion formula is:

$$\text{term } 1 = x$$

$$\text{term } 2, 4, 6, \cdots = 0$$

$$\text{term } n = \frac{-x^2}{(n)(n - 1)} (\text{term } n - 2)$$

which again is continued until a term is less in absolute value than $10^{-7}$. This is not representative of the methods used in high-speed machines for computing transcendental functions. Many short cuts would ordinarily be used (see Chapter 17).

With $x$ in accumulator in floating point and $e^x$ to be left in accumulator in floating point, the program is:

| LOCA-TION | OPERA-TION CODE | OPERATION ABBREVIATION | ADDRESS | REMARKS |
|---|---|---|---|---|
| 91.0000 | 40 | Store acc | 01.0010 | Store $x$ |
| 91.0001 | 10 | Clear add | 12.0000 | Floating 1.0 |
| 91.0002 | 40 | Store acc | 01.0011 | Term 0 |
| 91.0003 | 40 | Store acc | 01.0012 | Factorial |
| 91.0004 | 40 | Store acc | 01.0013 | Summation ($= e^x$ eventually) |
| 91.0005 | 10 | Clear add | 01.0011 | Term $n-1$ |
| 91.0006 | 73 | Fl div | 01.0012 | $\dfrac{\text{Term } n-1}{n}$ |
| 91.0007 | 72 | Fl mult | 01.0010 | $\dfrac{x}{n}(\text{term } n-1)$ |
| 91.0008 | 40 | Store acc | 01.0011 | New term $n$ |
| 91.0009 | 70 | Fl add | 01.0013 | New summation |
| 91.0010 | 40 | Store acc | 01.0013 | |
| 91.0011 | 10 | Clear add | 12.0000 | Floating 1.0 |
| 91.0012 | 70 | Fl add | 01.0012 | |
| 91.0013 | 40 | Store acc | 01.0012 | Add 1 to factorial counter |
| 91.0014 | 10 | Clear acc | 12.0003 | $10^{-7}$ |
| 91.0015 | 15 | Sub abs | 01.0011 | |
| 91.0016 | 03 | Acc plus jump | 91.0018 | Jump out if converged |
| 91.0017 | 01 | Un jump | 91.0005 | |
| 91.0018 | 10 | Clear add | 01.0013 | Put $e^x$ in accumulator |
| 91.0019 | 01 | Un jump | 00.0001, 00.0002 | |

With $x$ in floating in accumulator and sin $x$ to be left in accumulator in floating point, the program is:

| LOCA-TION | OPERA-TION CODE | OPERATION ABBREVIATION | ADDRESS | REMARKS |
|---|---|---|---|---|
| 92.0000 | 40 | Store acc | 01.0011 | Term 1 |
| 92.0001 | 40 | Store acc | 01.0013 | Summation |
| 92.0002 | 42 | Load MQ | 01.0011 | |
| 92.0003 | 72 | Fl mult | 01.0011 | $x^2$ |
| 92.0004 | 40 | Store acc | 01.0010 | |

(Continued on next page)

| 92.0005 | 10 | Clear add | 12.0001 | Floating 2.0 |
| 92.0006 | 40 | Store acc | 01.0014 | $n-1$ |
| 92.0007 | 10 | Clear add | 12.0002 | Floating 3.0 |
| 92.0008 | 40 | Store acc | 01.0015 | $n$ |
| 92.0009 | 13 | Clear sub | 01.0011 | $-\text{Term } n-2$ |
| 92.0010 | 73 | Fl div | 01.0014 | $\dfrac{-\text{Term } n-2}{(n-1)}$ |
| 92.0011 | 72 | Fl mult | 01.0010 | $\dfrac{-x^2(\text{term } n-2)}{(n-1)}$ |
| 92.0012 | 73 | Fl div | 01.0015 | $\dfrac{-x^2(\text{term } n-2)}{(n-1)(n)}$ |
| 92.0013 | 43 | Store MQ | 01.0011 | Term $n$ |
| 92.0014 | 10 | Clear add | 01.0013 | |
| 92.0015 | 70 | Fl add | 01.0011 | New summation |
| 92.0016 | 40 | Store acc | 01.0013 | |
| 92.0017 | 10 | Clear add | 12.0003 | $10^{-7}$ |
| 92.0018 | 15 | Sub abs | 01.0011 | Test convergence |
| 92.0019 | 03 | Acc plus jump | 92.0026 | |
| 92.0020 | 10 | Clear add | 01.0014 | Modify $n, n-1$ |
| 92.0021 | 70 | Fl add | 12.0001 | Floating 2.0 |
| 92.0022 | 40 | Store acc | 01.0014 | |
| 92.0023 | 70 | Fl add | 12.0000 | Floating 1.0 |
| 92.0024 | 40 | Store acc | 01.0015 | |
| 92.0025 | 01 | Un jump | 92.0009 | |
| 92.0026 | 10 | Clear add | 01.0013 | |
| 92.0027 | 01 | Un jump | 00.0001, 00.0002 | |

### Complex Exponential Routine

$$e^{(A+Bi)} = e^A \cos B + ie^A \sin B$$

| 76.0000 | 10 | Clear add | 30.0000 | $A$ |
| 76.0001 | 58 | Set ind jump | 91.0000, 00.0002 | $e^A$ |
| 76.0002 | 40 | Store acc | 01.0000 | |
| 76.0003 | 10 | Clear add | 30.0001 | $B$ |
| 76.0004 | 58 | Set ind jump | 92.0000, 00.0002 | $\sin B$ |
| 76.0005 | 40 | Store acc | 01.0001 | |
| 76.0006 | 10 | Clear add | 30.0001 | $B$ |
| 76.0007 | 70 | Fl add | 12.0004 | $B + \pi/2$ |
| 76.0008 | 58 | Set ind jump | 92.0000, 00.0002 | $\cos B$ |
| 76.0009 | 33 | Long right | 00.0010 | |
| 76.0010 | 72 | Fl mult | 01.0000 | $e^A \cos B$ |
| 76.0011 | 40 | Store acc | 30.0000 | Real part |
| 76.0012 | 42 | Load MQ | 01.0001 | $\sin B$ |
| 76.0013 | 72 | Fl mult | 01.0000 | $e^A \sin B$ |
| 76.0014 | 40 | Store acc | 30.0001 | Imag. part |
| 76.0015 | 01 | Un jump | 90.0000 | |

(*Continued on next page*)

### Sine Routine

$$\sin (A + Bi) = \frac{e^B + e^{-B}}{2} \sin A + i \cdot \frac{e^B - e^{-B}}{2} \cos A$$

| | | | | |
|---|---|---|---|---|
| 77.0000 | 10 | Clear add | 30.0000 | $A$ |
| 77.0001 | 58 | Set ind jump | 92.0000, 00.0002 | $\sin A$ |
| 77.0002 | 40 | Store acc | 01.0000 | |
| 77.0003 | 10 | Clear add | 30.0000 | $A$ |
| 77.0004 | 70 | Fl add | 12.0004 | $A + \pi/2$ |
| 77.0005 | 58 | Set ind jump | 92.0000, 00.0001 | $\cos A$ |
| 77.0006 | 40 | Store acc | 01.0001 | |
| 77.0007 | 10 | Clear add | 30.0001 | $B$ |
| 77.0008 | 58 | Set ind jump | 91.0000, 00.0001 | $e^B$ |
| 77.0009 | 40 | Store acc | 01.0002 | |
| 77.0010 | 10 | Clear add | 12.0000 | Floating 1.0 |
| 77.0011 | 73 | Fl div | 01.0002 | $1/e^B = e^{-B}$ |
| 77.0012 | 43 | Store MQ | 01.0003 | |
| 77.0013 | 10 | Clear add | 01.0002 | $e^B$ |
| 77.0014 | 70 | Fl add | 01.0003 | $e^B + e^{-B}$ |
| 77.0015 | 73 | Fl div | 12.0001 | $\dfrac{e^B + e^{-B}}{2}$ |
| 77.0016 | 72 | Fl mult | 01.0000 | Real part |
| 77.0017 | 40 | Store acc | 30.0000 | |
| 77.0018 | 10 | Clear add | 01.0002 | $e^B$ |
| 77.0019 | 71 | Fl sub | 01.0003 | $e^B - e^{-B}$ |
| 77.0020 | 73 | Fl div | 12.0001 | $\dfrac{e^B - e^{-B}}{2}$ |
| 77.0021 | 72 | Fl mult | 01.0001 | Imag. part |
| 77.0022 | 40 | Store acc | 30.0001 | |
| 77.0023 | 01 | Un jump | 90.0000 | |

### Unconditional Jump Routine

| | | | |
|---|---|---|---|
| 78.0000 | 50 | Mem to ind | 90.0009, 00.0001 |
| 78.0001 | 01 | Un jump | 90.0001 |

### Real Part Zero Jump

| | | | | |
|---|---|---|---|---|
| 79.0000 | 10 | Clear add | 30.0000 | $A$ |
| 79.0001 | 04 | Acc zero jump | 79.0003 | |
| 79.0002 | 01 | Un jump | 90.0000 | |
| 79.0003 | 50 | Mem to ind | 90.0009, 00.0001 | |
| 79.0004 | 01 | Un jump | 90.0001 | |

### Imaginary Part Zero Jump

| | | | | |
|---|---|---|---|---|
| 80.0000 | 10 | Clear add | 30.0001 | $B$ |
| 80.0001 | 04 | Acc zero jump | 80.0003 | |

(*Continued on next page*)

| 80.0002 | 01 | Un jump | 90.0000 |
| 80.0003 | 50 | Mem to ind | 90.0009, 00.0001 |
| 80.0004 | 01 | Un jump | 90.0001 |

### Store Complex Accumulator

| 81.0000 | 50 | Mem to ind | 90.0009, 00.0002 |
| 81.0001 | 10 | Clear add | 30.0000 |
| 81.0002 | 40 | Store acc | 00.0000, 00.0002 |
| 81.0003 | 50 | Mem to ind | 90.0011, 00.0002 |
| 81.0004 | 10 | Clear add | 30.0001 |
| 81.0005 | 40 | Store acc | 00.0000, 00.0002 |
| 81.0006 | 01 | Un jump | 90.0000 |

### Instructional Constant

| 03.0000 | 00 | Halt-jump | 11.0000 |

### Constants

| 12.0000 | 1.0 | Floating |
| 12.0001 | 2.0 | " |
| 12.0002 | 3.0 | " |
| 12.0003 | 0.0000001 | " |
| 12.0004 | $\pi/2$ | " |

An actual interpretive complex arithmetic might have a few more instructions. It was felt that these present the idea of how an interpretive routine works, and possibly provide a little insight into the work of "library" or utility programming.

## 15.3 Conclusion

It is worth pointing out that every interpretive instruction must be interpreted each time it is carried out. We have added about ten instructions (in the interpreter) for every complex operation simply to save the extra writing of calling sequences—which would be faster in machine time. There is another technique which is sometimes preferable, called *compiling;* this is discussed a little more fully in Chapter 18. In compiling, the interpretive instructions are interpreted only once, before actual execution of the problem, and the compiler substitutes calling sequences for the pseudo instructions. Once the pre-execution phase is done, we have both the advantage of a simple main program and efficient machine operation. On the other hand, this can run into large memory requirements, so large, in fact, that tapes must become an integral part of the system. If this happens, the compiling idea loses its attractiveness unless we are dealing with a machine where the arithmetic speed is not appreciably faster than tape transfer rates.  On recent large machines, the arithmetic speeds are so high (and often, memory so large) that it is more efficient to waste the time involved in interpreting each pseudo instruction each time it appears.

## Exercises

1. Using the interpretive complex arithmetic system in the text, write a program to evaluate:

$$x + yi = \frac{(A + Bi)e^{(C+Di)} - (E + Fi)\sin(G + Hi)}{(J + Ki)(L + Mi) \pm (P + Qi)}$$

The plus sign in the denominator is to be taken if $Q$ is positive, the minus if $Q$ is negative.  Assume locations for all the constants.

2. Using the text interpretive scheme and assuming any other subroutine which may be needed, write subroutines to convert between polar and rectangular forms, according to the formula:

$$(A + Bi) = Re^{i\theta}$$

where $R = +\sqrt{A^2 + B^2}$, $\theta = \tan^{-1} B/A$, $A = R\cos\theta$, and $B = R\sin\theta$.

(Is it possible to take the sine of a real number using the complex sine interpretive program?)

3. Set up an interpretive floating point system, using subroutines written as an exercise of Chapter 10.

4. A program to generate music on a high-speed computer might use an interpretive scheme like this:

| Set ind jump | loc prog, 1 |
|---|---|
| $n$ | $m$ |
| $n$ | $m$ |
| $n$ | $m$ |
| . | . |
| . | . |
| . | . |

In each interpretive instruction, $n$ determines the duration of the note and $m$ the pitch.  Each is basically controlled by repetitions of a loop. Write an interpreter for the duration (operation code) part only, as follows.  A loop which consists of exactly nine instructions, not including any multiplications or divisions, is to be repeated exactly $n$ times.  If nine instructions are not needed, pad the loop out somehow.

# 16 DOUBLE PRECISION ARITHMETIC

## 16.0 Introduction

There is a class of computer problems which cannot be handled satisfactorily using only eight or ten decimal digits in each arithmetic operation. Problem data are never that accurate, but the nature of the operations carried out may demand that more digits be kept in the intermediate stages—even though they will be discarded at the end. The typical situation where this arises is matrix work: matrix inversion, eigenvalue calculation, curve fitting, linear programming. It is not too unusual to find matrices of a hundred rows or columns or higher. In several of the matrix applications, the total number of arithmetic operations is proportional to the third power of number of rows or columns. An application requiring several million arithmetic operations can accumulate so much round-off error that the answers may have only one or two significant digits (if any) even though the input was good to four places and eight were kept at all intermediate steps. Depending on the exact numbers appearing in the problem, it is possible to lose *all* significance in just a few hundred arithmetic operations.

Another type of problem requiring more digits in the calculation involves the differences of very large numbers. Take a series like

$$J_1(x) = \frac{x}{2} - \frac{x^3}{2^3 2!} + \frac{x^5}{2^5 2! 3!} - \cdots$$

This series for a Bessel function converges for all $x$, but if we try to calculate $J_1(25)$, for example, from this series, we may find ourselves attempting to subtract numbers of the order of a million and still come out with seven decimals in the difference! In this example we would turn to an asymptotic expression, but there are cases where there is no choice but to try to evaluate the series.

What we need, then, is a simple way to carry twenty digits in each arithmetic operation in a machine built to hold only ten.* This

---

* Of course, this would be no problem at all in the IBM 702 or 705, since the length of numbers is completely variable.

is usually done by an interpretive program which takes two consecutive locations for each number and does simple arithmetic and possibly a little logic. The main work of the program, however, is doing one arithmetic operation on two numbers stored in four different places while keeping the signs straight.

Since twice as many digits as there are in one computer word are kept in each operation, and the number of digits is a measure of the *precision* of a number, this technique is called *double precision* arithmetic. *Triple precision* is used in some applications, particularly in machines with short words. Some double precision routines are floating point. We shall describe one which is fixed point.

## 16.1 Arithmetic Basis of Methods and TYDAC Codes

We shall denote the two numbers in an arithmetic operation as $A_1A_2$ and $B_1B_2$, where $A_1$ is the more significant ten digits in one storage location and $A_2$ is the less significant ten digits in the next higher numbered location. The twenty-digit numbers are all considered to be less than one, i.e., fractions.

The problem in addition and subtraction concerns signs.

$$(A_1A_2) + (B_1B_2) = (A_1 + B_1) + (A_2 + B_2)$$

The first problem is easily solved: what happens if $A_2 + B_2$ contains eleven digits? The addition can be arranged:

| | | |
|---|---|---|
| 10 | Clear add | Loc $A_2$ |
| 11 | Add | Loc $B_2$ |
| 33 | Long right | 10 |
| 11 | Add | Loc $A_1$ |
| 11 | Add | Loc $B_1$ |

If overflow does occur, the one will go into the overflow position and be shifted into the last position of the accumulator by the long right 10. If the two numbers have the same sign, the twenty-digit sum now appears in the accumulator and MQ. We have assumed that all numbers are less than one, which means that scaling has eliminated the possibility of overflow here. If overflow does occur, the machine must be programmed to stop.

The problem is a bit more complicated if the two numbers have different signs, either by subtraction or because the signs are different in an addition.

$$(A_1A_2) - (B_1B_2) = (A_1 - B_1) + (A_2 - B_2)$$

The problem is that the two parts of the answer may not be of the same sign. For instance, consider the subtraction

$$10000000009000000000$$
$$-40000000005000000000$$

which gives, in two parts,

$$(-3000000000) + (+4000000000)$$

The correct sum is, of course,

$$-29999999996000000000$$

but how do we generalize this and instruct the machine accordingly?

The rule is that if the two parts $(A_1 - B_1)$ and $(A_2 - B_2)$ are of different signs, $(A_2 - B_2)$ must be complemented, and one added to or subtracted from the last position of $(A_1 - B_1)$ depending on whether $(A_1 - B_1)$ is negative or positive respectively.

An outline program for double precision addition follows. Subtraction would require only a prior sign reversal of the subtrahend.

| LOCA-TION | OPERATION CODE | OPERATION ABBREVIATION | ADDRESS | REMARKS |
|---|---|---|---|---|
| 10.0000 | 10 | Clear add | Loc $A_2$ | |
| 10.0001 | 11 | Add | Loc $B_2$ | |
| 10.0002 | 33 | Long right | 00.0010 | |
| 10.0003 | 11 | Add | Loc $A_1$ | |
| 10.0004 | 11 | Add | Loc $B_1$ | |
| 10.0005 | 40 | Store acc | Loc $C_1$ | Store result; will be |
| 10.0006 | 43 | Store MQ | Loc $C_2$ | corrected if necessary |
| 10.0007 | 03 | Acc plus jump | 10.0010 | $(A_1 - B_1)$ positive |
| 10.0008 | 05 | MQ sign jump | 10.0019 | $(A_2 - B_2)$ positive |
| 10.0009 | 01 | Un jump | 10.0026 | Both negative; no corrections |
| 10.0010 | 05 | MQ sign jump | 10.0026 | Both positive; no correction |
| 10.0011 | 14 | Sub | Loc 1 | $(A_1 - B_1)$ positive and |
| 10.0012 | 02 | Ov jump | 10.0028 | $(A_2 - B_2)$ negative |
| 10.0013 | 40 | Store acc | Loc $C_1$ | Correction |
| 10.0014 | 10 | Clear add | Loc 1 | |
| 10.0015 | 30 | Acc left | 00.0010 | 1 into overflow pos. |
| 10.0016 | 11 | Add | Loc $C_2$ | Complement $C_2$ |
| 10.0017 | 40 | Store acc | Loc $C_2$ | |
| 10.0018 | 01 | Un jump | 10.0027 | Corrections finished |
| 10.0019 | 11 | Add | Loc 1 | $(A_1 - B_1)$ negative and |
| 10.0020 | 02 | Ov jump | 10.0028 | $(A_2 - B_2)$ positive |
| 10.0021 | 40 | Store acc | Loc $C_1$ | Correction |
| 10.0022 | 10 | Clear sub | Loc 1 | |
| 10.0023 | 30 | Acc left | 00.0010 | $-1$ into overflow pos. |

(Continued on next page)

| 10.0024 | 11 | Add | Loc $C_2$ | |
| 10.0025 | 40 | Store acc | Loc $C_2$ | Complement $C_2$ |
| 10.0026 | 02 | Ov jump | 10.0028 | |
| 10.0027 | 01 | Un jump | | Back to main prog. or interpreter |
| 10.0028 | 00 | Halt-jump | —— | |

In multiplication the sign control problem is taken care of by algebra and the machine, since the partial products will all be of the same sign. The formula is

$$(A_1 A_2)(B_1 B_2) = A_1 B_1 + A_1 B_2 + A_2 B_1$$

$A_2 B_2$ is omitted since it can at most have an effect of one in the twentieth digit. In some machines it is not difficult to include the effect, but in TYDAC it is not worth the trouble. The products $A_1 B_2$ and $A_2 B_1$ have ten zeros in front, with respect to the product $A_1 B_1$.

| LOCA-TION | OPERATION CODE | OPERATION ABBREVIATION | ADDRESS | REMARKS |
| --- | --- | --- | --- | --- |
| 11.0000 | 42 | Load MQ | Loc $A_1$ | |
| 11.0001 | 16 | Mult | Loc $B_1$ | |
| 11.0002 | 40 | Store acc | 01.0000 | Temporary |
| 11.0003 | 43 | Store MQ | 01.0001 | Temporary |
| 11.0004 | 42 | Load MQ | Loc $A_1$ | |
| 11.0005 | 17 | Mult round | Loc $B_2$ | |
| 11.0006 | 40 | Store acc | 01.0002 | Temporary |
| 11.0007 | 42 | Load MQ | Loc $B_1$ | |
| 11.0008 | 17 | Mult round | Loc $A_2$ | $A_2 B_1$ |
| 11.0009 | 11 | Add | 01.0002 | $+A_1 B_2$ |
| 11.0010 | 11 | Add | 01.0001 | Less significant half of $A_1 B_1$ |
| 11.0011 | 33 | Long right | 00.0010 | |
| 11.0012 | 11 | Add | 01.0000 | More significant half of $A_1 B_1$ |
| 11.0013 | 40 | Store acc | Loc $C_1$ | |
| 11.0014 | 43 | Store MQ | Loc $C_2$ | |
| 11.0015 | 01 | Un jump | Out | Finished |

Division is based on the approximation:

$$\frac{A}{B} = \frac{A}{B_1 + B_2} = \frac{A}{B_1}\left(\frac{1}{1 + \dfrac{B_2}{B_1}}\right) \cong \frac{A}{B_1}\left(1 - \frac{B_2}{B_1}\right)$$

Division of a double-length dividend by a single-length divisor is easily enough performed by a second division—dividing the remainder from a first division by the original divisor. Once $A/B_1$

and $(1 - B_2/B_1)$ have been calculated, the double precision multiplication routine can be used to multiply them and get the final
quotient.

| LOCA-TION | OPERATION CODE | OPERATION ABBREVIATION | ADDRESS | REMARKS |
|---|---|---|---|---|
| 12.0000 | 10 | Clear add | Loc $A_1$ | |
| 12.0001 | 42 | Load MQ | Loc $A_2$ | |
| 12.0002 | 18 | Divide | Loc $B_1$ | |
| 12.0003 | 43 | Store MQ | Loc $A_1$ | Prepare for double length multiplication |
| 12.0004 | 42 | Load MQ | Loc 0 | |
| 12.0005 | 18 | Divide | Loc $B_1$ | |
| 12.0006 | 43 | Store MQ | Loc $A_2$ | |
| 12.0007 | 10 | Clear add | Loc 0 | |
| 12.0008 | 42 | Load MQ | Loc $B_2$ | |
| 12.0009 | 18 | Divide | Loc $B_1$ | |
| 12.0010 | 43 | Store MQ | 01.0000 | Temporary |
| 12.0011 | 42 | Load MQ | Loc 0 | |
| 12.0012 | 18 | Divide | Loc $B_1$ | |
| 12.0013 | 43 | Store MQ | 01.0001 | |
| 12.0014 | 10 | Clear add | Loc 1 | |
| 12.0015 | 30 | Acc left | 10 | 1 into overflow pos. |
| 12.0016 | 14 | Sub | 01.0001 | |
| 12.0017 | 33 | Long right | 10 | |
| 12.0018 | 11 | Add | Loc 9999999999 | |
| 12.0019 | 14 | Sub | 01.0000 | $1 - (B_2/B_1)$ |
| 12.0020 | 40 | Store acc | Loc $B_1$ | |
| 12.0021 | 43 | Store MQ | Loc $B_2$ | |
| 12.0022 | 01 | Un jump | 11.0000 | Jump to multiply |

## 16.2 An Interpretive Routine

Such a system would almost always be written into an interpretive
system. The three routines above would be simply the working
sections of such a routine. Without writing the detailed code, which
would not be too different from the one in the last chapter, we may
describe a typical double precision routine.

All data addresses refer to the first of two consecutive locations.
The more significant ten digits are in the location specified by the
address; the less significant ten in the following location. Addresses
in the interpretive system are three digits only. The instructions are
"three-address," i.e., there are three locations in memory specified
in each instruction. Each instruction is made up of

| OPERATION | $A$ | $B$ | $C$ |
|---|---|---|---|
| X | XXX | XXX | XXX |

(The fact that this interpretive system is three-address is not necessarily typical.)

There might be eight operations:

| CODE | OPERATION | FUNCTION |
|---|---|---|
| 1 | Add | $C(A) + C(B) \rightarrow C(C)$ |
| 2 | Subtract | $C(A) - C(B) \rightarrow C(C)$ |
| 3 | Multiply | $C(A) \cdot C(B) \rightarrow C(C)$ |
| 4 | Divide | $C(A) \div C(B) \rightarrow C(C)$ |
| 5 | Plus jump | If $C(A) > 0$, take next instruction from $C$ |
| 6 | Zero jump | If $C(A) = 0$, take next instruction from $C$ |
| 7 | Shift right | Shift $C(A)$ $C$ places to right and place result in $B$ |
| 8 | Shift left | Shift $C(A)$ $C$ places to left and place result in $B$ |

A few notes are in order. $C(A) + C(B) \rightarrow C(C)$ means that the number specified by the first address $(A)$ is added to the number specified by the second address $(B)$ and the result is placed in location $C$. The jumps examine the number at $A$ and take the next (interpretive) instruction from $C$, not contents of $C$. In other words, $C$ is the usual address of a one-address jump instruction. The shifts operate on the $C(A)$ and place the shifted number in $B$; the number of shifts is specified by $C$. $A$ and $B$ can of course be the same. If $C$ is zero, the instruction simply moves a number from one location to another.

These instructions are the same total length as a regular TYDAC instruction, but they do require three addresses and a different format. The interpretive routine would not be especially complicated.

This program is fairly representative. It does depend to a certain extent on the particular features of a machine, such as addition with the overflow position and a conditional jump to test the sign of the MQ.

## Exercises

1. Using the interpretive system of Section 16.2, write a program to evaluate

$$y = \frac{a + \sqrt{1 + x^2}}{2}$$

All numbers are double length. Assume locations for these and any other needed constants. The heart of the problem is, of course, writing the double precision square root program.

2. Write the interpretive part of the system of Section 16.2.

3. Using the series for $J_1(x)$ mentioned in Section 16.0 and the interpretive system of Section 16.2, write a program to evaluate the series. Estimate the significance lost in calculating $J_1(100)$ due to subtraction of large, nearly equal numbers.

4. Write the approximation formulas and logic for a triple precision program. If desired, write the triple precision program also, either as subroutines or as an interpretive program.

# 17 MISCELLANEOUS PROGRAMMING TECHNIQUES

## 17.0 Introduction

This chapter is a collection of various methods in programming and coding which do not fall logically into other chapters. The items are all fairly common problems in computing. Although the ideas presented are not complex, they do represent a considerable amount of effort to a person who may have to rediscover them.

## 17.1 Using a Code Number to Pick One of *n* Alternatives

It is not too uncommon to find situations where there are several alternative paths at a given point in a problem, of which one must be chosen on the basis of some number in memory. An example occurred in Chapter 15 in the complex arithmetic interpretive routine, where one of thirteen subroutines had to be chosen on the basis of a code number between zero and twelve. Another might be a choice of several computational procedures to be made on the basis of which of several intervals brackets a number. Another might be a choice of where to store a tally, depending on the size of a number.

All of these come under the general heading of branches or forks. In terms of flow charts, the situation is that we have some type of comparison block, out of which proceed two or more arrows for the *n* alternatives. Several techniques are available in this area, which will be illustrated by examples. The method used with each example is not meant to be the only applicable method, or even the best one. The choice of a method must, as usual, be based on the economic balance of computer memory space, computer time and cost, and programming time and cost.

### FUNCTIONAL RELATIONSHIP BETWEEN CODE NUMBER AND ADDRESS

About the simplest case is a set of alternatives which can be related to the controlling code number by a simple formula. An example occurred in Chapter 5 on address computation. Suppose that one of ten constants stored in 02.0000 through 02.0009 must be placed in 01.0010, depending on whether the code number in 01.0005 is 0 through 9. This is simplicity itself, since the functional relationship is simply: address of clear add instruction = 02.0000 + contents of 01.0005.

| LOCATION | OPERATION CODE | OPERATION ABBREVIATION | ADDRESS |
|---|---|---|---|
| 10.0000 | 10 | Clear add | 01.0005 |
| 10.0001 | 11 | Add | 03.0000 |
| 10.0002 | 41 | Store address | 10.0003 |
| 10.0003 | 10 | Clear add | [00.0000] |
| 10.0004 | 40 | Store acc | 01.0010 |

where 03.0000 contains

| | OPERATION CODE | OPERATION ABBREVIATION | ADDRESS |
|---|---|---|---|
| | 00 | Halt-jump | 02.0000 |

Many applications of this technique apply where the functional relationship is more complicated. The primary task is recognizing and defining the relationship.

## ZERO-JUMP TESTING OF A CODE NUMBER

Take the situation where a jump must be made to one of four sections of a program, starting at 11.0000, 12.0000, 13.0000, or 14.0000, depending on whether a code number in 01.0000 is 4, 5, 6, or 7 respectively. The starting points are not separated by equal amounts, so there is no possible formula defining the jump address. For no more than this many possibilities, the shortest method is to make a zero-jump test of the size of the code number:

| LOCATION | OPERATION CODE | OPERATION ABBREVIATION | ADDRESS |
|---|---|---|---|
| 10.0000 | 10 | Clear add | 01.0000 |
| 10.0001 | 14 | Sub | 02.0002 |
| 10.0002 | 04 | Acc zero jump | 11.0000 |
| 10.0003 | 14 | Sub | 02.0001 |
| 10.0004 | 04 | Acc zero jump | 12.0000 |
| 10.0005 | 14 | Sub | 02.0001 |
| 10.0006 | 04 | Acc zero jump | 13.0000 |
| 10.0007 | 14 | Sub | 02.0001 |
| 10.0008 | 04 | Acc zero jump | 14.0000 |

Contents of 02.0002 = 4 with same decimal point as code
Content of 02.0001 = 1 with same decimal point as code

## JUMP TABLE

If the list of possibilities in the above is much longer, the jump table method of Chapter 15 is shorter in space and certainly in time. Since such a scheme typically appears in the heart of an interpretive system which is used a great many times in one problem, time savings of a few milliseconds can become very important.

The idea is simply to synthesize a functional relationship by setting up a table of jumps to the appropriate sections. There will still be no equal amounts between the starting locations of the various sections, but there will be a simple system to the locations of the jumps in the jump table. The code on page 183 is an adequate example of this technique.

## TABLE LOOK-UP WITH MORE COMPLICATED CODE

These methods are satisfactory if the code is a simple integer. Suppose now that on the basis of a fractional number in 01.0000 we have to make the following choice:

| IF THE NUMBER IS BETWEEN: | JUMP TO: |
|---|---|
| 0.000 and 0.175 | 22.0000 |
| 0.175 and 0.347 | 23.0000 |
| 0.347 and 0.689 | 24.0000 |
| 0.689 and 0.900 | 25.0000 |
| 0.900 and 0.999 | 26.0000 |

This is not in the least farfetched. An immediate example that comes to mind is the determination of step rates in a pension calculation. On at least one machine, the IBM 650, such a problem is no problem at all. The table look-up feature allows us to store two tables in memory. The code number is placed in one of the arithmetic registers and a table look-up instruction given. The machine automatically searches through the table of arguments until it finds an argument from the table which is equal to or larger than the given code (argument). The address of this location is placed in another of the arithmetic registers. Knowing the relative locations of the two tables (arguments and functions), the address of the correct function can easily be computed. The same problem may also be handled by the following method.

## STRAIGHT SEARCH WITH MORE COMPLICATED CODE

When table look-up is not available, other techniques may be used. The most straightforward is to test the code size by subtraction and plus jumps. For instance, with the above example:

| LOCATION | OPERATION CODE | OPERATION ABBREVIATION | ADDRESS | REMARKS |
|---|---|---|---|---|
| 10.0001 | 10 | Clear add | Loc 0.175 | |
| 10.0002 | 14 | Sub | 01.0000 | Code |
| 10.0003 | 03 | Acc plus jump | 22.0000 | |
| 10.0004 | 10 | Clear add | Loc 0.347 | |
| 10.0005 | 14 | Sub | 01.0000 | Code |
| 10.0006 | 03 | Acc plus jump | 23.0000 | |
| 10.0007 | 10 | Clear add | Loc 0.689 | |
| 10.0008 | 14 | Sub | 01.0000 | Code |
| 10.0009 | 03 | Acc plus jump | 24.0000 | |
| 10.0010 | 10 | Clear add | Loc 0.900 | |
| 10.0011 | 14 | Sub | 01.0000 | Code |
| 10.0012 | 03 | Acc plus jump | 25.0000 | |
| 10.0013 | 01 | Un jump | 26.0000 | |

This last assumes that the number *is* less than 1.0000, and therefore if not less than 0.900 it must be between 0.900 and 0.999.

A few instructions may be saved in such a program by omitting all but the first Clear add and adding in only the *differences* between adjacent table values:

| 10.0001 | 10 | Clear add | Loc 0.175 | |
|---|---|---|---|---|
| 10.0002 | 14 | Sub | 01.0000 | Code |
| 10.0003 | 03 | Acc plus jump | 22.0000 | |
| 10.0004 | 11 | Add | Loc 0.172 | $0.347 - 0.175$ |
| 10.0005 | 03 | Acc plus jump | 23.0000 | |
| 10.0006 | 11 | Add | Loc 0.342 | $0.689 - 0.347$ |
| 10.0007 | 03 | Acc plus jump | 24.0000 | |
| 10.0008 | 11 | Add | Loc 0.211 | $0.900 - 0.689$ |
| 10.0009 | 03 | Acc plus jump | 25.0000 | |
| 10.0010 | 01 | Un jump | 26.0000 | |

## BINARY SEARCH

The above is satisfactory until the table gets long and we realize that if the code happens to lie near the high end of the table, we shall spend considerable time looking in the wrong place. The next method continually splits the table in half and decides which of these halves it should look in next. This can never require more than $\log_2 n$ tests, where $n$ is the next power of 2 larger than the number of items in the table. Thus for a table with fifty items we never have to make more than six tests, where by the previous method we would expect to average twenty-five. The larger the table, the more attractive this becomes, obviously.

The actual coding of the method is a bit more complicated, however. For concreteness, suppose we have a table like that on page 200, except that there are sixty-five entries (64 intervals), in ascending order in 20.0000 through 20.0064. A code which is known to be within the range of the table is stored in 21.0000. The binary search requires us to determine whether the code is larger or smaller than the number in 20.0032. If smaller, then we wish to know whether it is larger or smaller than the number in 20.0016; if larger, whether it is larger or smaller than the number in 20.0048, etc. This can be done with a loop but perhaps it will be simpler to follow if we write it out in straight-line fashion.

| LOCATION | OPERATION CODE | OPERATION ABBREVIATION | ADDRESS | REMARKS |
|---|---|---|---|---|
| 10.0000 | 13 | Clear sub | 20.0032 | |
| 10.0001 | 11 | Add | 21.0000 | |
| 10.0002 | 33 | Long right | 00.0000 | |
| 10.0003 | 10 | Clear add | 02.0002 | Loc 16 |
| 10.0004 | 32 | Long left | 00.0000 | |
| 10.0005 | 11 | Add | 10.0000 | |
| 10.0006 | 41 | Store address | 10.0007 | |
| 10.0007 | 13 | Clear sub | [0000] | |
| 10.0008 | 11 | Add | 21.0000 | |
| 10.0009 | 33 | Long right | 00.0000 | |
| 10.0010 | 10 | Clear add | 02.0003 | Loc 8 |
| 10.0011 | 32 | Long left | 00.0000 | |
| 10.0012 | 11 | Add | 10.0007 | |
| 10.0013 | 41 | Store address | 10.0014 | |
| 10.0014 | 13 | Clear sub | [0000] | |
| 10.0015 | 11 | Add | 21.0000 | |
| 10.0016 | 33 | Long right | 00.0000 | |
| 10.0017 | 10 | Clear add | 02.0004 | Loc 4 |
| 10.0018 | 32 | Long left | 00.0000 | |
| 10.0019 | 11 | Add | 10.0014 | |
| 10.0020 | 41 | Store address | 10.0021 | |
| 10.0021 | 13 | Clear sub | [0000] | |
| 10.0022 | 11 | Add | 21.0000 | |
| 10.0023 | 33 | Long right | 00.0000 | |
| 10.0024 | 10 | Clear add | 02.0005 | Loc 2 |
| 10.0025 | 32 | Long left | 00.0000 | |
| 10.0026 | 11 | Add | 10.0021 | |
| 10.0027 | 41 | Store address | 10.0028 | |
| 10.0028 | 13 | Clear sub | [0000] | |
| 10.0029 | 11 | Add | 21.0000 | |
| 10.0030 | 33 | Long right | 00.0000 | |
| 10.0031 | 10 | Clear add | 02.0006 | Loc 1 |
| 10.0032 | 32 | Long left | 00.0000 | |
| 10.0033 | 11 | Add | 10.0028 | |
| 10.0034 | 41 | Store address | 10.0035 | |

(*Continued on next page*)

| 10.0035 | 10 | Clear add | [0000] | |
| 10.0036 | 14 | Sub | 21.0000 | |
| 10.0037 | 33 | Long right | 00.0000 | |
| 10.0038 | 10 | Clear add | 10.0035 | |
| 10.0039 | 05 | MQ sign jump | 10.0041 | |
| 10.0040 | 11 | Add | 02.0001 | Loc 1 |

The address of the table value just larger than the code is now in the address part of the accumulator. Note that the long right and left shifts are simply for the purpose of attaching a sign to a number. The address of zero means that no shift takes place—only the sign changes. This is an illustration of the old saying about skinning cats: the obvious way to do this job was with plus jumps, but the program would have been five steps longer. Note also that this program is self-initializing. The address of the first instruction is never changed, and all of the computed addresses "bootstrap" from that one. This actually would not be so hard to work into a loop, particularly with indexing to get the 16, 8, 4, 2, and 1, but it would be a little hard to follow.

## DECISION ON BASIS OF A MORE COMPLEX FUNCTION OF CODE

Sometimes a functional relationship can be established which is a bit more cumbersome than the examples above, but which is still worth the trouble. Suppose for an example that one of the answers in a Monte Carlo calculation is the cosine of an angle. Since in this type of problem there may be thousands or even millions of individual cases, we need a tabulation of how many of the cosines fall into the range 0.000–0.025, how many fall in the range 0.025–0.050, etc., up to 0.975–1.000. Suppose that the tally of the number of cosines falling into the first range is stored in 15.0000, the tally of the number falling into the second range is stored in 15.0001, etc. What sort of a functional relationship can be set up here? Consider the formula:

Tally address = 15.0000 + integral part of: (40)(cosine)

If the cosine is less than 0.025, 40 times it will be less than one and the integral part of the product will be zero. If the cosine is equal to or greater than 0.025 but less than 0.050, the integral part of the product will be one, etc. So if the cosine is in the accumulator as a fixed point fraction and we are required to add a tally of one in the appropriate location, the following program will do the job:

| 10.0000 | 33 | Long right | 00.0010 | Into MQ |
| 10.0001 | 16 | Mult | 02.0010 | = Loc 40 |
| 10.0002 | 11 | Add | 03.0000 | = Loc 15.0000 |
| 10.0003 | 41 | Store address | 10.0005 | |
| 10.0004 | 10 | Clear add | 02.0001 | Loc 1 |
| 10.0005 | 19 | Add to mem | [0000] | |

02.0010 is assumed to be the location of 40, stored as 000040.0000, which will place the decimal point of the product between the sixth and seventh position of the accumulator; in other words, the integral part of the product will end up already in the address part of the accumulator.

## 17.2 Alternators

Sometimes it is necessary to carry out an operation only *every other* time through a section of the program. It is possible to test a counter for evenness or count to two in a simple loop, but there is a trick which is so simple as to be almost elegant. Suppose 16.0000 contains a $+1$ at the start of the program. The second, fourth, sixth, etc., times through, we are required to jump to 32.0000; the other times to continue in sequence. This program does the job:

| 13 | Clear sub | 16.0000 | $+1$ to start |
| 40 | Store acc | 16.0000 | |
| 03 | Acc plus jump | 32.0000 | |
| | Continuation | | |

The first time through, the Clear subtract of the positive number will give a negative number in the accumulator at the third step. Next time, Clear subtract of what is now a negative number leaves a positive number there and the plus jump is taken.

## 17.3 Floating to Fixed Point Conversion

Sometimes it is necessary to convert a number from floating form to fixed. For instance, it may be more convenient to enter all numbers in a calculation in floating point form, either for uniformity in filling out data sheets or because of the requirements of the loading program which must be used. But if one of the input numbers is actually a code number which must be used in address computation, usually the form must be changed.

In some computers there are special-purpose instructions which make this very simple. We have not assumed any such instruction in TYDAC, and it may be instructive to see how it could be done by programming. For concreteness, suppose the code number is actually an integer. If it is between 0 and 9, its form in memory will be 51.X000 0000. If it is between 10 and 99, its form will be 52.XX00 0000. If it is between 10,000,000 and 99,999,999 its form will be 58.XXXXXXXX. This last is not likely, to say the least, but if it should happen, we would need only to delete the exponent to have the number already in fixed point form with the units digit in the units position in a word. This suggests that to do the conversion, we need to shift the fractional part to the right a number of places equal to the difference between 58 and the number's exponent. A program like the following would do the trick:

| LOCATION | OPERATION CODE | OPERATION ABBREVIATION | ADDRESS | REMARKS |
|---|---|---|---|---|
| 10.0000 | 10 | Clear add | Loc 61 0000 0000 | |
| 10.0001 | 15 | Sub abs | Loc code | |
| 10.0002 | 31 | Acc right | 00.0004 | Into address |
| 10.0003 | 41 | Store address | 10.0006 | part |
| 10.0004 | 10 | Clear add | Loc code | |
| 10.0005 | 30 | Acc left | 00.0003 | To delete |
| 10.0006 | 31 | Acc right | [0000] | exponent |

The fixed point integer is now in the accumulator with its units digit in the last position of the accumulator. The exponent of the code was subtracted from 61 rather than 58 to compensate for the left shift of 3 which was necessary to delete the exponent. Note also that, as written, the conversion will work whether the code is positive or negative.

The converse problem of converting a fixed point integer to floating point form is handled quite simply by the feature of the built-in floating point addition which shifts the fractional part of the sum left, if it has leading zeros after the addition. The only point to watch is the possibility of a negative code.

| 10.0000 | 10 | Clear add | Loc 58 0000 0000 |
|---|---|---|---|
| 10.0001 | 12 | Add abs | Loc code |
| 10.0002 | 70 | Fl add | Loc 58 0000 0000 |
| 10.0003 | 42 | Load MQ | Loc code |
| 10.0004 | 32 | Long left | 00.0000 |

The first two steps convert the code number into an unnormalized floating point form. The third does nothing but normalize it, i.e., it brings the first nonzero digit into position three of the accumulator. The last two instructions put the sign back if it was negative.

If the number is not an integer, analysis can show in a similar manner how many shifts are necessary.

## 17.4 Function Evaluation

In any scientific calculation there are almost always transcendental functions to be evaluated. Several alternative methods are available.

### TABLE LOOK-UP

In some applications and using certain equipment, the best way may be to store a table of values of the function at certain values of the argument—which is also in memory. Usually interpolation is used, either linear or a higher order formula. It may be feasible to store entries at closer spaced values of the argument where the function is changing rapidly. The locating of the values in the table which surround the argument of current interest may be done by any of the methods of Section 17.1—which now appears in a more general light.

### POWER SERIES EVALUATION

Many functions of interest are defined quite simply by Maclaurin or Taylor series. For any function which converges as one over $n$ factorial, this is about the best way in most calculators. In the functions commonly encountered, this includes the exponential, sine, cosine, hyperbolic sine and cosine, and some of the Bessel functions. Other functions *may* be evaluated this way, but there is usually a better way: logarithm and inverse trigonometric functions, particularly.

For any of these, a reduction of the size of the argument is usually worth the trouble because it speeds convergence and requires fewer terms. Some of the many identities which may be used for the purpose are:

$$\sin x = \sin (2k\pi + x)$$

$$e^x = (e^{x/n})^n$$

$$\tan^{-1} x = \pi/2 - \tan^{-1}\frac{1}{x}$$

$$\tan^{-1} x = \pi/6 - \tan^{-1}\frac{1/\sqrt{3} - x}{1 + x/\sqrt{3}}$$

$$\log_n (a \cdot n^p) = p + \log_n a$$

There are at least three approaches to evaluating these series. The first is to start at the "front" and compute until a term too small to have any significance appears. This is a sort of running test of convergence which guarantees that no more terms will be computed than are needed. On the other hand, the loops involve more operations than the next method. This method requires an estimate of the maximum number of terms based on the maximum anticipated size of the argument. The truncated series is factored:

$$e^x = 1 + \frac{x}{1!} + \frac{x^2}{2!} + \frac{x^3}{3!} + \frac{x^4}{4!} + \frac{x^5}{5!} + \frac{x^6}{6!}$$

$$= 1 + x \left[ 1 + \frac{x}{2} \left[ 1 + \frac{x}{3} \left[ 1 + \frac{x}{4} \left[ 1 + \frac{x}{5} \left[ 1 + \frac{x}{6} \right] \right] \right] \right] \right]$$

The factored series is then evaluated "from the inside out," which is also called *nesting*.

If this method is used on a series which converges as $1/n$, such as inverse tangent, the factored form is:

$$\tan^{-1} x = x - \frac{x^3}{3} + \frac{x^5}{5} - \frac{x^7}{7}$$

$$= x[1 - x^2[\tfrac{1}{3} - x^2[\tfrac{1}{5} - x^2[\tfrac{1}{7}]]]]$$

There are many such factorizations, which may be discovered by a little experimentation.

The third approach is a variant of either of these. It is the question of whether to obtain the integers needed in any of these approaches by computing them in the loop or by storing them. Of course, storing costs space, but it can save three or more steps each time through if indexing is available. If not, there is little gain in storing the integers.

Often these series can be made to do double duty. By changing all the signs to plus in the sine series, we get the hyperbolic sine. By dividing the argument by 2 and making a minor change in the form of the series, the sine becomes a Bessel function. Sometimes it is more convenient to program the change in the series than to write out both forms.

## CONTINUED FRACTIONS

An expession which for many functions converges faster and over a wider interval than does the continued product or series above is the continued fraction. This technique is fully discussed in reference 20;* an example may be given to illustrate the form.

$$\tan^{-1} x = \cfrac{x}{1 + \cfrac{x^2}{3 + \cfrac{(2x)^2}{5 + \cfrac{(3x)^2}{7 + \cfrac{(4x)^2}{\text{etc.}}}}}}$$

Only ten terms are required to get $\tan^{-1} x$ to eight places for $x$ between 0 and 1. Several hundred terms of the power series would be required to get the same accuracy.

## RATIONAL APPROXIMATION

It is possible to find reasonably short rational algebraic expressions which will represent a function to some degree of accuracy over a certain range of the argument. For instance,

$$\tan^{-1} x = 0.9999,7726x - 0.3326,2347x^3$$
$$+ 0.1935,4346x^5 - 0.1164,3287x^7$$
$$+ 0.0526,5332x^9 - 0.0117,2120x^{11}$$

is good to six decimals for $x$ between $-1$ and $+1$.† This is, of course, enormously shorter than the power series, and about a tossup with the continued fraction.

*As a small example of the technique, we may note the derivation of the continued fraction for $\sqrt{2}$.

$$\sqrt{2} = 1 + \sqrt{2} - 1$$
$$= 1 + (\sqrt{2} - 1)(\sqrt{2} + 1)/(\sqrt{2} + 1)$$
$$= 1 + (2 - 1)/(\sqrt{2} + 1)$$
$$= 1 + 1/(\sqrt{2} + 1)$$
$$= 1 + \cfrac{1}{2 + \cfrac{1}{\sqrt{2} + 1}}$$
$$= 1 + \cfrac{1}{2 + \cfrac{1}{2 + \cfrac{1}{2 + \cdots}}}$$

† From *Approximations for Digital Computers*, Cecil Hastings, RAND Corporation, Santa Monica, Calif., 1955. This book describes the methods of finding rational approximations to functions, and contains a valuable collection of many functions which have already been approximated.

Depending on the difficulty of evaluating other formulas for the same function, and particularly on memory restrictions, rational approximations may be very attractive. It seems to most of us to be no easy task to obtain the coefficients, but fortunately much of this has already been done.

## NEWTON'S METHOD

Again depending on the relative case of evaluating certain forms, it may be desirable to evaluate some functions by Newton's method. For instance, a logarithm can be calculated by repeated application of the formula:

$$x_{i+1} = x_i + \frac{a - e^{x_i}}{e^{x_i}}$$

$$x_n = \log_e a$$

Since an exponential is often considerably easier to evaluate than a logarithm, this may be the best way out in some situations. It obviously is most effective when the inverse of the desired function is very much easier to calculate than the function itself.

## Exercises

1. Write a subroutine to make a binary search of a table in memory which is in ascending order. The calling sequence is:

| | |
|---|---|
| Set ind jump | Loc program, 1 |
| Halt-jump | Loc given $x$ |
| Halt-jump | IA |
| Halt-jump | FA |

The table starts at IA (initial address) and ends at FA (final address). The address of the table value just larger than the given $x$ should be left in the address part of the accumulator. The table values are all positive and distinct, but nothing is known about the size of the table. It may be a few words long or a few hundred. Note that the table may have a number of entries which is not simply related to a power of 2. This must be written as a loop, and a thorough flow chart will be necessary.

2. A fraction $x$ in location 500 may be between $-1$ and $+1$. If it is:

$$-1.0 \leq x < -0.9, \text{ tally 1 in 600}$$
$$-0.9 \leq x < -0.8, \text{ tally 1 in 601}$$
$$-0.8 \leq x < -0.7, \text{ tally 1 in 602}$$

$$\cdot$$
$$\cdot$$
$$\cdot$$

$$+0.9 \leq x < 1.0, \text{ tally 1 in ?}$$

3. Devise a three-way "alternator" which will jump to 1800 the third, sixth, ninth, etc., times through the program but will continue in sequence otherwise.

4. Find a factorization and write a loop to evaluate:

$$\sin x = x - \frac{x^3}{3!} + \frac{x^5}{5!} - \frac{x^7}{7!} + \cdots$$

$$\ln x = (x - 1) - \frac{(x-1)^2}{2} + \frac{(x-1)^3}{3} - \frac{(x-1)^4}{4} + \cdots$$

where $(0 < x \leq 2)$

$$\sin^{-1} x = x + \frac{x^3}{2 \cdot 3} + \frac{1 \cdot 3 x^5}{2 \cdot 4 \cdot 5} + \frac{1 \cdot 3 \cdot 5 x^7}{2 \cdot 4 \cdot 6 \cdot 7} + \cdots$$

$$J_0(x) = 1 - \frac{(x/2)^2}{1^2} + \frac{(x/2)^4}{1^2 \cdot 2^2} - \frac{(x/2)^6}{1^2 \cdot 2^2 \cdot 3^2} + \cdots$$

5. Write a loop to evaluate the continued fraction expansion for $\tan^{-1} x$ given in the text.

6. Develop a formula and write a program to evaluate $\sin^{-1} x$ by Newton's method.

# 18 AUTOMATIC CODING

## 18.0 Introduction

In most scientific computing, the personnel costs are roughly equal to the machine costs. As another generalization we may say that half the computer time is spent in checkout, the other half in actual production running to get answers. These statements are subject to many qualifications, but it is probably safe to say that more of the cost of scientific computing comes before the start of production than after.

Since this is true, it seems reasonable to try to find ways of reducing the effort of problem preparation and checkout. We have discussed at some length the checkout problem, and how special-purpose programs can be used to assist in the process. The intention of this chapter's subject matter is similar: to develop ways of making the machine do as much as possible of the routine work of coding, which is what machines should be doing anyway.

There are various definitions of automatic coding. Under the broadest definition, automatic coding is any technique which makes coding easier or faster. Under a more restrictive definition, automatic coding is a process whereby instructions to the machine are written in a "language" which is somewhat like the working language of the user, such as mathematics or ordinary English. This "language" may be nothing like the machine's instructions, and the computer has to be programmed to make the translation. In between these two definitions are tool programs which have the broad requirement that the instructions have at least a vague resemblance to machine instructions, but which will do considerably more than simply translate to actual machine language from a notation slightly more convenient for the coder.

## 18.1 Coding Aids

Under the heading of techniques which are of assistance in writing code are included some of the techniques already discussed. For instance, any interpretive system is in a sense automatic coding. After all, by simply writing one pseudo instruction, the machine is directed to carry out many actual instructions, and certainly the task of coding has been simplified—but that hardly constitutes automatic coding. Some interpretive systems are designed to do much more per interpretive instruction than the example in Chapter 15. It is fairly common to find interpretive systems which do some combination of the following:

1. "Change" a one-address machine to multiple address.
2. Provide floating point in a machine which does not have it built in.
3. Provide indexing where it is not built in.

All of these make coding easier and shorter. Most such systems are considerably easier to learn than is actual machine language coding.

A relatively minor technique which might be mentioned under this heading is the fairly common practice of writing a two-or-three-letter code instead of the actual numerical code. Rather than writing 10 Clear add, we might simply write CLA. This would serve as a reminder of what the operation is, and later be translated, by the computer, to the required 10.

Another technique in this category is the writing of data in a convenient form. A floating decimal 2.0 in TYDAC eventually appears as 5120000000 in memory. With suitable programs it is possible to write numbers in ordinary form, including exponents if desired.

$$2.0$$
$$-.0002$$
$$2, 3(=2 \cdot 10^3)$$
$$2000$$
$$2, -6(=2 \cdot 10^{-6})$$

The use of relative addresses is sometimes included under the heading of automatic coding. As applied to the form presented in this text, this is stretching the definition slightly. As applied to the next section it is perhaps appropriate.

## 18.2 Higher Level Assistance

The second general classification of automatic coding consists of programs which do more than merely simplify the task, but which require instructions somewhat like machine instructions. These include the more complete assembly programs, compilers, and generators, or some combination of these.

The advanced-type assembly programs are, generally speaking, "professionals'" programs. Once understood, they are very powerful in the hands of an experienced programmer, and produce fast-running, efficient programs. On the other hand, to the completely uninitiated, they can be fairly difficult to learn.

All of these intermediate-type tools allow relative addresses. On some, this means only that numerical addresses are written—but these are not the *actual* locations which are eventually used. In others, the system is along the lines of the relative addressing described in Chapter 14, with occasionally a little more or less flexibility. Sometimes a special code is used to indicate the type of addresses. In the most flexible assemblies, a variable size alphanumeric address is used. For instance, acceptable addresses might be A, HERE, PT/PS, ALPHA, TEMP, EQUAT, DATA, P2, T4, 14Q87, EQU14, etc. In addition, it might be allowable to write symbols such as the above followed by a plus or minus sign and an integer. For instance, if TEMP is the symbol for the start of a region of temporary storage, addresses for the following locations could be written TEMP + 1, TEMP + 2, TEMP + 3, etc. On some systems it is possible to refer to an instruction shortly before or after the current location by some such symbol as *+ 2 or *— 4. That is, a sequence might read:

| | |
|---|---|
| Clear add | LOCN |
| Sub | LOC2 |
| Store address | *+ 1 |
| Clear add | [    ] |

The address of the third instruction simply means that the address is to be stored in the next instruction.

In most of these systems, little need be done to establish the meaning of the symbols. Often it is necessary only that every symbol appear as the location part of some instruction. It is usually possible, if desired, to specify the absolute equivalent of any symbol. In almost all of these assembly programs the operation code is written as a mnemonic code which is interpreted and translated by the assembly program.

A *compiler* is a program (often a part of an assembly program) which can bring many instructions into the final program when signaled by a single instruction in the original program. As an example, there may be provision for a special pseudo instruction to the compiler which says in effect, "At this point bring the specified subroutine into the final program, and consider this as the absolute equivalent of the symbol used for this subroutine." This implies that at any point in the program where a subroutine is needed, the programmer must write a linkage: a Set index jump type, or whatever is required in the particular machine. In the more sophisticated compilers, the programmer need only write a pseudo instruction; the compiler program brings in the required subroutine at some point where space is available and sets up the necessary linkage or return address. The compiler will take into account the fact that there may be many references to the same subroutine.

This difference in the operation of compilers points up another fact. What the programmer writes may be translated into machine instructions in a one-to-one fashion with a few exceptions, or it may be translated in a one-to-many fashion. If the latter, the compiling program is essentially interpreting the original program, but producing a final program which is not interpretive when it finally runs on the machine. See the comment in Section 15.3.

A *generator* is a program, working as part of an assembler or compiler, which produces a subroutine from certain basic information. For instance, if the programmer wants to print some answers, he may be required to specify only where the numbers are in memory, how many columns he wants, the spacing on the page, how many decimals he wishes, and perhaps how he wants the rows identified. This information can be condensed into two or three words in a calling sequence or a pseudo instruction. Then the generator takes over, decodes the information in the calling sequence and produces a subroutine to print as specified. The required subroutine is entered into the program at some convenient point. Actually, the same thing may be done by a subroutine which is part of the operating program and which is called each time it is needed. The latter is slower, but takes less memory space.

## 18.3 True Automatic Coding

A few programs are available, and more are proposed, which accept information in a form which looks nothing like machine instructions, and translate it into machine instructions which will solve the problem. There are several areas where such work is being done, but it has seemed best not to describe any of the operating programs in detail. So much is being done currently that any description would be badly outdated before it could get into print. Some reports available at the time of writing are listed in the bibliography. Some of the features of these may be illustrated with examples.

The automatic coding systems directed toward scientific calculations accept problem statements in a form similar to ordinary mathematical language. An example is given in the manual for FORTRAN (Mathematical FORmula TRANslating System), developed largely by John Backus and his associates at IBM. The problem is to find the largest of a set of numbers entered from cards into the IBM 704, and print the largest value.

The entire input to FORTRAN is:

```
        DIMENSION A(999)
        FREQUENCY 30(2,1,10), 5(100)
        READ 1, N, (A(I), I = 1,N)
1       FORMAT (I3/(12F6.2))
        BIGA = A(1)
5       DO 20 I = 2,N
30      IF (BIGA-A(I)) 10,20,20
10      BIGA = A(I)
20      CONTINUE
        PRINT 2, N, BIGA
2       FORMAT (22H1 THE LARGEST OF THESE I3, 12H NUMBERS
        IS F7.2)
        STOP 77777
```

This would specify input, the loop which finds the largest value, and output.

The automatic coding systems for commercial data processing are aimed at accepting a problem statement in ordinary business English, although in a necessarily restricted vocabulary. An example of input to such a program might be:

TABULATE AMOUNT-OF-INSURANCE PREMIUM NUMBER-OF-
POLICIES BY POLICY-ACCOUNT BRANCH YEAR PLAN AGE.

This statement would be translated by a compiler-generator program into a set of actual machine instructions for the particular computer involved. This program is one of many produced under the direction of Dr. Grace Hopper at the Remington Rand Univac Division of Sperry Rand Corporation. This particular program, however, is probably not typical of the automatic programming systems which are actually being used in the data-processing area; most programs in actual use are somewhat less ambitious.

This has been a most sketchy description of some very interesting work which may well bring about a revolution in programming.

## 18.4 Algebra Programs

There have been a few experiments, to the time of writing, in the area of entering algebraic symbols, performing algebraic operations, and putting out algebraic symbols. No numerical constants need appear anywhere; the work is actually algebraic manipulation of literal quantities. The best publicized effort in this area is the Analytical Differentiator, developed by Harry Kahramanian. It accepts coded information describing formulas in differential calculus, and computes (again in literal symbols) the successive derivatives of the expressions. Further work is being done in this area, as well as in other branches of nonnumerical calculation.

## 18.5 Conclusion

The ultimate goal of automatic coding or programming is to free the computer user completely from all the detailed work of coding. It should eventually be possible, for many problems at least, to write ordinary English or mathematics and have the machine prepare its own detailed programs. Some problems will probably always be outside the scope of such tools, and there will always be some rules about how to present the English or mathematics to the machine, but a great deal of the burden should some day be removed.

The reader need not feel, however, that this is an anticlimactic ending to a book on the details of computer programming. It will be some time before such programs are in general use. It may be a very long time indeed before a completely versatile automatic programming system is available for medium-sized machines like the IBM 650 and the DATATRON. And remember that the writing of the translation programs themselves requires very highly skilled coding. The techniques presented in this text will be of value to many computer users for some time to come.

## NUMERICAL OPERATION CODES FOR TYDAC

| INSTRUCTION TYPE | CODE | ABBREVIATION | OPERATION |
|---|---|---|---|
| JUMP | 00 | Halt-jump | Halt and jump |
| | 01 | Un jump | Unconditional jump |
| | 02 | Ov jump | Overflow jump |
| | 03 | Acc plus jump | Accumulator plus jump |
| | 04 | Acc zero jump | Accumulator zero jump |
| | 05 | MQ sign jump | Multiplier-quotient sign jump |
| | 06 | Break jump | Break point jump |
| | 07 | Switch jump | Switch jump |
| ARITHMETIC | 10 | Clear add | Clear and add |
| | 11 | Add | Add |
| | 12 | Add abs | Add absolute value |
| | 13 | Clear sub | Clear and subtract |
| | 14 | Sub | Subtract |
| | 15 | Sub abs | Subtract absolute value |
| | 16 | Mult | Multiply |
| | 17 | Mult round | Multiply and round |
| | 18 | Divide | Divide |
| | 19 | Add to mem | Add to memory |
| SHIFT | 30 | Acc left | Accumulator left shift |
| | 31 | Acc right | Accumulator right shift |
| | 32 | Long left | Long left shift |
| | 33 | Long right | Long right shift |
| ROUND, STORE, MQ, TRANSFER | 35 | Round | Round |
| | 40 | Store acc | Store accumulator |
| | 41 | Store address | Store address |
| | 42 | Load MQ | Load multiplier-quotient |
| | 43 | Store MQ | Store multiplier-quotient |
| | 44 | Block tr | Block transfer |
| INDEX | 50 | Mem to ind | Load index from memory |
| | 51 | Acc to ind | Load index from accumulator |
| | 52 | Ind to mem | Store index in memory |
| | 53 | Ind to acc | Store index in accumulator |
| | 54 | Raise ind | Raise index |
| | 55 | Lower ind | Lower index |
| | 56 | Zero ind jump | Zero index jump |
| | 57 | Eq ind jump | Equal index jump |
| | 58 | Set ind jump | Set index and jump |
| INPUT, OUTPUT | 60 | Select | Select |
| | 61 | Read | Read |
| | 62 | Write | Write |
| | 63 | Rewind | Rewind tape |
| | 64 | Write mark | Write tape mark |
| FLOATING POINT | 70 | Fl add | Floating add |
| | 71 | Fl sub | Floating subtract |
| | 72 | Fl mult | Floating multiply |
| | 73 | Fl div | Floating divide |

# Appendix

# 1 SUMMARY OF TYDAC INSTRUCTIONS

The first line of the description of each instruction consists of the full name, the abbreviation which is used in the text, an A to signify the address, an I if an index register may be specified, a B if the last four digits are used for some other purpose than to specify an index register, and the numerical operation code of the instruction. The operation codes were chosen arbitrarily and have no significance in themselves. The term *effective address* (for which the symbol E is used) means the address A plus the contents of the index register I. If no index register is specified, then the terms *address* and *effective address* are equivalent.

| OPERATION | ABBREVIATION | CODE |
|---|---|---|
| Halt and jump | Halt-jump A | 00 |

The machine stops. When the start button on the console is pressed the next operation is taken from location A.

| | | |
|---|---|---|
| Unconditional jump | Un jump A, I | 01 |

The next instruction is taken from location E, regardless of where the current instruction is located.

| | | |
|---|---|---|
| Overflow jump | Ov jump A, I | 02 |

If the overflow position contains any digit but zero, the next instruction is taken from location E; if it is a zero, the next instruction is taken in normal sequence.

| | | |
|---|---|---|
| Accumulator plus jump | Acc plus jump A, I | 03 |

If the sign of the accumulator is plus, the next instruction is taken from location E; if it is negative, the next instruction is taken in normal sequence. Zero is always positive in TYDAC.

Accumulator zero jump          Acc zero jump A, I          04

If the accumulator contains all zeros, including the overflow position, the next instruction is taken from location E; otherwise, in normal sequence.

Multiplier-quotient sign jump          MQ sign jump A, I          05

If the sign of the MQ is plus, the next instruction is taken from location E; if negative, in normal sequence.

Break point jump          Break jump A, B          06

A "break point switch" on the console has ten positions, 0 through 9. One of the nine positions 0 through 9 may be specified by B. If the switch is set to the position specified by B, this instruction will cause the machine to stop. When the start button on the console is pressed, the next instruction is taken from location A. If the switch is not set to position B, the next instruction is taken in normal sequence.

Switch jump          Switch jump A, B          07

There are ten switches on the console, numbered 0 through 9. If the switch specified by B is down, the next instruction is taken from location A. If the switch is up, the next instruction is taken in normal sequence. This is the same as Break point jump except that the machine does not stop before jumping, and more than one switch may be down at one time.

Clear and add          Clear add A, I          10

The word at the effective address replaces the contents of the accumulator. The overflow position is cleared; the word at the effective address is unchanged.

Add          Add A, I          11

The word at the effective address is added algebraically to the contents of the accumulator. Overflow is possible. The word at the effective address is unchanged.

Add absolute value          Add abs A, I          12

The word at the effective address is treated as a positive number and added algebraically to the contents of the accumulator. Overflow is possible. The word at the effective address is unchanged.

Clear and subtract          Clear sub A, I          13

The negative of the word at the effective address replaces the contents of the accumulator. The word at the effective address is unchanged.

Subtract                          Sub A, I                          14

The word at the effective address is subtracted algebraically from the contents of the accumulator. Overflow is possible. The word at the effective address is unchanged.

Subtract absolute value          Sub abs A, I                      15

The word at the effective address is treated as a positive number and subtracted algebraically from the contents of the accumulator. Overflow is possible. The word at the effective address is unchanged.

Multiply                          Mult A, I                         16

The accumulator is cleared. The word at the effective address is multiplied algebraically by the contents of the MQ. The product is formed in the accumulator and MQ, the more significant digits being in the accumulator. The accumulator and MQ both have the correct sign, i.e., positive if both factors were of same sign, negative otherwise. The original contents of the MQ are lost in the process of multiplication. Overflow is not possible. The word at the effective address is unchanged.

Multiply and round               Mult round A, I                   17

Same as Multiply except that a ten-digit rounded product is formed in the accumulator. Rounding is accomplished by adding (subtracting if accumulator is negative) one to the last position of the accumulator if the first digit in the MQ is five or greater.

Divide                            Divide A, I                       18

The contents of the accumulator and MQ, taken as one twenty-digit register, are divided by the word at the effective address. The quotient appears in the MQ with correct algebraic sign; the remainder appears in the accumulator with the sign of the dividend. Division will take place only if the divisor is larger in absolute value than the contents of the accumulator; otherwise, the MQ is cleared, the division is not attempted, and the machine stops with the divide stop light on.

Add to memory                    Add to mem A, I                   19

The number at the effective address is added to the accumulator and the sum stored at the effective address. Accumulator overflow is possible; if it occurs, the "sum" in memory is incorrect.

Accumulator left shift          Acc left A, I          30

The contents of the accumulator, including the overflow position, are shifted left E places. Digits shifted out of the overflow position are lost. The accumulator sign is unchanged. Zeros are entered at the right as the number is shifted. E may not exceed 99.

Accumulator right shift          Acc right A, I          31

The contents of the accumulator, including the overflow position, are shifted right E places. Digits shifted past the right end of the accumulator are lost. Zeros are entered at the left. The accumulator sign is unchanged. E may not exceed 99.

Long left shift          Long left A, I          32

The contents of the accumulator and MQ, taken as one twenty-one–digit register, are shifted left E places. The sign of the accumulator is made the same as that of the MQ. Digits shifted out of the first position of the MQ enter the last position of the accumulator. Digits shifted out of the overflow position are lost. Zeros are entered at the right. E may not exceed 99.

Long right shift          Long right A, I          33

The contents of the accumulator and MQ, taken as one twenty-one–digit register, are shifted E places to the right. The sign of the MQ is made the same as that of the accumulator. Digits shifted out of the last position of the accumulator enter the first position of the MQ. Digits shifted out of the last position of the MQ are lost. Zeros are entered at the left. E may not exceed 99.

Round          Round          35

If the high order digit of the MQ is five or greater, *one* is added to the last position of the accumulator; otherwise, nothing is done. If the accumulator is negative, the one is subtracted instead of added. No address is needed.

Store accumulator          Store acc A, I          40

The contents of the accumulator, including the sign position, but *not* including the overflow position, replace the word at the effective address. The accumulator is unchanged, but whatever was at the effective address is lost.

Store address          Store address A, I          41

The address part (positions 3–6, counting from the left) of the accumulator replaces the corresponding positions of the word at the effective address. The accumulator, as well as the other positions of the word at the effective address, are unchanged. The sign of the accumulator is immaterial.

Load multiplier-quotient          Load MQ A, I          42

The word at the effective address replaces the contents of the MQ. The word at the effective address is unchanged.

Store multiplier-quotient          Store MQ A, I          43

The contents of the MQ, including sign, replace the word at the effective address. What was at the effective address is lost.

Block transfer          Block tr A, B          44

The eight words starting at A are transferred to the eight locations starting at B. The accumulator and MQ are unchanged.

Load index from memory          Mem to ind A, B          50

The number in the address part (positions 3–6) of the word at A replaces the contents of index register B. The word at A is unchanged.

Load index from accumulator          Acc to ind A, B          51

The number in the address part (positions 3–6) of the accumulator replaces the contents of index register B. The accumulator is unchanged. The "address" A is not used on this instruction; any number may be written in these positions.

Store index in memory          Ind to mem A, B          52

The contents of index register B replace the address part (positions 3–6) of the word at A. The index register, the accumulator, and the other positions of the word at A are unchanged.

Store index in accumulator          Ind to acc A, B          53

The contents of index register B replace the address part (positions 3–6) of the accumulator. The index register and other positions of the accumulator are unchanged. The address A is immaterial.

Raise index          Raise ind A, B          54

The number A (not contents of A) is added to index register B. For this purpose, the next number after 9999 is 0.

Lower index          Lower ind A, B          55

The number A (not contents of A) is subtracted from index register

B.  If the result would normally be negative, the index register will contain 9999 minus the difference, i.e., the ten's complement.

| Zero index jump | Zero ind jump A, B | 56 |
|---|---|---|

If index register B does not contain zero, the next instruction is taken from location A; otherwise in normal sequence.

| Equal index jump | Equal ind jump A | 57 |
|---|---|---|

If the two index registers do not contain the same number, the next instruction is taken from location A; otherwise in normal sequence.

| Set index and jump | Set ind jump A, B | 58 |
|---|---|---|

The contents of the location counter replace the contents of index register B.  The next instruction is taken from location A.

| Select | Select A | 60 |
|---|---|---|

The input or output device designated by A is readied to transmit information to or from high-speed memory.  No information is transferred by this instruction alone; the circuits are established and the mechanical parts begin to move.

The designations are:

| A | INPUT–OUTPUT DEVICE |
|---|---|
| 1 | Card reader |
| 2 | Card punch |
| 3 | Typewriter |
| 11 | Tape unit 1 |
| 12 | Tape unit 2 |
| 13 | Tape unit 3 |
| 14 | Tape unit 4 |

Note that A is not an "address" in the sense of specifying a location in memory.  Only one input-output device may be selected at one time.

| Read | Read A, I | 61 |
|---|---|---|

An eight-word block is brought into the eight locations beginning at the effective address, from whichever device was specified by the last Select operation.  This is either: one IBM card, one eight-word block from any tape unit, or eight words from the typewriter. Whatever was at the locations specified is of course lost.

The instruction following a read instruction is normally a jump. This is automatically skipped unless (a) a tape mark is sensed on tape, or (*b*) no more cards are in the reader, or (*c*) there is blank paper tape in the tape reader on the typewriter.

Write                              Write A, I                              62

An eight-word block beginning at the effective address is transferred to whichever output device was specified by the last select operation. This is either: one IBM card punched; one eight-word block written on any tape unit, or one line typed on the typewriter. The words in memory are unaffected.

Rewind tape                        Rewind A                                63

The tape specified by A (11, 12, 13, or 14) is rewound to the beginning of the reel.

Write tape mark                    Write mark A                            64

A symbol is written on the tape specified by A, to indicate that no more information is to be written on the tape. The tape mark is sensed by the tape unit and controls whether the instruction immediately following a read instruction is executed.

Floating add                       Fl add A, I                             70

The augend is assumed to be in the accumulator. The word at the effective address is added algebraically to the augend in the accumulator. The word at the effective address is unchanged. The MQ is used during the operation and any previous contents will be destroyed. If the two numbers are equal in absolute value but of opposite sign, the result will be all zeros—both exponent and fractional part. If the result is larger in absolute value than $10^{50}$, the machine will stop with the "exponent" light on and the arithmetic registers will contain numbers which cannot be used meaningfully in any further operations. The result is always in normalized form; i.e., the first digit of the fractional part is nonzero.

Floating subtract                  Fl sub A, I                             71

Same as floating add except that the word at the effective address is subtracted algebraically.

Floating multiply                  Fl mult A, I                            72

The multiplier is assumed to be in the MQ. The word at the effective address is multiplied algebraically by the word in the MQ. The word at the effective address is unchanged. The product appears in the accumulator; the multiplier (in the MQ) is lost in the operation. If either factor is zero, the result will be a floating point zero.  If the result is outside the allowable exponent range (too large or small), the machine will stop with the "exponent" light on and the arithmetic registers will contain numbers which cannot be used meaningfully in any further operations.

Floating divide                    Fl div A, I                    73

The dividend is assumed to be in the accumulator, and is divided algebraically by the word at the effective address.  The word at the effective address is unchanged.  The quotient appears in the MQ; the dividend in the accumulator is lost during the operation.  If the dividend is zero, the quotient will be zero, regardless of the size of the divisor—which is the exception to the next statement.  If the result lies outside the allowable exponent range (too large or small), the machine will stop with the "exponent" light on and the arithmetic registers will contain numbers which cannot be used meaningfully in any further operations.  If division by zero is attempted, the division will not be performed, the MQ will be cleared, and the machine will stop with the divide stop light on.

# Appendix

# 2 MINIMUM ACCESS PROGRAMMING

## A2.0 Introduction

In any machine using a delay or recirculating-type memory, an ordinary program wastes considerable time. A magnetic drum takes a certain length of time to make a complete revolution. If the particular address specified by an instruction is not just ready to go under the reading head when it is called for, the arithmetic and control circuits must simply wait for the drum to turn. If no efforts are made to avoid this situation, the average wait will be half the time required for one drum revolution. The same considerations apply to a sonic or acoustic (mercury tank) memory, and to a lumped-parameter delay-line memory.

From an idealistic viewpoint the solution is to use magnetic cores and avoid the whole problem. Unfortunately, however, these are more expensive than a drum memory of the same size. Many medium-sized machines use magnetic drums as main memory and will no doubt continue to do so for many years to come. What can be done to eliminate or reduce the lost time?

There are two methods at present, which will be described briefly. Both are in the class of things which depend in large measure on the details of particular computers. We can only outline the principles, and observe that the individual manufacturers have published methods for their equipment.

## A2.1 Fast Access Loops

The first method to be described depends on the availability in the computer of small sections of memory which have considerably lower access time than the main memory. "Access time" is the time required to get a number from memory into the arithmetic or control circuits, after the control circuits have called for it.

In a mercury delay-line memory, a small part of the storage may consist of tanks which are physically shorter than the main memory.

The time required for a sound wave to travel from one end to the other is shorter, of course, as is the *average* access time. In a magnetic drum, it is possible to place a reading head quite close to a writing head, and arrange the associated circuitry so that information read is returned back to the writing head. This is interrupted only when information is being read into the loop. The effect is to provide the equivalent of a much faster drum, with possibly one-fifth the delay of the main drum. The high-speed section may actually be a different type of memory, such as magnetic cores.

However the fast access loop may be built, it is used to speed up operation by placing much-used parts of the program in it. There are usually single instructions which transfer a block of instructions from the main memory to the rapid access portion. Thus a subroutine may be read over to the rapid access section just before it is executed. The transfer takes time, but not nearly as long as the time which would be wasted by waiting in main memory.

The high-speed loops may also be used to store certain constants which are frequently used, but this requires more planning, along the lines of the next section.

## A2.2 Minimum Access Techniques

The second technique for reducing operating time in a delay-type memory is not independent of the first, if both are available. It is the technique of placing data and instructions, so far as possible, in

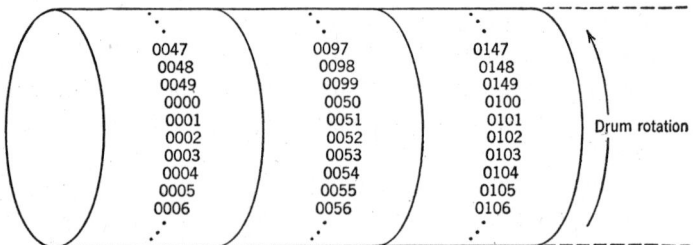

Figure 1. Schematic of the arrangement of information on a typical magnetic drum.

the locations where there will be the least delay when they are needed. This seems fairly obvious, but it turns out to be a bit of work, and is often done only when the problem is fairly large.

To understand the principle of the method consider Figure 1, showing an enlarged section of a magnetic drum. This schematic of drum addresses shows that numbers are recorded on the drum in parallel "tracks." Each track has a reading and a writing head. Typically, there are twenty tracks on the drum, with fifty numbers recorded in each track. The figure shows a small section of three tracks. The first track starts at 0000 and runs through 0049; track two runs from 0050 to 0099. Details of design can differ here, but usually the timing is such that corresponding addresses in the twenty tracks are all available for reading at the same time. That is, the addresses 0013, 0063, 0113, 0163, etc., are exactly equivalent from a timing standpoint.*

This is the first essential of minimum access programming. The second is knowledge of the time required by each operation. (Time is usually measured in something like "word times," which is the time required to execute one basic machine function.) Then, knowing where the current instruction is located, and how much time will elapse between reading the instruction off the drum and needing the data specified by the address, we can plan the optimum location for the data. If, in addition, the machine is built on the one-plus-one address system where the second address specifies the location of the next instruction, we can calculate the time required by the current instruction and plan the optimum location for the next instruction also. "Planning the optimum location" means to calculate the amount of turning of the drum until a number or instruction is needed. Then one of the twenty equivalent drum addresses is chosen for the data—an address which will appear under the reading heads at just exactly the right time to require no waiting. The process is the same for the next instruction unless the instructions are taken sequentially. Of course, the data and instructions will be scrambled all over memory and must be loaded accordingly. This confuses the input problem somewhat.

There are other complications. Certain instructions require a variable amount of time, depending on either the address or the size of the data. A shift instruction takes more or less time, depending on the number of shifts. In most decimal machines, the time for multiplication or division depends on the particular digits of the multiplier or quotient. This cannot in general be predicted, except perhaps in making estimates that a certain multiplier will always

* On some drums used in big machines, the drum locations are not individually addressable. However, a drum in such a machine is not used to store instructions while they are being executed.

The addresses in a track need not be located sequentially. It may facilitate the minimum access problem to "interlace" the addresses, so that sequential addresses are located at wider intervals around the drum. This may be done whether the drum is used for main or auxiliary memory.

have six leading zeros, and therefore the upper bound on the multiplication time can be estimated.  A conditional jump instruction often cannot be made optimum with respect to both alternatives.  The jumps to subroutines, which have to be in fixed locations, cannot usually be optimum.  Certain much-used constants may be placed in the drum in four or five places to reduce waiting for them, but even then there will ordinarily be some delay.

This process can be tied in with the use of rapid access memory if available.  Sometimes this adds complications because there are two things to worry about instead of one.  On the other hand, the use of rapid access loops *alone* may represent enough saving of time by itself that optimum programming of the slow memory is ignored.

In any case, minimum access programming adds considerably to the complexity of programming.  It is used only where it holds promise of enough saving of machine time to be worth the trouble.  Prime examples are any library program: floating decimal, function evaluation, etc.  In these cases, very great pains may be taken to save time.  As an example, an estimate may be made of the *average* time in a multiplication or division so as to try to optimize the program even in a part which is inherently unpredictable.

The ideal procedure is to design a program which translates a program written sequentially (no attempt to optimize) into a minimum access program.  This is done as a preliminary step, and may include some of the features of relative programming and an assembly program.

# Appendix

# 3 EXTERNALLY PROGRAMMED COMPUTERS

## A3.0 Introduction

The early computers were all externally programmed machines. From Babbage's Analytical Engine to Mark I to the ENIAC to the SSEC, "programming" was effected by external wiring or paper tapes or cards. As mentioned previously, the biggest single advance in computer design was the stored program principle, on which all large-scale general-purpose machines are now based.

There is a point in the size spectrum, however, below which it is not economical to build a stored program machine. There is a definite need for machines with about a hundred words of data storage and speeds between three and a hundred operations per second, including data access. Several computers in this category are very widely used; there are some few thousands of them in existence.

These machines are built on three or four principles. One of these is fairly unimportant now—the punched paper tape. It is used only on some older machines, and as a strictly auxiliary control for some of the smaller machines.

## A3.1 Wired Program Computers

A number of the small machines are controlled by a removable plugboard which contains many wires. The wires are flexible connectors with metal tips which extend through to the back of the board and touch spring contacts in the machine. The plugboards are removable; there are ordinarily many of them with each machine, one for each recurring problem.

Storage is much more limited than in the stored program machines, for three reasons: (1) no instructions are stored in memory, (2) ordinarily a single group of calculations is done for each card *as the card is read* so that there is need for less storage, and (3) being in an in-between category, it is not feasible to use memories which have a low cost-per-digit, so memory is quite expensive.

Basically, these machines carry out a group of arithmetic operations on each card. There may be ten or twenty or a hundred arithmetic operations, which calculate a man's net pay or a cosine. With certain exceptions noted below, it is usual for the machine to do about the same calculation on *each* card. The calculation is completed in the time between reading successive cards. In most machines, data are read from one card at the same time the results for the previous card are being punched. Answers thus are punched back on the same card from which the data were read. There are many exceptions, however.

A calculation is carried out by a series of steps, each of which is set up by a few wires on the plugboard. A typical section of a program might be:

1. Reset accumulator
2. Add                    Storage 6
3. Subtract               Storage 8
4. Store and reset        Storage 10
5. Load MQ                Storage 4
6. Multiply               Storage 5
7. Round                  Position 4
8. Add                    Storage 10      Position 5
9. Store                  Storage 11      Position 5

Each step would require from one to three wires. On the plugboard, there are three or four holes corresponding to each step; wires are run from these holes to other holes which control storage or shifting or the arithmetic registers.

There may be from twenty to something over a hundred of these steps. Two variations of this basic one-step-after-the-other scheme are possible. First are the suppression tests. Details vary, but it is usually possible to make a test for zero, plus, or minus. If the test is satisfied, then a wire from a "suppression exit" to holes for following steps will cause those steps to be suppressed, i.e., not executed. By this means it is possible to set up two or more alternative programs, then choose which to execute by a suppression test.

The second variation is to repeat a basic set of steps, after making some change in the numbers in storage. For instance, the square root iteration can be set up very nicely on such a machine. A few "initializing" steps at the start are suppressed on the repetition. Repeating is stopped as soon as suppression tests show that the process has converged.

Comparing this with the stored program machines, we see that "instructions" here consist of wires. These obviously cannot be "modified." "Loops" consist of repeating the entire program, and suppressing unwanted sections. This almost precludes any extensive loops-within-loops. Storage is *very* limited, so that scientific problems requiring extensive storage have to be set up with complicated card-handling procedures. (Much very good work was done this way, however, before the large machines were available.) And finally, the number of steps is quite limited. If more steps are required, intermediate answers must be punched out and the new cards run through with a different board—which is obviously a clumsy process. Today, most such machines are used in "commercial" applications: payroll, utility billing, inventory records, etc.

## A3.2 Card Programmed Calculators

In the broadest sense, a card programmed calculator is any card machine which does a particular operation as called for by an instruction card, and concurrently with card reading. This can include any small card machine. Several operations such as arithmetic and elementary functions can be wired into a general-purpose control panel; a control punch on each card specifies which operation to perform on this card.

However, the name in just this form almost always implies a combination of several pieces of IBM equipment. The name is usually capitalized and usually abbreviated to CPC. While the intention of this book has not been to describe existing equipment, this particular machine is in such wide use that a page in this connection would not be out of order.

The IBM CPC consists of four units:

1. A modified tabulator, which reads cards, prints answers, stores seven or eight numbers, and performs much of the logic of decoding the operation code and controlling the rest of the machine.

2. An electronic calculator unit which does practically all the arithmetic (usually floating) and function evaluation. It has only enough internal electronic storage for the manipulations required in the floating point, etc., and just barely enough for that.

3. A card punch which can punch the results stored in the tabulator.

4. From one to five separate storage units, each capable of storing sixteen numbers of ten digits each. These are universally called *iceboxes*.

These are the basic components. Exactly how they function in a computing system depends entirely on how three plugboards are wired. A great many different systems have been devised in the time the CPC has been operating. The differences are largely matters of varying needs in diverse applications.

A scientific CPC application is usually built around a three- or four-address programming system. Each instruction card has punched on it an operation and several addresses; the important thing to remember is that the specified operation is carried out *as* the card is read by the tabulator. Never are instructions stored in memory as in stored program machines, except in a special case or two which are not representative. This does mean that the machine can operate no faster than cards can be read, but then such machines are much cheaper and somewhat easier to program than stored program machines.

The only logic possible is to conditionally switch over to another set of instructions on the same cards. In other words, a certain card may call for a test of the sign of the last result: if positive, columns 21–30 may be read for instructions; if negative, columns 51–60 may be read. Often this means simply that under one of the conditions some cards are simply skipped over, as with a stored program jump instruction. In the CPC, the big difference is that we "skip over" by reading the cards anyway, at the usual speed, without doing anything. This again illustrates the major advantage of stored program computers.

This is not to say, however, that wired program and card programmed machines are on their way out. It simply means that if the machine is big enough to support the expense of stored program storage and control elements, then it should be stored program. For many smaller applications the earlier machines are still more economical; they are fast enough, and are very reliable. There are literally thousands of these in operation and more are being built.

## A3.3 Pinboard Machines

This last illustration is not too different from the wired program machines described in Section A3.1. To the author's knowledge, only one machine is built on this idea, the Burroughs E101. Here, a "step" consists of a line on a removable board. Rather than inserting wires, however, it is only necessary to insert pins into appropriate holes to call for the desired functions and storage. It is capable of about the same amount of logical manipulation as the typical wired program equipment, aided by some special operations.

Speed is intermediate between the card programmed and wired program machines. Floating decimal does not seem to be feasible, although the way the machine is used, floating decimal is not really needed. Numbers are entered into a keyboard which looks like an ordinary desk calculator. Answers print on typewriter-type carriage. Magnetic tapes are optional. The pinboard machine is actually something of a cross between a very large desk calculator and a medium-sized electronic calculator.

# APPENDIX 4. OCTAL-DECIMAL INTEGER CONVERSION TABLE

| 0000 to 0777 (Octal) | 0000 to 0511 (Decimal) |
|---|---|

|  | 0 | 1 | 2 | 3 | 4 | 5 | 6 | 7 |
|---|---|---|---|---|---|---|---|---|
| 0000 | 0000 | 0001 | 0002 | 0003 | 0004 | 0005 | 0006 | 0007 |
| 0010 | 0008 | 0009 | 0010 | 0011 | 0012 | 0013 | 0014 | 0015 |
| 0020 | 0016 | 0017 | 0018 | 0019 | 0020 | 0021 | 0022 | 0023 |
| 0030 | 0024 | 0025 | 0026 | 0027 | 0028 | 0029 | 0030 | 0031 |
| 0040 | 0032 | 0033 | 0034 | 0035 | 0036 | 0037 | 0038 | 0039 |
| 0050 | 0040 | 0041 | 0042 | 0043 | 0044 | 0045 | 0046 | 0047 |
| 0060 | 0048 | 0049 | 0050 | 0051 | 0052 | 0053 | 0054 | 0055 |
| 0070 | 0056 | 0057 | 0058 | 0059 | 0060 | 0061 | 0062 | 0063 |
| 0100 | 0064 | 0065 | 0066 | 0067 | 0068 | 0069 | 0070 | 0071 |
| 0110 | 0072 | 0073 | 0074 | 0075 | 0076 | 0077 | 0078 | 0079 |
| 0120 | 0080 | 0081 | 0082 | 0083 | 0084 | 0085 | 0086 | 0087 |
| 0130 | 0088 | 0089 | 0090 | 0091 | 0092 | 0093 | 0094 | 0095 |
| 0140 | 0096 | 0097 | 0098 | 0099 | 0100 | 0101 | 0102 | 0103 |
| 0150 | 0104 | 0105 | 0106 | 0107 | 0108 | 0109 | 0110 | 0111 |
| 0160 | 0112 | 0113 | 0114 | 0115 | 0116 | 0117 | 0118 | 0119 |
| 0170 | 0120 | 0121 | 0122 | 0123 | 0124 | 0125 | 0126 | 0127 |
| 0200 | 0128 | 0129 | 0130 | 0131 | 0132 | 0133 | 0134 | 0135 |
| 0210 | 0136 | 0137 | 0138 | 0139 | 0140 | 0141 | 0142 | 0143 |
| 0220 | 0144 | 0145 | 0146 | 0147 | 0148 | 0149 | 0150 | 0151 |
| 0230 | 0152 | 0153 | 0154 | 0155 | 0156 | 0157 | 0158 | 0159 |
| 0240 | 0160 | 0161 | 0162 | 0163 | 0164 | 0165 | 0166 | 0167 |
| 0250 | 0168 | 0169 | 0170 | 0171 | 0172 | 0173 | 0174 | 0175 |
| 0260 | 0176 | 0177 | 0178 | 0179 | 0180 | 0181 | 0182 | 0183 |
| 0270 | 0184 | 0185 | 0186 | 0187 | 0188 | 0189 | 0190 | 0191 |
| 0300 | 0192 | 0193 | 0194 | 0195 | 0196 | 0197 | 0198 | 0199 |
| 0310 | 0200 | 0201 | 0202 | 0203 | 0204 | 0205 | 0206 | 0207 |
| 0320 | 0208 | 0209 | 0210 | 0211 | 0212 | 0213 | 0214 | 0215 |
| 0330 | 0216 | 0217 | 0218 | 0219 | 0220 | 0221 | 0222 | 0223 |
| 0340 | 0224 | 0225 | 0226 | 0227 | 0228 | 0229 | 0230 | 0231 |
| 0350 | 0232 | 0233 | 0234 | 0235 | 0236 | 0237 | 0238 | 0239 |
| 0360 | 0240 | 0241 | 0242 | 0243 | 0244 | 0245 | 0246 | 0247 |
| 0370 | 0248 | 0249 | 0250 | 0251 | 0252 | 0253 | 0254 | 0255 |

|  | 0 | 1 | 2 | 3 | 4 | 5 | 6 | 7 |
|---|---|---|---|---|---|---|---|---|
| 0400 | 0256 | 0257 | 0258 | 0259 | 0260 | 0261 | 0262 | 0263 |
| 0410 | 0264 | 0265 | 0266 | 0267 | 0268 | 0269 | 0270 | 0271 |
| 0420 | 0272 | 0273 | 0274 | 0275 | 0276 | 0277 | 0278 | 0279 |
| 0430 | 0280 | 0281 | 0282 | 0283 | 0284 | 0285 | 0286 | 0287 |
| 0440 | 0288 | 0289 | 0290 | 0291 | 0292 | 0293 | 0294 | 0295 |
| 0450 | 0296 | 0297 | 0298 | 0299 | 0300 | 0301 | 0302 | 0303 |
| 0460 | 0304 | 0305 | 0306 | 0307 | 0308 | 0309 | 0310 | 0311 |
| 0470 | 0312 | 0313 | 0314 | 0315 | 0316 | 0317 | 0318 | 0319 |
| 0500 | 0320 | 0321 | 0322 | 0323 | 0324 | 0325 | 0326 | 0327 |
| 0510 | 0328 | 0329 | 0330 | 0331 | 0332 | 0333 | 0334 | 0335 |
| 0520 | 0336 | 0337 | 0338 | 0339 | 0340 | 0341 | 0342 | 0343 |
| 0530 | 0344 | 0345 | 0346 | 0347 | 0348 | 0349 | 0350 | 0351 |
| 0540 | 0352 | 0353 | 0354 | 0355 | 0356 | 0357 | 0358 | 0359 |
| 0550 | 0360 | 0361 | 0362 | 0363 | 0364 | 0365 | 0366 | 0367 |
| 0560 | 0368 | 0369 | 0370 | 0371 | 0372 | 0373 | 0374 | 0375 |
| 0570 | 0376 | 0377 | 0378 | 0379 | 0380 | 0381 | 0382 | 0383 |
| 0600 | 0384 | 0385 | 0386 | 0387 | 0388 | 0389 | 0390 | 0391 |
| 0610 | 0392 | 0393 | 0394 | 0395 | 0396 | 0397 | 0398 | 0399 |
| 0620 | 0400 | 0401 | 0402 | 0403 | 0404 | 0405 | 0406 | 0407 |
| 0630 | 0408 | 0409 | 0410 | 0411 | 0412 | 0413 | 0414 | 0415 |
| 0640 | 0416 | 0417 | 0418 | 0419 | 0420 | 0421 | 0422 | 0423 |
| 0650 | 0424 | 0425 | 0426 | 0427 | 0428 | 0429 | 0430 | 0431 |
| 0660 | 0432 | 0433 | 0434 | 0435 | 0436 | 0437 | 0438 | 0439 |
| 0670 | 0440 | 0441 | 0442 | 0443 | 0444 | 0445 | 0446 | 0447 |
| 0700 | 0448 | 0449 | 0450 | 0451 | 0452 | 0453 | 0454 | 0455 |
| 0710 | 0456 | 0457 | 0458 | 0459 | 0460 | 0461 | 0462 | 0463 |
| 0720 | 0464 | 0465 | 0466 | 0467 | 0468 | 0469 | 0470 | 0471 |
| 0730 | 0472 | 0473 | 0474 | 0475 | 0476 | 0477 | 0478 | 0479 |
| 0740 | 0480 | 0481 | 0482 | 0483 | 0484 | 0485 | 0486 | 0487 |
| 0750 | 0488 | 0489 | 0490 | 0491 | 0492 | 0493 | 0494 | 0495 |
| 0760 | 0496 | 0497 | 0498 | 0499 | 0500 | 0501 | 0502 | 0503 |
| 0770 | 0504 | 0505 | 0506 | 0507 | 0508 | 0509 | 0510 | 0511 |

Courtesy International Business Machines Corporation

|      | 0 | 1 | 2 | 3 | 4 | 5 | 6 | 7 |
|------|------|------|------|------|------|------|------|------|
| 1000 | 0512 | 0513 | 0514 | 0515 | 0516 | 0517 | 0518 | 0519 |
| 1010 | 0520 | 0521 | 0522 | 0523 | 0524 | 0525 | 0526 | 0527 |
| 1020 | 0528 | 0529 | 0530 | 0531 | 0532 | 0533 | 0534 | 0535 |
| 1030 | 0536 | 0537 | 0538 | 0539 | 0540 | 0541 | 0542 | 0543 |
| 1040 | 0544 | 0545 | 0546 | 0547 | 0548 | 0549 | 0550 | 0551 |
| 1050 | 0552 | 0553 | 0554 | 0555 | 0556 | 0557 | 0558 | 0559 |
| 1060 | 0560 | 0561 | 0562 | 0563 | 0564 | 0565 | 0566 | 0567 |
| 1070 | 0568 | 0569 | 0570 | 0571 | 0572 | 0573 | 0574 | 0575 |
| 1100 | 0576 | 0577 | 0578 | 0579 | 0580 | 0581 | 0582 | 0583 |
| 1110 | 0584 | 0585 | 0586 | 0587 | 0588 | 0589 | 0590 | 0591 |
| 1120 | 0592 | 0593 | 0594 | 0595 | 0596 | 0597 | 0598 | 0599 |
| 1130 | 0600 | 0601 | 0602 | 0603 | 0604 | 0605 | 0606 | 0607 |
| 1140 | 0608 | 0609 | 0610 | 0611 | 0612 | 0613 | 0614 | 0615 |
| 1150 | 0616 | 0617 | 0618 | 0619 | 0620 | 0621 | 0622 | 0623 |
| 1160 | 0624 | 0625 | 0626 | 0627 | 0628 | 0629 | 0630 | 0631 |
| 1170 | 0632 | 0633 | 0634 | 0635 | 0636 | 0637 | 0638 | 0639 |
| 1200 | 0640 | 0641 | 0642 | 0643 | 0644 | 0645 | 0646 | 0647 |
| 1210 | 0648 | 0649 | 0650 | 0651 | 0652 | 0653 | 0654 | 0655 |
| 1220 | 0656 | 0657 | 0658 | 0659 | 0660 | 0661 | 0662 | 0663 |
| 1230 | 0664 | 0665 | 0666 | 0667 | 0668 | 0669 | 0670 | 0671 |
| 1240 | 0672 | 0673 | 0674 | 0675 | 0676 | 0677 | 0678 | 0679 |
| 1250 | 0680 | 0681 | 0682 | 0683 | 0684 | 0685 | 0686 | 0687 |
| 1260 | 0688 | 0689 | 0690 | 0691 | 0692 | 0693 | 0694 | 0695 |
| 1270 | 0696 | 0697 | 0698 | 0699 | 0700 | 0701 | 0702 | 0703 |
| 1300 | 0704 | 0705 | 0706 | 0707 | 0708 | 0709 | 0710 | 0711 |
| 1310 | 0712 | 0713 | 0714 | 0715 | 0716 | 0717 | 0718 | 0719 |
| 1320 | 0720 | 0721 | 0722 | 0723 | 0724 | 0725 | 0726 | 0727 |
| 1330 | 0728 | 0729 | 0730 | 0731 | 0732 | 0733 | 0734 | 0735 |
| 1340 | 0736 | 0737 | 0738 | 0739 | 0740 | 0741 | 0742 | 0743 |
| 1350 | 0744 | 0745 | 0746 | 0747 | 0748 | 0749 | 0750 | 0751 |
| 1360 | 0752 | 0753 | 0754 | 0755 | 0756 | 0757 | 0758 | 0759 |
| 1370 | 0760 | 0761 | 0762 | 0763 | 0764 | 0765 | 0766 | 0767 |

|      | 0 | 1 | 2 | 3 | 4 | 5 | 6 | 7 |
|------|------|------|------|------|------|------|------|------|
| 1400 | 0768 | 0769 | 0770 | 0771 | 0772 | 0773 | 0774 | 0775 |
| 1410 | 0776 | 0777 | 0778 | 0779 | 0780 | 0781 | 0782 | 0783 |
| 1420 | 0784 | 0785 | 0786 | 0787 | 0788 | 0789 | 0790 | 0791 |
| 1430 | 0792 | 0793 | 0794 | 0795 | 0796 | 0797 | 0798 | 0799 |
| 1440 | 0800 | 0801 | 0802 | 0803 | 0804 | 0805 | 0806 | 0807 |
| 1450 | 0808 | 0809 | 0810 | 0811 | 0812 | 0813 | 0814 | 0815 |
| 1460 | 0816 | 0817 | 0818 | 0819 | 0820 | 0821 | 0822 | 0823 |
| 1470 | 0824 | 0825 | 0826 | 0827 | 0828 | 0829 | 0830 | 0831 |
| 1500 | 0832 | 0833 | 0834 | 0835 | 0836 | 0837 | 0838 | 0839 |
| 1510 | 0840 | 0841 | 0842 | 0843 | 0844 | 0845 | 0846 | 0847 |
| 1520 | 0848 | 0849 | 0850 | 0851 | 0852 | 0853 | 0854 | 0855 |
| 1530 | 0856 | 0857 | 0858 | 0859 | 0860 | 0861 | 0862 | 0863 |
| 1540 | 0864 | 0865 | 0866 | 0867 | 0868 | 0869 | 0870 | 0871 |
| 1550 | 0872 | 0873 | 0874 | 0875 | 0876 | 0877 | 0878 | 0879 |
| 1560 | 0880 | 0881 | 0882 | 0883 | 0884 | 0885 | 0886 | 0887 |
| 1570 | 0888 | 0889 | 0890 | 0891 | 0892 | 0893 | 0894 | 0895 |
| 1600 | 0896 | 0897 | 0898 | 0899 | 0900 | 0901 | 0902 | 0903 |
| 1610 | 0904 | 0905 | 0906 | 0907 | 0908 | 0909 | 0910 | 0911 |
| 1620 | 0912 | 0913 | 0914 | 0915 | 0916 | 0917 | 0918 | 0919 |
| 1630 | 0920 | 0921 | 0922 | 0923 | 0924 | 0925 | 0926 | 0927 |
| 1640 | 0928 | 0929 | 0930 | 0931 | 0932 | 0933 | 0934 | 0935 |
| 1650 | 0936 | 0937 | 0938 | 0939 | 0940 | 0941 | 0942 | 0943 |
| 1660 | 0944 | 0945 | 0946 | 0947 | 0948 | 0949 | 0950 | 0951 |
| 1670 | 0952 | 0953 | 0954 | 0955 | 0956 | 0957 | 0958 | 0959 |
| 1700 | 0960 | 0961 | 0962 | 0963 | 0964 | 0965 | 0966 | 0967 |
| 1710 | 0968 | 0969 | 0970 | 0971 | 0972 | 0973 | 0974 | 0975 |
| 1720 | 0976 | 0977 | 0978 | 0979 | 0980 | 0981 | 0982 | 0983 |
| 1730 | 0984 | 0985 | 0986 | 0987 | 0988 | 0989 | 0990 | 0991 |
| 1740 | 0992 | 0993 | 0994 | 0995 | 0996 | 0997 | 0998 | 0999 |
| 1750 | 1000 | 1001 | 1002 | 1003 | 1004 | 1005 | 1006 | 1007 |
| 1760 | 1008 | 1009 | 1010 | 1011 | 1012 | 1013 | 1014 | 1015 |
| 1770 | 1016 | 1017 | 1018 | 1019 | 1020 | 1021 | 1022 | 1023 |

| 1000 to 1777 (Octal) | 0512 to 1023 (Decimal) |

## OCTAL-DECIMAL INTEGER CONVERSION TABLE

|  | 2000 to 2777 (Octal) | 1024 to 1535 (Decimal) |
|---|---|---|

|      | 0    | 1    | 2    | 3    | 4    | 5    | 6    | 7    |
|------|------|------|------|------|------|------|------|------|
| 2000 | 1024 | 1025 | 1026 | 1027 | 1028 | 1029 | 1030 | 1031 |
| 2010 | 1032 | 1033 | 1034 | 1035 | 1036 | 1037 | 1038 | 1039 |
| 2020 | 1040 | 1041 | 1042 | 1043 | 1044 | 1045 | 1046 | 1047 |
| 2030 | 1048 | 1049 | 1050 | 1051 | 1052 | 1053 | 1054 | 1055 |
| 2040 | 1056 | 1057 | 1058 | 1059 | 1060 | 1061 | 1062 | 1063 |
| 2050 | 1064 | 1065 | 1066 | 1067 | 1068 | 1069 | 1070 | 1071 |
| 2060 | 1072 | 1073 | 1074 | 1075 | 1076 | 1077 | 1078 | 1079 |
| 2070 | 1080 | 1081 | 1082 | 1083 | 1084 | 1085 | 1086 | 1087 |
| 2100 | 1088 | 1089 | 1090 | 1091 | 1092 | 1093 | 1094 | 1095 |
| 2110 | 1096 | 1097 | 1098 | 1099 | 1100 | 1101 | 1102 | 1103 |
| 2120 | 1104 | 1105 | 1106 | 1107 | 1108 | 1109 | 1110 | 1111 |
| 2130 | 1112 | 1113 | 1114 | 1115 | 1116 | 1117 | 1118 | 1119 |
| 2140 | 1120 | 1121 | 1122 | 1123 | 1124 | 1125 | 1126 | 1127 |
| 2150 | 1128 | 1129 | 1130 | 1131 | 1132 | 1133 | 1134 | 1135 |
| 2160 | 1136 | 1137 | 1138 | 1139 | 1140 | 1141 | 1142 | 1143 |
| 2170 | 1144 | 1145 | 1146 | 1147 | 1148 | 1149 | 1150 | 1151 |
| 2200 | 1152 | 1153 | 1154 | 1155 | 1156 | 1157 | 1158 | 1159 |
| 2210 | 1160 | 1161 | 1162 | 1163 | 1164 | 1165 | 1166 | 1167 |
| 2220 | 1168 | 1169 | 1170 | 1171 | 1172 | 1173 | 1174 | 1175 |
| 2230 | 1176 | 1177 | 1178 | 1179 | 1180 | 1181 | 1182 | 1183 |
| 2240 | 1184 | 1185 | 1186 | 1187 | 1188 | 1189 | 1190 | 1191 |
| 2250 | 1192 | 1193 | 1194 | 1195 | 1196 | 1197 | 1198 | 1199 |
| 2260 | 1200 | 1201 | 1202 | 1203 | 1204 | 1205 | 1206 | 1207 |
| 2270 | 1208 | 1209 | 1210 | 1211 | 1212 | 1213 | 1214 | 1215 |
| 2300 | 1216 | 1217 | 1218 | 1219 | 1220 | 1221 | 1222 | 1223 |
| 2310 | 1224 | 1225 | 1226 | 1227 | 1228 | 1229 | 1230 | 1231 |
| 2320 | 1232 | 1233 | 1234 | 1235 | 1236 | 1237 | 1238 | 1239 |
| 2330 | 1240 | 1241 | 1242 | 1243 | 1244 | 1245 | 1246 | 1247 |
| 2340 | 1248 | 1249 | 1250 | 1251 | 1252 | 1253 | 1254 | 1255 |
| 2350 | 1256 | 1257 | 1258 | 1259 | 1260 | 1261 | 1262 | 1263 |
| 2360 | 1264 | 1265 | 1266 | 1267 | 1268 | 1269 | 1270 | 1271 |
| 2370 | 1272 | 1273 | 1274 | 1275 | 1276 | 1277 | 1278 | 1279 |

|      | 0    | 1    | 2    | 3    | 4    | 5    | 6    | 7    |
|------|------|------|------|------|------|------|------|------|
| 2400 | 1280 | 1281 | 1282 | 1283 | 1284 | 1285 | 1286 | 1287 |
| 2410 | 1288 | 1289 | 1290 | 1291 | 1292 | 1293 | 1294 | 1295 |
| 2420 | 1296 | 1297 | 1298 | 1299 | 1300 | 1301 | 1302 | 1303 |
| 2430 | 1304 | 1305 | 1306 | 1307 | 1308 | 1309 | 1310 | 1311 |
| 2440 | 1312 | 1313 | 1314 | 1315 | 1316 | 1317 | 1318 | 1319 |
| 2450 | 1320 | 1321 | 1322 | 1323 | 1324 | 1325 | 1326 | 1327 |
| 2460 | 1328 | 1329 | 1330 | 1331 | 1332 | 1333 | 1334 | 1335 |
| 2470 | 1336 | 1337 | 1338 | 1339 | 1340 | 1341 | 1342 | 1343 |
| 2500 | 1344 | 1345 | 1346 | 1347 | 1348 | 1349 | 1350 | 1351 |
| 2510 | 1352 | 1353 | 1354 | 1355 | 1356 | 1357 | 1358 | 1359 |
| 2520 | 1360 | 1361 | 1362 | 1363 | 1364 | 1365 | 1366 | 1367 |
| 2530 | 1368 | 1369 | 1370 | 1371 | 1372 | 1373 | 1374 | 1375 |
| 2540 | 1376 | 1377 | 1378 | 1379 | 1380 | 1381 | 1382 | 1383 |
| 2550 | 1384 | 1385 | 1386 | 1387 | 1388 | 1389 | 1390 | 1391 |
| 2560 | 1392 | 1393 | 1394 | 1395 | 1396 | 1397 | 1398 | 1399 |
| 2570 | 1400 | 1401 | 1402 | 1403 | 1404 | 1405 | 1406 | 1407 |
| 2600 | 1408 | 1409 | 1410 | 1411 | 1412 | 1413 | 1414 | 1415 |
| 2610 | 1416 | 1417 | 1418 | 1419 | 1420 | 1421 | 1422 | 1423 |
| 2620 | 1424 | 1425 | 1426 | 1427 | 1428 | 1429 | 1430 | 1431 |
| 2630 | 1432 | 1433 | 1434 | 1435 | 1436 | 1437 | 1438 | 1439 |
| 2640 | 1440 | 1441 | 1442 | 1443 | 1444 | 1445 | 1446 | 1447 |
| 2650 | 1448 | 1449 | 1450 | 1451 | 1452 | 1453 | 1454 | 1455 |
| 2660 | 1456 | 1457 | 1458 | 1459 | 1460 | 1461 | 1462 | 1463 |
| 2670 | 1464 | 1465 | 1466 | 1467 | 1468 | 1469 | 1470 | 1471 |
| 2700 | 1472 | 1473 | 1474 | 1475 | 1476 | 1477 | 1478 | 1479 |
| 2710 | 1480 | 1481 | 1482 | 1483 | 1484 | 1485 | 1486 | 1487 |
| 2720 | 1488 | 1489 | 1490 | 1491 | 1492 | 1493 | 1494 | 1495 |
| 2730 | 1496 | 1497 | 1498 | 1499 | 1500 | 1501 | 1502 | 1503 |
| 2740 | 1504 | 1505 | 1506 | 1507 | 1508 | 1509 | 1510 | 1511 |
| 2750 | 1512 | 1513 | 1514 | 1515 | 1516 | 1517 | 1518 | 1519 |
| 2760 | 1520 | 1521 | 1522 | 1523 | 1524 | 1525 | 1526 | 1527 |
| 2770 | 1528 | 1529 | 1530 | 1531 | 1532 | 1533 | 1534 | 1535 |

| 3000 to 3777 (Octal) | 1536 to 2047 (Decimal) |
|---|---|

|  | 0 | 1 | 2 | 3 | 4 | 5 | 6 | 7 |
|---|---|---|---|---|---|---|---|---|
| 3000 | 1536 | 1537 | 1538 | 1539 | 1540 | 1541 | 1542 | 1543 |
| 3010 | 1544 | 1545 | 1546 | 1547 | 1548 | 1549 | 1550 | 1551 |
| 3020 | 1552 | 1553 | 1554 | 1555 | 1556 | 1557 | 1558 | 1559 |
| 3030 | 1560 | 1561 | 1562 | 1563 | 1564 | 1565 | 1566 | 1567 |
| 3040 | 1568 | 1569 | 1570 | 1571 | 1572 | 1573 | 1574 | 1575 |
| 3050 | 1576 | 1577 | 1578 | 1579 | 1580 | 1581 | 1582 | 1583 |
| 3060 | 1584 | 1585 | 1586 | 1587 | 1588 | 1589 | 1590 | 1591 |
| 3070 | 1592 | 1593 | 1594 | 1595 | 1596 | 1597 | 1598 | 1599 |
| 3100 | 1600 | 1601 | 1602 | 1603 | 1604 | 1605 | 1606 | 1607 |
| 3110 | 1608 | 1609 | 1610 | 1611 | 1612 | 1613 | 1614 | 1615 |
| 3120 | 1616 | 1617 | 1618 | 1619 | 1620 | 1621 | 1622 | 1623 |
| 3130 | 1624 | 1625 | 1626 | 1627 | 1628 | 1629 | 1630 | 1631 |
| 3140 | 1632 | 1633 | 1634 | 1635 | 1636 | 1637 | 1638 | 1639 |
| 3150 | 1640 | 1641 | 1642 | 1643 | 1644 | 1645 | 1646 | 1647 |
| 3160 | 1648 | 1649 | 1650 | 1651 | 1652 | 1653 | 1654 | 1655 |
| 3170 | 1656 | 1657 | 1658 | 1659 | 1660 | 1661 | 1662 | 1663 |
| 3200 | 1664 | 1665 | 1666 | 1667 | 1668 | 1669 | 1670 | 1671 |
| 3210 | 1672 | 1673 | 1674 | 1675 | 1676 | 1677 | 1678 | 1679 |
| 3220 | 1680 | 1681 | 1682 | 1683 | 1684 | 1685 | 1686 | 1687 |
| 3230 | 1688 | 1689 | 1690 | 1691 | 1692 | 1693 | 1694 | 1695 |
| 3240 | 1696 | 1697 | 1698 | 1699 | 1700 | 1701 | 1702 | 1703 |
| 3250 | 1704 | 1705 | 1706 | 1707 | 1708 | 1709 | 1710 | 1711 |
| 3260 | 1712 | 1713 | 1714 | 1715 | 1716 | 1717 | 1718 | 1719 |
| 3270 | 1720 | 1721 | 1722 | 1723 | 1724 | 1725 | 1726 | 1727 |
| 3300 | 1728 | 1729 | 1730 | 1731 | 1732 | 1733 | 1734 | 1735 |
| 3310 | 1736 | 1737 | 1738 | 1739 | 1740 | 1741 | 1742 | 1743 |
| 3320 | 1744 | 1745 | 1746 | 1747 | 1748 | 1749 | 1750 | 1751 |
| 3330 | 1752 | 1753 | 1754 | 1755 | 1756 | 1757 | 1758 | 1759 |
| 3340 | 1760 | 1761 | 1762 | 1763 | 1764 | 1765 | 1766 | 1767 |
| 3350 | 1768 | 1769 | 1770 | 1771 | 1772 | 1773 | 1774 | 1775 |
| 3360 | 1776 | 1777 | 1778 | 1779 | 1780 | 1781 | 1782 | 1783 |
| 3370 | 1784 | 1785 | 1786 | 1787 | 1788 | 1789 | 1790 | 1791 |

|  | 0 | 1 | 2 | 3 | 4 | 5 | 6 | 7 |
|---|---|---|---|---|---|---|---|---|
| 3400 | 1792 | 1793 | 1794 | 1795 | 1796 | 1797 | 1798 | 1799 |
| 3410 | 1800 | 1801 | 1802 | 1803 | 1804 | 1805 | 1806 | 1807 |
| 3420 | 1808 | 1809 | 1810 | 1811 | 1812 | 1813 | 1814 | 1815 |
| 3430 | 1816 | 1817 | 1818 | 1819 | 1820 | 1821 | 1822 | 1823 |
| 3440 | 1824 | 1825 | 1826 | 1827 | 1828 | 1829 | 1830 | 1831 |
| 3450 | 1832 | 1833 | 1834 | 1835 | 1836 | 1837 | 1838 | 1839 |
| 3460 | 1840 | 1841 | 1842 | 1843 | 1844 | 1845 | 1846 | 1847 |
| 3470 | 1848 | 1849 | 1850 | 1851 | 1852 | 1853 | 1854 | 1855 |
| 3500 | 1856 | 1857 | 1858 | 1859 | 1860 | 1861 | 1862 | 1863 |
| 3510 | 1864 | 1865 | 1866 | 1867 | 1868 | 1869 | 1870 | 1871 |
| 3520 | 1872 | 1873 | 1874 | 1875 | 1876 | 1877 | 1878 | 1879 |
| 3530 | 1880 | 1881 | 1882 | 1883 | 1884 | 1885 | 1886 | 1887 |
| 3540 | 1888 | 1889 | 1890 | 1891 | 1892 | 1893 | 1894 | 1895 |
| 3550 | 1896 | 1897 | 1898 | 1899 | 1900 | 1901 | 1902 | 1903 |
| 3560 | 1904 | 1905 | 1906 | 1907 | 1908 | 1909 | 1910 | 1911 |
| 3570 | 1912 | 1913 | 1914 | 1915 | 1916 | 1917 | 1918 | 1919 |
| 3600 | 1920 | 1921 | 1922 | 1923 | 1924 | 1925 | 1926 | 1927 |
| 3610 | 1928 | 1929 | 1930 | 1931 | 1932 | 1933 | 1934 | 1935 |
| 3620 | 1936 | 1937 | 1938 | 1939 | 1940 | 1941 | 1942 | 1943 |
| 3630 | 1944 | 1945 | 1946 | 1947 | 1948 | 1949 | 1950 | 1951 |
| 3640 | 1952 | 1953 | 1954 | 1955 | 1956 | 1957 | 1958 | 1959 |
| 3650 | 1960 | 1961 | 1962 | 1963 | 1964 | 1965 | 1966 | 1967 |
| 3660 | 1968 | 1969 | 1970 | 1971 | 1972 | 1973 | 1974 | 1975 |
| 3670 | 1976 | 1977 | 1978 | 1979 | 1980 | 1981 | 1982 | 1983 |
| 3700 | 1984 | 1985 | 1986 | 1987 | 1988 | 1989 | 1990 | 1991 |
| 3710 | 1992 | 1993 | 1994 | 1995 | 1996 | 1997 | 1998 | 1999 |
| 3720 | 2000 | 2001 | 2002 | 2003 | 2004 | 2005 | 2006 | 2007 |
| 3730 | 2008 | 2009 | 2010 | 2011 | 2012 | 2013 | 2014 | 2015 |
| 3740 | 2016 | 2017 | 2018 | 2019 | 2020 | 2021 | 2022 | 2023 |
| 3750 | 2024 | 2025 | 2026 | 2027 | 2028 | 2029 | 2030 | 2031 |
| 3760 | 2032 | 2033 | 2034 | 2035 | 2036 | 2037 | 2038 | 2039 |
| 3770 | 2040 | 2041 | 2042 | 2043 | 2044 | 2045 | 2046 | 2047 |

## OCTAL-DECIMAL INTEGER CONVERSION TABLE

| 4000 to 4777 (Octal) | 2048 to 2559 (Decimal) |

|      | 0    | 1    | 2    | 3    | 4    | 5    | 6    | 7    |
|------|------|------|------|------|------|------|------|------|
| 4000 | 2048 | 2049 | 2050 | 2051 | 2052 | 2053 | 2054 | 2055 |
| 4010 | 2056 | 2057 | 2058 | 2059 | 2060 | 2061 | 2062 | 2063 |
| 4020 | 2064 | 2065 | 2066 | 2067 | 2068 | 2069 | 2070 | 2071 |
| 4030 | 2072 | 2073 | 2074 | 2075 | 2076 | 2077 | 2078 | 2079 |
| 4040 | 2080 | 2081 | 2082 | 2083 | 2084 | 2085 | 2086 | 2087 |
| 4050 | 2088 | 2089 | 2090 | 2091 | 2092 | 2093 | 2094 | 2095 |
| 4060 | 2096 | 2097 | 2098 | 2099 | 2100 | 2101 | 2102 | 2103 |
| 4070 | 2104 | 2105 | 2106 | 2107 | 2108 | 2109 | 2110 | 2111 |
| 4100 | 2112 | 2113 | 2114 | 2115 | 2116 | 2117 | 2118 | 2119 |
| 4110 | 2120 | 2121 | 2122 | 2123 | 2124 | 2125 | 2126 | 2127 |
| 4120 | 2128 | 2129 | 2130 | 2131 | 2132 | 2133 | 2134 | 2135 |
| 4130 | 2136 | 2137 | 2138 | 2139 | 2140 | 2141 | 2142 | 2143 |
| 4140 | 2144 | 2145 | 2146 | 2147 | 2148 | 2149 | 2150 | 2151 |
| 4150 | 2152 | 2153 | 2154 | 2155 | 2156 | 2157 | 2158 | 2159 |
| 4160 | 2160 | 2161 | 2162 | 2163 | 2164 | 2165 | 2166 | 2167 |
| 4170 | 2168 | 2169 | 2170 | 2171 | 2172 | 2173 | 2174 | 2175 |
| 4200 | 2176 | 2177 | 2178 | 2179 | 2180 | 2181 | 2182 | 2183 |
| 4210 | 2184 | 2185 | 2186 | 2187 | 2188 | 2189 | 2190 | 2191 |
| 4220 | 2192 | 2193 | 2194 | 2195 | 2196 | 2197 | 2198 | 2199 |
| 4230 | 2200 | 2201 | 2202 | 2203 | 2204 | 2205 | 2206 | 2207 |
| 4240 | 2208 | 2209 | 2210 | 2211 | 2212 | 2213 | 2214 | 2215 |
| 4250 | 2216 | 2217 | 2218 | 2219 | 2220 | 2221 | 2222 | 2223 |
| 4260 | 2224 | 2225 | 2226 | 2227 | 2228 | 2229 | 2230 | 2231 |
| 4270 | 2232 | 2233 | 2234 | 2235 | 2236 | 2237 | 2238 | 2239 |
| 4300 | 2240 | 2241 | 2242 | 2243 | 2244 | 2245 | 2246 | 2247 |
| 4310 | 2248 | 2249 | 2250 | 2251 | 2252 | 2253 | 2254 | 2255 |
| 4320 | 2256 | 2257 | 2258 | 2259 | 2260 | 2261 | 2262 | 2263 |
| 4330 | 2264 | 2265 | 2266 | 2267 | 2268 | 2269 | 2270 | 2271 |
| 4340 | 2272 | 2273 | 2274 | 2275 | 2276 | 2277 | 2278 | 2279 |
| 4350 | 2280 | 2281 | 2282 | 2283 | 2284 | 2285 | 2286 | 2287 |
| 4360 | 2288 | 2289 | 2290 | 2291 | 2292 | 2293 | 2294 | 2295 |
| 4370 | 2296 | 2297 | 2298 | 2299 | 2300 | 2301 | 2302 | 2303 |

|      | 0    | 1    | 2    | 3    | 4    | 5    | 6    | 7    |
|------|------|------|------|------|------|------|------|------|
| 4400 | 2304 | 2305 | 2306 | 2307 | 2308 | 2309 | 2310 | 2311 |
| 4410 | 2312 | 2313 | 2314 | 2315 | 2316 | 2317 | 2318 | 2319 |
| 4420 | 2320 | 2321 | 2322 | 2323 | 2324 | 2325 | 2326 | 2327 |
| 4430 | 2328 | 2329 | 2330 | 2331 | 2332 | 2333 | 2334 | 2335 |
| 4440 | 2336 | 2337 | 2338 | 2339 | 2340 | 2341 | 2342 | 2343 |
| 4450 | 2344 | 2345 | 2346 | 2347 | 2348 | 2349 | 2350 | 2351 |
| 4460 | 2352 | 2353 | 2354 | 2355 | 2356 | 2357 | 2358 | 2359 |
| 4470 | 2360 | 2361 | 2362 | 2363 | 2364 | 2365 | 2366 | 2367 |
| 4500 | 2368 | 2369 | 2370 | 2371 | 2372 | 2373 | 2374 | 2375 |
| 4510 | 2376 | 2377 | 2378 | 2379 | 2380 | 2381 | 2382 | 2383 |
| 4520 | 2384 | 2385 | 2386 | 2387 | 2388 | 2389 | 2390 | 2391 |
| 4530 | 2392 | 2393 | 2394 | 2395 | 2396 | 2397 | 2398 | 2399 |
| 4540 | 2400 | 2401 | 2402 | 2403 | 2404 | 2405 | 2406 | 2407 |
| 4550 | 2408 | 2409 | 2410 | 2411 | 2412 | 2413 | 2414 | 2415 |
| 4560 | 2416 | 2417 | 2418 | 2419 | 2420 | 2421 | 2422 | 2423 |
| 4570 | 2424 | 2425 | 2426 | 2427 | 2428 | 2429 | 2430 | 2431 |
| 4600 | 2432 | 2433 | 2434 | 2435 | 2436 | 2437 | 2438 | 2439 |
| 4610 | 2440 | 2441 | 2442 | 2443 | 2444 | 2445 | 2446 | 2447 |
| 4620 | 2448 | 2449 | 2450 | 2451 | 2452 | 2453 | 2454 | 2455 |
| 4630 | 2456 | 2457 | 2458 | 2459 | 2460 | 2461 | 2462 | 2463 |
| 4640 | 2464 | 2465 | 2466 | 2467 | 2468 | 2469 | 2470 | 2471 |
| 4650 | 2472 | 2473 | 2474 | 2475 | 2476 | 2477 | 2478 | 2479 |
| 4660 | 2480 | 2481 | 2482 | 2483 | 2484 | 2485 | 2486 | 2487 |
| 4670 | 2488 | 2489 | 2490 | 2491 | 2492 | 2493 | 2494 | 2495 |
| 4700 | 2496 | 2497 | 2498 | 2499 | 2500 | 2501 | 2502 | 2503 |
| 4710 | 2504 | 2505 | 2506 | 2507 | 2508 | 2509 | 2510 | 2511 |
| 4720 | 2512 | 2513 | 2514 | 2515 | 2516 | 2517 | 2518 | 2519 |
| 4730 | 2520 | 2521 | 2522 | 2523 | 2524 | 2525 | 2526 | 2527 |
| 4740 | 2528 | 2529 | 2530 | 2531 | 2532 | 2533 | 2534 | 2535 |
| 4750 | 2536 | 2537 | 2538 | 2539 | 2540 | 2541 | 2542 | 2543 |
| 4760 | 2544 | 2545 | 2546 | 2547 | 2548 | 2549 | 2550 | 2551 |
| 4770 | 2552 | 2553 | 2554 | 2555 | 2556 | 2557 | 2558 | 2559 |

5000 to 5777 (Octal) | 2560 to 3071 (Decimal)

| | 0 | 1 | 2 | 3 | 4 | 5 | 6 | 7 |
|---|---|---|---|---|---|---|---|---|
| 5000 | 2560 | 2561 | 2562 | 2563 | 2564 | 2565 | 2566 | 2567 |
| 5010 | 2568 | 2569 | 2570 | 2571 | 2572 | 2573 | 2574 | 2575 |
| 5020 | 2576 | 2577 | 2578 | 2579 | 2580 | 2581 | 2582 | 2583 |
| 5030 | 2584 | 2585 | 2586 | 2587 | 2588 | 2589 | 2590 | 2591 |
| 5040 | 2592 | 2593 | 2594 | 2595 | 2596 | 2597 | 2598 | 2599 |
| 5050 | 2600 | 2601 | 2602 | 2603 | 2604 | 2605 | 2606 | 2607 |
| 5060 | 2608 | 2609 | 2610 | 2611 | 2612 | 2613 | 2614 | 2615 |
| 5070 | 2616 | 2617 | 2618 | 2619 | 2620 | 2621 | 2622 | 2623 |
| 5100 | 2624 | 2625 | 2626 | 2627 | 2628 | 2629 | 2630 | 2631 |
| 5110 | 2632 | 2633 | 2634 | 2635 | 2636 | 2637 | 2638 | 2639 |
| 5120 | 2640 | 2641 | 2642 | 2643 | 2644 | 2645 | 2646 | 2647 |
| 5130 | 2648 | 2649 | 2650 | 2651 | 2652 | 2653 | 2654 | 2655 |
| 5140 | 2656 | 2657 | 2658 | 2659 | 2660 | 2661 | 2662 | 2663 |
| 5150 | 2664 | 2665 | 2666 | 2667 | 2668 | 2669 | 2670 | 2671 |
| 5160 | 2672 | 2673 | 2674 | 2675 | 2676 | 2677 | 2678 | 2679 |
| 5170 | 2680 | 2681 | 2682 | 2683 | 2684 | 2685 | 2686 | 2687 |
| 5200 | 2688 | 2689 | 2690 | 2691 | 2692 | 2693 | 2694 | 2695 |
| 5210 | 2696 | 2697 | 2698 | 2699 | 2700 | 2701 | 2702 | 2703 |
| 5220 | 2704 | 2705 | 2706 | 2707 | 2708 | 2709 | 2710 | 2711 |
| 5230 | 2712 | 2713 | 2714 | 2715 | 2716 | 2717 | 2718 | 2719 |
| 5240 | 2720 | 2721 | 2722 | 2723 | 2724 | 2725 | 2726 | 2727 |
| 5250 | 2728 | 2729 | 2730 | 2731 | 2732 | 2733 | 2734 | 2735 |
| 5260 | 2736 | 2737 | 2738 | 2739 | 2740 | 2741 | 2742 | 2743 |
| 5270 | 2744 | 2745 | 2746 | 2747 | 2748 | 2749 | 2750 | 2751 |
| 5300 | 2752 | 2753 | 2754 | 2755 | 2756 | 2757 | 2758 | 2759 |
| 5310 | 2760 | 2761 | 2762 | 2763 | 2764 | 2765 | 2766 | 2767 |
| 5320 | 2768 | 2769 | 2770 | 2771 | 2772 | 2773 | 2774 | 2775 |
| 5330 | 2776 | 2777 | 2778 | 2779 | 2780 | 2781 | 2782 | 2783 |
| 5340 | 2784 | 2785 | 2786 | 2787 | 2788 | 2789 | 2790 | 2791 |
| 5350 | 2792 | 2793 | 2794 | 2795 | 2796 | 2797 | 2798 | 2799 |
| 5360 | 2800 | 2801 | 2802 | 2803 | 2804 | 2805 | 2806 | 2807 |
| 5370 | 2808 | 2809 | 2810 | 2811 | 2812 | 2813 | 2814 | 2815 |

| | 0 | 1 | 2 | 3 | 4 | 5 | 6 | 7 |
|---|---|---|---|---|---|---|---|---|
| 5400 | 2816 | 2817 | 2818 | 2819 | 2820 | 2821 | 2822 | 2823 |
| 5410 | 2824 | 2825 | 2826 | 2827 | 2828 | 2829 | 2830 | 2831 |
| 5420 | 2832 | 2833 | 2834 | 2835 | 2836 | 2837 | 2838 | 2839 |
| 5430 | 2840 | 2841 | 2842 | 2843 | 2844 | 2845 | 2846 | 2847 |
| 5440 | 2848 | 2849 | 2850 | 2851 | 2852 | 2853 | 2854 | 2855 |
| 5450 | 2856 | 2857 | 2858 | 2859 | 2860 | 2861 | 2862 | 2863 |
| 5460 | 2864 | 2865 | 2866 | 2867 | 2868 | 2869 | 2870 | 2871 |
| 5470 | 2872 | 2873 | 2874 | 2875 | 2876 | 2877 | 2878 | 2879 |
| 5500 | 2880 | 2881 | 2882 | 2883 | 2884 | 2885 | 2886 | 2887 |
| 5510 | 2888 | 2889 | 2890 | 2891 | 2892 | 2893 | 2894 | 2895 |
| 5520 | 2896 | 2897 | 2898 | 2899 | 2900 | 2901 | 2902 | 2903 |
| 5530 | 2904 | 2905 | 2906 | 2907 | 2908 | 2909 | 2910 | 2911 |
| 5540 | 2912 | 2913 | 2914 | 2915 | 2916 | 2917 | 2918 | 2919 |
| 5550 | 2920 | 2921 | 2922 | 2923 | 2924 | 2925 | 2926 | 2927 |
| 5560 | 2928 | 2929 | 2930 | 2931 | 2932 | 2933 | 2934 | 2935 |
| 5570 | 2936 | 2937 | 2938 | 2939 | 2940 | 2941 | 2942 | 2943 |
| 5600 | 2944 | 2945 | 2946 | 2947 | 2948 | 2949 | 2950 | 2951 |
| 5610 | 2952 | 2953 | 2954 | 2955 | 2956 | 2957 | 2958 | 2959 |
| 5620 | 2960 | 2961 | 2962 | 2963 | 2964 | 2965 | 2966 | 2967 |
| 5630 | 2968 | 2969 | 2970 | 2971 | 2972 | 2973 | 2974 | 2975 |
| 5640 | 2976 | 2977 | 2978 | 2979 | 2980 | 2981 | 2982 | 2983 |
| 5650 | 2984 | 2985 | 2986 | 2987 | 2988 | 2989 | 2990 | 2991 |
| 5660 | 2992 | 2993 | 2994 | 2995 | 2996 | 2997 | 2998 | 2999 |
| 5670 | 3000 | 3001 | 3002 | 3003 | 3004 | 3005 | 3006 | 3007 |
| 5700 | 3008 | 3009 | 3010 | 3011 | 3012 | 3013 | 3014 | 3015 |
| 5710 | 3016 | 3017 | 3018 | 3019 | 3020 | 3021 | 3022 | 3023 |
| 5720 | 3024 | 3025 | 3026 | 3027 | 3028 | 3029 | 3030 | 3031 |
| 5730 | 3032 | 3033 | 3034 | 3035 | 3036 | 3037 | 3038 | 3039 |
| 5740 | 3040 | 3041 | 3042 | 3043 | 3044 | 3045 | 3046 | 3047 |
| 5750 | 3048 | 3049 | 3050 | 3051 | 3052 | 3053 | 3054 | 3055 |
| 5760 | 3056 | 3057 | 3058 | 3059 | 3060 | 3061 | 3062 | 3063 |
| 5770 | 3064 | 3065 | 3066 | 3067 | 3068 | 3069 | 3070 | 3071 |

## OCTAL-DECIMAL INTEGER CONVERSION TABLE

| 6000 to 6777 (Octal) | 3072 to 3583 (Decimal) |
|---|---|

|      | 0 | 1 | 2 | 3 | 4 | 5 | 6 | 7 |
|------|------|------|------|------|------|------|------|------|
| 6000 | 3072 | 3073 | 3074 | 3075 | 3076 | 3077 | 3078 | 3079 |
| 6010 | 3080 | 3081 | 3082 | 3083 | 3084 | 3085 | 3086 | 3087 |
| 6020 | 3088 | 3089 | 3090 | 3091 | 3092 | 3093 | 3094 | 3095 |
| 6030 | 3096 | 3097 | 3098 | 3099 | 3100 | 3101 | 3102 | 3103 |
| 6040 | 3104 | 3105 | 3106 | 3107 | 3108 | 3109 | 3110 | 3111 |
| 6050 | 3112 | 3113 | 3114 | 3115 | 3116 | 3117 | 3118 | 3119 |
| 6060 | 3120 | 3121 | 3122 | 3123 | 3124 | 3125 | 3126 | 3127 |
| 6070 | 3128 | 3129 | 3130 | 3131 | 3132 | 3133 | 3134 | 3135 |
| 6100 | 3136 | 3137 | 3138 | 3139 | 3140 | 3141 | 3142 | 3143 |
| 6110 | 3144 | 3145 | 3146 | 3147 | 3148 | 3149 | 3150 | 3151 |
| 6120 | 3152 | 3153 | 3154 | 3155 | 3156 | 3157 | 3158 | 3159 |
| 6130 | 3160 | 3161 | 3162 | 3163 | 3164 | 3165 | 3166 | 3167 |
| 6140 | 3168 | 3169 | 3170 | 3171 | 3172 | 3173 | 3174 | 3175 |
| 6150 | 3176 | 3177 | 3178 | 3179 | 3180 | 3181 | 3182 | 3183 |
| 6160 | 3184 | 3185 | 3186 | 3187 | 3188 | 3189 | 3190 | 3191 |
| 6170 | 3192 | 3193 | 3194 | 3195 | 3196 | 3197 | 3198 | 3199 |
| 6200 | 3200 | 3201 | 3202 | 3203 | 3204 | 3205 | 3206 | 3207 |
| 6210 | 3208 | 3209 | 3210 | 3211 | 3212 | 3213 | 3214 | 3215 |
| 6220 | 3216 | 3217 | 3218 | 3219 | 3220 | 3221 | 3222 | 3223 |
| 6230 | 3224 | 3225 | 3226 | 3227 | 3228 | 3229 | 3230 | 3231 |
| 6240 | 3232 | 3233 | 3234 | 3235 | 3236 | 3237 | 3238 | 3239 |
| 6250 | 3240 | 3241 | 3242 | 3243 | 3244 | 3245 | 3246 | 3247 |
| 6260 | 3248 | 3249 | 3250 | 3251 | 3252 | 3253 | 3254 | 3255 |
| 6270 | 3256 | 3257 | 3258 | 3259 | 3260 | 3261 | 3262 | 3263 |
| 6300 | 3264 | 3265 | 3266 | 3267 | 3268 | 3269 | 3270 | 3271 |
| 6310 | 3272 | 3273 | 3274 | 3275 | 3276 | 3277 | 3278 | 3279 |
| 6320 | 3280 | 3281 | 3282 | 3283 | 3284 | 3285 | 3286 | 3287 |
| 6330 | 3288 | 3289 | 3290 | 3291 | 3292 | 3293 | 3294 | 3295 |
| 6340 | 3296 | 3297 | 3298 | 3299 | 3300 | 3301 | 3302 | 3303 |
| 6350 | 3304 | 3305 | 3306 | 3307 | 3308 | 3309 | 3310 | 3311 |
| 6360 | 3312 | 3313 | 3314 | 3315 | 3316 | 3317 | 3318 | 3319 |
| 6370 | 3320 | 3321 | 3322 | 3323 | 3324 | 3325 | 3326 | 3327 |

|      | 0 | 1 | 2 | 3 | 4 | 5 | 6 | 7 |
|------|------|------|------|------|------|------|------|------|
| 6400 | 3328 | 3329 | 3330 | 3331 | 3332 | 3333 | 3334 | 3335 |
| 6410 | 3336 | 3337 | 3338 | 3339 | 3340 | 3341 | 3342 | 3343 |
| 6420 | 3344 | 3345 | 3346 | 3347 | 3348 | 3349 | 3350 | 3351 |
| 6430 | 3352 | 3353 | 3354 | 3355 | 3356 | 3357 | 3358 | 3359 |
| 6440 | 3360 | 3361 | 3362 | 3363 | 3364 | 3365 | 3366 | 3367 |
| 6450 | 3368 | 3369 | 3370 | 3371 | 3372 | 3373 | 3374 | 3375 |
| 6460 | 3376 | 3377 | 3378 | 3379 | 3380 | 3381 | 3382 | 3383 |
| 6470 | 3384 | 3385 | 3386 | 3387 | 3388 | 3389 | 3390 | 3391 |
| 6500 | 3392 | 3393 | 3394 | 3395 | 3396 | 3397 | 3398 | 3399 |
| 6510 | 3400 | 3401 | 3402 | 3403 | 3404 | 3405 | 3406 | 3407 |
| 6520 | 3408 | 3409 | 3410 | 3411 | 3412 | 3413 | 3414 | 3415 |
| 6530 | 3416 | 3417 | 3418 | 3419 | 3420 | 3421 | 3422 | 3423 |
| 6540 | 3424 | 3425 | 3426 | 3427 | 3428 | 3429 | 3430 | 3431 |
| 6550 | 3432 | 3433 | 3434 | 3435 | 3436 | 3437 | 3438 | 3439 |
| 6560 | 3440 | 3441 | 3442 | 3443 | 3444 | 3445 | 3446 | 3447 |
| 6570 | 3448 | 3449 | 3450 | 3451 | 3452 | 3453 | 3454 | 3455 |
| 6600 | 3456 | 3457 | 3458 | 3459 | 3460 | 3461 | 3462 | 3463 |
| 6610 | 3464 | 3465 | 3466 | 3467 | 3468 | 3469 | 3470 | 3471 |
| 6620 | 3472 | 3473 | 3474 | 3475 | 3476 | 3477 | 3478 | 3479 |
| 6630 | 3480 | 3481 | 3482 | 3483 | 3484 | 3485 | 3486 | 3487 |
| 6640 | 3488 | 3489 | 3490 | 3491 | 3492 | 3493 | 3494 | 3495 |
| 6650 | 3496 | 3497 | 3498 | 3499 | 3500 | 3501 | 3502 | 3503 |
| 6660 | 3504 | 3505 | 3506 | 3507 | 3508 | 3509 | 3510 | 3511 |
| 6670 | 3512 | 3513 | 3514 | 3515 | 3516 | 3517 | 3518 | 3519 |
| 6700 | 3520 | 3521 | 3522 | 3523 | 3524 | 3525 | 3526 | 3527 |
| 6710 | 3528 | 3529 | 3530 | 3531 | 3532 | 3533 | 3534 | 3535 |
| 6720 | 3536 | 3537 | 3538 | 3539 | 3540 | 3541 | 3542 | 3543 |
| 6730 | 3544 | 3545 | 3546 | 3547 | 3548 | 3549 | 3550 | 3551 |
| 6740 | 3552 | 3553 | 3554 | 3555 | 3556 | 3557 | 3558 | 3559 |
| 6750 | 3560 | 3561 | 3562 | 3563 | 3564 | 3565 | 3566 | 3567 |
| 6760 | 3568 | 3569 | 3570 | 3571 | 3572 | 3573 | 3574 | 3575 |
| 6770 | 3576 | 3577 | 3578 | 3579 | 3580 | 3581 | 3582 | 3583 |

7000 to 7777 (Octal) | 3584 to 4095 (Decimal)

| | 0 | 1 | 2 | 3 | 4 | 5 | 6 | 7 |
|---|---|---|---|---|---|---|---|---|
| 7000 | 3584 | 3585 | 3586 | 3587 | 3588 | 3589 | 3590 | 3591 |
| 7010 | 3592 | 3593 | 3594 | 3595 | 3596 | 3597 | 3598 | 3599 |
| 7020 | 3600 | 3601 | 3602 | 3603 | 3604 | 3605 | 3606 | 3607 |
| 7030 | 3608 | 3609 | 3610 | 3611 | 3612 | 3613 | 3614 | 3615 |
| 7040 | 3616 | 3617 | 3618 | 3619 | 3620 | 3621 | 3622 | 3623 |
| 7050 | 3624 | 3625 | 3626 | 3627 | 3628 | 3629 | 3630 | 3631 |
| 7060 | 3632 | 3633 | 3634 | 3635 | 3636 | 3637 | 3638 | 3639 |
| 7070 | 3640 | 3641 | 3642 | 3643 | 3644 | 3645 | 3646 | 3647 |
| 7100 | 3648 | 3649 | 3650 | 3651 | 3652 | 3653 | 3654 | 3655 |
| 7110 | 3656 | 3657 | 3658 | 3659 | 3660 | 3661 | 3662 | 3663 |
| 7120 | 3664 | 3665 | 3666 | 3667 | 3668 | 3669 | 3670 | 3671 |
| 7130 | 3672 | 3673 | 3674 | 3675 | 3676 | 3677 | 3678 | 3679 |
| 7140 | 3680 | 3681 | 3682 | 3683 | 3684 | 3685 | 3686 | 3687 |
| 7150 | 3688 | 3689 | 3690 | 3691 | 3692 | 3693 | 3694 | 3695 |
| 7160 | 3696 | 3697 | 3698 | 3699 | 3700 | 3701 | 3702 | 3703 |
| 7170 | 3704 | 3705 | 3706 | 3707 | 3708 | 3709 | 3710 | 3711 |
| 7200 | 3712 | 3713 | 3714 | 3715 | 3716 | 3717 | 3718 | 3719 |
| 7210 | 3720 | 3721 | 3722 | 3723 | 3724 | 3725 | 3726 | 3727 |
| 7220 | 3728 | 3729 | 3730 | 3731 | 3732 | 3733 | 3734 | 3735 |
| 7230 | 3736 | 3737 | 3738 | 3739 | 3740 | 3741 | 3742 | 3743 |
| 7240 | 3744 | 3745 | 3746 | 3747 | 3748 | 3749 | 3750 | 3751 |
| 7250 | 3752 | 3753 | 3754 | 3755 | 3756 | 3757 | 3758 | 3759 |
| 7260 | 3760 | 3761 | 3762 | 3763 | 3764 | 3765 | 3766 | 3767 |
| 7270 | 3768 | 3769 | 3770 | 3771 | 3772 | 3773 | 3774 | 3775 |
| 7300 | 3776 | 3777 | 3778 | 3779 | 3780 | 3781 | 3782 | 3783 |
| 7310 | 3784 | 3785 | 3786 | 3787 | 3788 | 3789 | 3790 | 3791 |
| 7320 | 3792 | 3793 | 3794 | 3795 | 3796 | 3797 | 3798 | 3799 |
| 7330 | 3800 | 3801 | 3802 | 3803 | 3804 | 3805 | 3806 | 3807 |
| 7340 | 3808 | 3809 | 3810 | 3811 | 3812 | 3813 | 3814 | 3815 |
| 7350 | 3816 | 3817 | 3818 | 3819 | 3820 | 3821 | 3822 | 3823 |
| 7360 | 3824 | 3825 | 3826 | 3827 | 3828 | 3829 | 3830 | 3831 |
| 7370 | 3832 | 3833 | 3834 | 3835 | 3836 | 3837 | 3838 | 3839 |

| | 0 | 1 | 2 | 3 | 4 | 5 | 6 | 7 |
|---|---|---|---|---|---|---|---|---|
| 7400 | 3840 | 3841 | 3842 | 3843 | 3844 | 3845 | 3846 | 3847 |
| 7410 | 3848 | 3849 | 3850 | 3851 | 3852 | 3853 | 3854 | 3855 |
| 7420 | 3856 | 3857 | 3858 | 3859 | 3860 | 3861 | 3862 | 3863 |
| 7430 | 3864 | 3865 | 3866 | 3867 | 3868 | 3869 | 3870 | 3871 |
| 7440 | 3872 | 3873 | 3874 | 3875 | 3876 | 3877 | 3878 | 3879 |
| 7450 | 3880 | 3881 | 3882 | 3883 | 3884 | 3885 | 3886 | 3887 |
| 7460 | 3888 | 3889 | 3890 | 3891 | 3892 | 3893 | 3894 | 3895 |
| 7470 | 3896 | 3897 | 3898 | 3899 | 3900 | 3901 | 3902 | 3903 |
| 7500 | 3904 | 3905 | 3906 | 3907 | 3908 | 3909 | 3910 | 3911 |
| 7510 | 3912 | 3913 | 3914 | 3915 | 3916 | 3917 | 3918 | 3919 |
| 7520 | 3920 | 3921 | 3922 | 3923 | 3924 | 3925 | 3926 | 3927 |
| 7530 | 3928 | 3929 | 3930 | 3931 | 3932 | 3933 | 3934 | 3935 |
| 7540 | 3936 | 3937 | 3938 | 3939 | 3940 | 3941 | 3942 | 3943 |
| 7550 | 3944 | 3945 | 3946 | 3947 | 3948 | 3949 | 3950 | 3951 |
| 7560 | 3952 | 3953 | 3954 | 3955 | 3956 | 3957 | 3958 | 3959 |
| 7570 | 3960 | 3961 | 3962 | 3963 | 3964 | 3965 | 3966 | 3967 |
| 7600 | 3968 | 3969 | 3970 | 3971 | 3972 | 3973 | 3974 | 3975 |
| 7610 | 3976 | 3977 | 3978 | 3979 | 3980 | 3981 | 3982 | 3983 |
| 7620 | 3984 | 3985 | 3986 | 3987 | 3988 | 3989 | 3990 | 3991 |
| 7630 | 3992 | 3993 | 3994 | 3995 | 3996 | 3997 | 3998 | 3999 |
| 7640 | 4000 | 4001 | 4002 | 4003 | 4004 | 4005 | 4006 | 4007 |
| 7650 | 4008 | 4009 | 4010 | 4011 | 4012 | 4013 | 4014 | 4015 |
| 7660 | 4016 | 4017 | 4018 | 4019 | 4020 | 4021 | 4022 | 4023 |
| 7670 | 4024 | 4025 | 4026 | 4027 | 4028 | 4029 | 4030 | 4031 |
| 7700 | 4032 | 4033 | 4034 | 4035 | 4036 | 4037 | 4038 | 4039 |
| 7710 | 4040 | 4041 | 4042 | 4043 | 4044 | 4045 | 4046 | 4047 |
| 7720 | 4048 | 4049 | 4050 | 4051 | 4052 | 4053 | 4054 | 4055 |
| 7730 | 4056 | 4057 | 4058 | 4059 | 4060 | 4061 | 4062 | 4063 |
| 7740 | 4064 | 4065 | 4066 | 4067 | 4068 | 4069 | 4070 | 4071 |
| 7750 | 4072 | 4073 | 4074 | 4075 | 4076 | 4077 | 4078 | 4079 |
| 7760 | 4080 | 4081 | 4082 | 4083 | 4084 | 4085 | 4086 | 4087 |
| 7770 | 4088 | 4089 | 4090 | 4091 | 4092 | 4093 | 4094 | 4095 |

## APPENDIX 5. OCTAL-DECIMAL FRACTION CONVERSION TABLE

| OCTAL | DEC. | OCTAL | DEC. | OCTAL | DEC. | OCTAL | DEC. |
|---|---|---|---|---|---|---|---|
| .000 | .000000 | .100 | .125000 | .200 | .250000 | .300 | .375000 |
| .001 | .001953 | .101 | .126953 | .201 | .251953 | .301 | .376953 |
| .002 | .003906 | .102 | .128906 | .202 | .253906 | .302 | .378906 |
| .003 | .005859 | .103 | .130859 | .203 | .255859 | .303 | .380859 |
| .004 | .007812 | .104 | .132812 | .204 | .257812 | .304 | .382812 |
| .005 | .009765 | .105 | .134765 | .205 | .259765 | .305 | .384765 |
| .006 | .011718 | .106 | .136718 | .206 | .261718 | .306 | .386718 |
| .007 | .013671 | .107 | .138671 | .207 | .263671 | .307 | .388671 |
| .010 | .015625 | .110 | .140625 | .210 | .265625 | .310 | .390625 |
| .011 | .017578 | .111 | .142578 | .211 | .267578 | .311 | .392578 |
| .012 | .019531 | .112 | .144531 | .212 | .269531 | .312 | .394531 |
| .013 | .021484 | .113 | .146484 | .213 | .271484 | .313 | .396484 |
| .014 | .023437 | .114 | .148437 | .214 | .273437 | .314 | .398437 |
| .015 | .025390 | .115 | .150390 | .215 | .275390 | .315 | .400390 |
| .016 | .027343 | .116 | .152343 | .216 | .277343 | .316 | .402343 |
| .017 | .029296 | .117 | .154296 | .217 | .279296 | .317 | .404296 |
| .020 | .031250 | .120 | .156250 | .220 | .281250 | .320 | .406250 |
| .021 | .033203 | .121 | .158203 | .221 | .283203 | .321 | .408203 |
| .022 | .035156 | .122 | .160156 | .222 | .285156 | .322 | .410156 |
| .023 | .037109 | .123 | .162109 | .223 | .287109 | .323 | .412109 |
| .024 | .039062 | .124 | .164062 | .224 | .289062 | .324 | .414062 |
| .025 | .041015 | .125 | .166015 | .225 | .291015 | .325 | .416015 |
| .026 | .042968 | .126 | .167968 | .226 | .292968 | .326 | .417968 |
| .027 | .044921 | .127 | .169921 | .227 | .294921 | .327 | .419921 |
| .030 | .046875 | .130 | .171875 | .230 | .296875 | .330 | .421875 |
| .031 | .048828 | .131 | .173828 | .231 | .298828 | .331 | .423828 |
| .032 | .050781 | .132 | .175781 | .232 | .300781 | .332 | .425781 |
| .033 | .052734 | .133 | .177734 | .233 | .302734 | .333 | .427734 |
| .034 | .054687 | .134 | .179687 | .234 | .304687 | .334 | .429687 |
| .035 | .056640 | .135 | .181640 | .235 | .306640 | .335 | .431640 |
| .036 | .058593 | .136 | .183593 | .236 | .308593 | .336 | .433593 |
| .037 | .060546 | .137 | .185546 | .237 | .310546 | .337 | .435546 |
| .040 | .062500 | .140 | .187500 | .240 | .312500 | .340 | .437500 |
| .041 | .064453 | .141 | .189453 | .241 | .314453 | .341 | .439453 |
| .042 | .066406 | .142 | .191406 | .242 | .316406 | .342 | .441406 |
| .043 | .068359 | .143 | .193359 | .243 | .318359 | .343 | .443359 |
| .044 | .070312 | .144 | .195312 | .244 | .320312 | .344 | .445312 |
| .045 | .072265 | .145 | .197265 | .245 | .322265 | .345 | .447265 |
| .046 | .074218 | .146 | .199218 | .246 | .324218 | .346 | .449218 |
| .047 | .076171 | .147 | .201171 | .247 | .326171 | .347 | .451171 |
| .050 | .078125 | .150 | .203125 | .250 | .328125 | .350 | .453125 |
| .051 | .080078 | .151 | .205078 | .251 | .330078 | .351 | .455078 |
| .052 | .082031 | .152 | .207031 | .252 | .332031 | .352 | .457031 |
| .053 | .083984 | .153 | .208984 | .253 | .333984 | .353 | .458984 |
| .054 | .085937 | .154 | .210937 | .254 | .335937 | .354 | .460937 |
| .055 | .087890 | .155 | .212890 | .255 | .337890 | .355 | .462890 |
| .056 | .089843 | .156 | .214843 | .256 | .339843 | .356 | .464843 |
| .057 | .091796 | .157 | .216796 | .257 | .341796 | .357 | .466796 |
| .060 | .093750 | .160 | .218750 | .260 | .343750 | .360 | .468750 |
| .061 | .095703 | .161 | .220703 | .261 | .345703 | .361 | .470703 |
| .062 | .097656 | .162 | .222656 | .262 | .347656 | .362 | .472656 |
| .063 | .099609 | .163 | .224609 | .263 | .349609 | .363 | .474609 |
| .064 | .101562 | .164 | .226562 | .264 | .351562 | .364 | .476562 |
| .065 | .103515 | .165 | .228515 | .265 | .353515 | .365 | .478515 |
| .066 | .105468 | .166 | .230468 | .266 | .355468 | .366 | .480468 |
| .067 | .107421 | .167 | .232421 | .267 | .357421 | .367 | .482421 |
| .070 | .109375 | .170 | .234375 | .270 | .359375 | .370 | .484375 |
| .071 | .111328 | .171 | .236328 | .271 | .361328 | .371 | .486328 |
| .072 | .113281 | .172 | .238281 | .272 | .363281 | .372 | .488281 |
| .073 | .115234 | .173 | .240234 | .273 | .365234 | .373 | .490234 |
| .074 | .117187 | .174 | .242187 | .274 | .367187 | .374 | .492187 |
| .075 | .119140 | .175 | .244140 | .275 | .369140 | .375 | .494140 |
| .076 | .121093 | .176 | .246093 | .276 | .371093 | .376 | .496093 |
| .077 | .123046 | .177 | .248046 | .277 | .373046 | .377 | .498046 |

## OCTAL-DECIMAL FRACTION CONVERSION TABLE

| OCTAL | DEC. | OCTAL | DEC. | OCTAL | DEC. | OCTAL | DEC. |
|---|---|---|---|---|---|---|---|
| .000000 | .000000 | .000100 | .000244 | .000200 | .000488 | .000300 | .000732 |
| .000001 | .000003 | .000101 | .000247 | .000201 | .000492 | .000301 | .000736 |
| .000002 | .000007 | .000102 | .000251 | .000202 | .000495 | .000302 | .000740 |
| .000003 | .000011 | .000103 | .000255 | .000203 | .000499 | .000303 | .000743 |
| .000004 | .000015 | .000104 | .000259 | .000204 | .000503 | .000304 | .000747 |
| .000005 | .000019 | .000105 | .000263 | .000205 | .000507 | .000305 | .000751 |
| .000006 | .000022 | .000106 | .000267 | .000206 | .000511 | .000306 | .000755 |
| .000007 | .000026 | .000107 | .000270 | .000207 | .000514 | .000307 | .000759 |
| .000010 | .000030 | .000110 | .000274 | .000210 | .000518 | .000310 | .000762 |
| .000011 | .000034 | .000111 | .000278 | .000211 | .000522 | .000311 | .000766 |
| .000012 | .000038 | .000112 | .000282 | .000212 | .000526 | .000312 | .000770 |
| .000013 | .000041 | .000113 | .000286 | .000213 | .000530 | .000313 | .000774 |
| .000014 | .000045 | .000114 | .000289 | .000214 | .000534 | .000314 | .000778 |
| .000015 | .000049 | .000115 | .000293 | .000215 | .000537 | .000315 | .000782 |
| .000016 | .000053 | .000116 | .000297 | .000216 | .000541 | .000316 | .000785 |
| .000017 | .000057 | .000117 | .000301 | .000217 | .000545 | .000317 | .000789 |
| .000020 | .000061 | .000120 | .000305 | .000220 | .000549 | .000320 | .000793 |
| .000021 | .000064 | .000121 | .000308 | .000221 | .000553 | .000321 | .000797 |
| .000022 | .000068 | .000122 | .000312 | .000222 | .000556 | .000322 | .000801 |
| .000023 | .000072 | .000123 | .000316 | .000223 | .000560 | .000323 | .000805 |
| .000024 | .000076 | .000124 | .000320 | .000224 | .000564 | .000324 | .000808 |
| .000025 | .000080 | .000125 | .000324 | .000225 | .000568 | .000325 | .000812 |
| .000026 | .000083 | .000126 | .000328 | .000226 | .000572 | .000326 | .000816 |
| .000027 | .000087 | .000127 | .000331 | .000227 | .000576 | .000327 | .000820 |
| .000030 | .000091 | .000130 | .000335 | .000230 | .000579 | .000330 | .000823 |
| .000031 | .000095 | .000131 | .000339 | .000231 | .000583 | .000331 | .000827 |
| .000032 | .000099 | .000132 | .000343 | .000232 | .000587 | .000332 | .000831 |
| .000033 | .000102 | .000133 | .000347 | .000233 | .000591 | .000333 | .000835 |
| .000034 | .000106 | .000134 | .000350 | .000234 | .000595 | .000334 | .000839 |
| .000035 | .000110 | .000135 | .000354 | .000235 | .000598 | .000335 | .000843 |
| .000036 | .000114 | .000136 | .000358 | .000236 | .000602 | .000336 | .000846 |
| .000037 | .000118 | .000137 | .000362 | .000237 | .000606 | .000337 | .000850 |
| .000040 | .000122 | .000140 | .000366 | .000240 | .000610 | .000340 | .000854 |
| .000041 | .000125 | .000141 | .000370 | .000241 | .000614 | .000341 | .000858 |
| .000042 | .000129 | .000142 | .000373 | .000242 | .000617 | .000342 | .000862 |
| .000043 | .000133 | .000143 | .000377 | .000243 | .000621 | .000343 | .000865 |
| .000044 | .000137 | .000144 | .000381 | .000244 | .000625 | .000344 | .000869 |
| .000045 | .000141 | .000145 | .000385 | .000245 | .000629 | .000345 | .000873 |
| .000046 | .000144 | .000146 | .000389 | .000246 | .000633 | .000346 | .000877 |
| .000047 | .000148 | .000147 | .000392 | .000247 | .000637 | .000347 | .000881 |
| .000050 | .000152 | .000150 | .000396 | .000250 | .000640 | .000350 | .000885 |
| .000051 | .000156 | .000151 | .000400 | .000251 | .000644 | .000351 | .000888 |
| .000052 | .000160 | .000152 | .000404 | .000252 | .000648 | .000352 | .000892 |
| .000053 | .000164 | .000153 | .000408 | .000253 | .000652 | .000353 | .000896 |
| .000054 | .000167 | .000154 | .000411 | .000254 | .000656 | .000354 | .000900 |
| .000055 | .000171 | .000155 | .000415 | .000255 | .000659 | .000355 | .000904 |
| .000056 | .000175 | .000156 | .000419 | .000256 | .000663 | .000356 | .000907 |
| .000057 | .000179 | .000157 | .000423 | .000257 | .000667 | .000357 | .000911 |
| .000060 | .000183 | .000160 | .000427 | .000260 | .000671 | .000360 | .000915 |
| .000061 | .000186 | .000161 | .000431 | .000261 | .000675 | .000361 | .000919 |
| .000062 | .000190 | .000162 | .000434 | .000262 | .000679 | .000362 | .000923 |
| .000063 | .000194 | .000163 | .000438 | .000263 | .000682 | .000363 | .000926 |
| .000064 | .000198 | .000164 | .000442 | .000264 | .000686 | .000364 | .000930 |
| .000065 | .000202 | .000165 | .000446 | .000265 | .000690 | .000365 | .000934 |
| .000066 | .000205 | .000166 | .000450 | .000266 | .000694 | .000366 | .000938 |
| .000067 | .000209 | .000167 | .000453 | .000267 | .000698 | .000367 | .000942 |
| .000070 | .000213 | .000170 | .000457 | .000270 | .000701 | .000370 | .000946 |
| .000071 | .000217 | .000171 | .000461 | .000271 | .000705 | .000371 | .000949 |
| .000072 | .000221 | .000172 | .000465 | .000272 | .000709 | .000372 | .000953 |
| .000073 | .000225 | .000173 | .000469 | .000273 | .000713 | .000373 | .000957 |
| .000074 | .000228 | .000174 | .000473 | .000274 | .000717 | .000374 | .000961 |
| .000075 | .000232 | .000175 | .000476 | .000275 | .000720 | .000375 | .000965 |
| .000076 | .000236 | .000176 | .000480 | .000276 | .000724 | .000376 | .000968 |
| .000077 | .000240 | .000177 | .000484 | .000277 | .000728 | .000377 | .000972 |

## OCTAL-DECIMAL FRACTION CONVERSION TABLE

| OCTAL | DEC. | OCTAL | DEC. | OCTAL | DEC. | OCTAL | DEC. |
|---|---|---|---|---|---|---|---|
| .000400 | .000976 | .000500 | .001220 | .000600 | .001464 | .000700 | .001708 |
| .000401 | .000980 | .000501 | .001224 | .000601 | .001468 | .000701 | .001712 |
| .000402 | .000984 | .000502 | .001228 | .000602 | .001472 | .000702 | .001716 |
| .000403 | .000988 | .000503 | .001232 | .000603 | .001476 | .000703 | .001720 |
| .000404 | .000991 | .000504 | .001235 | .000604 | .001480 | .000704 | .001724 |
| .000405 | .000995 | .000505 | .001239 | .000605 | .001483 | .000705 | .001728 |
| .000406 | .000999 | .000506 | .001243 | .000606 | .001487 | .000706 | .001731 |
| .000407 | .001003 | .000507 | .001247 | .000607 | .001491 | .000707 | .001735 |
| .000410 | .001007 | .000510 | .001251 | .000610 | .001495 | .000710 | .001739 |
| .000411 | .001010 | .000511 | .001255 | .000611 | .001499 | .000711 | .001743 |
| .000412 | .001014 | .000512 | .001258 | .000612 | .001502 | .000712 | .001747 |
| .000413 | .001018 | .000513 | .001262 | .000613 | .001506 | .000713 | .001750 |
| .000414 | .001022 | .000514 | .001266 | .000614 | .001510 | .000714 | .001754 |
| .000415 | .001026 | .000515 | .001270 | .000615 | .001514 | .000715 | .001758 |
| .000416 | .001029 | .000516 | .001274 | .000616 | .001518 | .000716 | .001762 |
| .000417 | .001033 | .000517 | .001277 | .000617 | .001522 | .000717 | .001766 |
| .000420 | .001037 | .000520 | .001281 | .000620 | .001525 | .000720 | .001770 |
| .000421 | .001041 | .000521 | .001285 | .000621 | .001529 | .000721 | .001773 |
| .000422 | .001045 | .000522 | .001289 | .000622 | .001533 | .000722 | .001777 |
| .000423 | .001049 | .000523 | .001293 | .000623 | .001537 | .000723 | .001781 |
| .000424 | .001052 | .000524 | .001296 | .000624 | .001541 | .000724 | .001785 |
| .000425 | .001056 | .000525 | .001300 | .000625 | .001544 | .000725 | .001789 |
| .000426 | .001060 | .000526 | .001304 | .000626 | .001548 | .000726 | .001792 |
| .000427 | .001064 | .000527 | .001308 | .000627 | .001552 | .000727 | .001796 |
| .000430 | .001068 | .000530 | .001312 | .000630 | .001556 | .000730 | .001800 |
| .000431 | .001071 | .000531 | .001316 | .000631 | .001560 | .000731 | .001804 |
| .000432 | .001075 | .000532 | .001319 | .000632 | .001564 | .000732 | .001808 |
| .000433 | .001079 | .000533 | .001323 | .000633 | .001567 | .000733 | .001811 |
| .000434 | .001083 | .000534 | .001327 | .000634 | .001571 | .000734 | .001815 |
| .000435 | .001087 | .000535 | .001331 | .000635 | .001575 | .000735 | .001819 |
| .000436 | .001091 | .000536 | .001335 | .000636 | .001579 | .000736 | .001823 |
| .000437 | .001094 | .000537 | .001338 | .000637 | .001583 | .000737 | .001827 |
| .000440 | .001098 | .000540 | .001342 | .000640 | .001586 | .000740 | .001831 |
| .000441 | .001102 | .000541 | .001346 | .000641 | .001590 | .000741 | .001834 |
| .000442 | .001106 | .000542 | .001350 | .000642 | .001594 | .000742 | .001838 |
| .000443 | .001110 | .000543 | .001354 | .000643 | .001598 | .000743 | .001842 |
| .000444 | .001113 | .000544 | .001358 | .000644 | .001602 | .000744 | .001846 |
| .000445 | .001117 | .000545 | .001361 | .000645 | .001605 | .000745 | .001850 |
| .000446 | .001121 | .000546 | .001365 | .000646 | .001609 | .000746 | .001853 |
| .000447 | .001125 | .000547 | .001369 | .000647 | .001613 | .000747 | .001857 |
| .000450 | .001129 | .000550 | .001373 | .000650 | .001617 | .000750 | .001861 |
| .000451 | .001132 | .000551 | .001377 | .000651 | .001621 | .000751 | .001865 |
| .000452 | .001136 | .000552 | .001380 | .000652 | .001625 | .000752 | .001869 |
| .000453 | .001140 | .000553 | .001384 | .000653 | .001628 | .000753 | .001873 |
| .000454 | .001144 | .000554 | .001388 | .000654 | .001632 | .000754 | .001876 |
| .000455 | .001148 | .000555 | .001392 | .000655 | .001636 | .000755 | .001880 |
| .000456 | .001152 | .000556 | .001396 | .000656 | .001640 | .000756 | .001884 |
| .000457 | .001155 | .000557 | .001399 | .000657 | .001644 | .000757 | .001888 |
| .000460 | .001159 | .000560 | .001403 | .000660 | .001647 | .000760 | .001892 |
| .000461 | .001163 | .000561 | .001407 | .000661 | .001651 | .000761 | .001895 |
| .000462 | .001167 | .000562 | .001411 | .000662 | .001655 | .000762 | .001899 |
| .000463 | .001171 | .000563 | .001415 | .000663 | .001659 | .000763 | .001903 |
| .000464 | .001174 | .000564 | .001419 | .000664 | .001663 | .000764 | .001907 |
| .000465 | .001178 | .000565 | .001422 | .000665 | .001667 | .000765 | .001911 |
| .000466 | .001182 | .000566 | .001426 | .000666 | .001670 | .000766 | .001914 |
| .000467 | .001186 | .000567 | .001430 | .000667 | .001674 | .000767 | .001918 |
| .000470 | .001190 | .000570 | .001434 | .000670 | .001678 | .000770 | .001922 |
| .000471 | .001194 | .000571 | .001438 | .000671 | .001682 | .000771 | .001926 |
| .000472 | .001197 | .000572 | .001441 | .000672 | .001686 | .000772 | .001930 |
| .000473 | .001201 | .000573 | .001445 | .000673 | .001689 | .000773 | .001934 |
| .000474 | .001205 | .000574 | .001449 | .000674 | .001693 | .000774 | .001937 |
| .000475 | .001209 | .000575 | .001453 | .000675 | .001697 | .000775 | .001941 |
| .000476 | .001213 | .000576 | .001457 | .000676 | .001701 | .000776 | .001945 |
| .000477 | .001216 | .000577 | .001461 | .000677 | .001705 | .000777 | .001949 |

# Appendix

# 6 BIBLIOGRAPHY

1. *Proceedings* of the Joint Computer Conferences. Published by American Institute of Electrical Engineers, 33 West 39th Street, New York 18, N. Y. (Reprints of the papers presented at the Joint Computer Conferences of the American Institute of Electrical Engineers, Institute of Radio Engineers, and Association for Computing Machinery, which are currently being held twice a year. Papers cover every phase of computing: design, application, digital, analog, new product announcements, etc.)

## Periodicals

2. *Proceedings of the IRE.* Published monthly by Institute of Radio Engineers, 1 East 79th Street, New York 21, N. Y.

3. *Journal of the Association for Computing Machinery.* Published quarterly by the Association, 2 East 63rd Street, New York 21, N. Y.

4. *Journal of the Operations Research Society of America.* Published quarterly by the Society, Mount Royal and Guilford Avenues, Baltimore 2, Md.

5. *Automatic Control.* Published monthly at 430 Park Avenue, New York 22, N. Y.

6. *Control Engineering.* Published monthly by McGraw-Hill Publishing Company, 330 West 42nd Street, New York 36, N. Y.

7. *Automation.* Published monthly by Penton Publications, Penton Building, Cleveland 12, Ohio.

8. *Computers and Automation.* Published ten times a year by Edmund C. Berkeley and Associates, 36 West 11th Street, New York 11, N. Y.

9. *Data Processing Digest.* Published monthly by Canning, Sisson and Associates, 1140 South Robertson Boulevard, Los Angeles 35, Calif.

10. *Computing News,* published semimonthly by Jackson W. Granholm, 12805 64th Avenue South, Seattle 88, Wash.

## Books and Other Publications

11. Berkeley, Edmund C., *Giant Brains, or Machines That Think,* John Wiley and Sons, New York, 1949. (General description of computing equipment available at time of writing.)

12. Berkeley, Edmund C., and Lawrence Wainwright, *Computers, Their Operation and Applications,* Reinhold Publishing Corporation, New York, 1956. (In many ways a sequel to *Giant Brains,* brought up to date and with more emphasis on applications.)

13. Booth, Andrew D., and Kathleen H. V. Booth, *Automatic Digital Computers*, Butterworths Scientific Publications, London, 1953. (Design and applications.)

14. Bowden, B. V., editor, *Faster than Thought*, Sir Isaac Pitman & Sons, Ltd., London, 1953. (History, theory, descriptions, applications. A symposium.)

15. Canning, Richard G., *Electronic Data Processing for Business and Industry*, John Wiley and Sons, New York, 1956. (Management-language discussion of how to select and use computers in the data-processing area.)

16. Eckert, Wallace J., and Rebecca Jones, *Faster, Faster*, International Business Machines Corporation, New York, 1955. (Nontechnical description of the NORC, a very large and fast scientific computer.)

17. Kozmetsky, George, and Paul Kircher, *Electronic Computers and Management Control*, McGraw-Hill Book Company, Inc., New York, 1956. (Discusses the impact of computers and other information-handling devices on management.)

18. Levin, Howard S., *Office Work and Automation*, John Wiley and Sons, New York, 1956. (Discusses the effect of automation on the information-gathering and -processing function of business.)

19. Richards, R. K., *Arithmetic Operations in Digital Computers*, D. Van Nostrand Company, New York, 1955. (Mostly logical design, i.e., the flow of *information* through the circuits of a computer, rather than actual electronic circuit design.)

20. Wall, H. S., *The Analytic Theory of Continued Fractions*, D. Van Nostrand Company, New York, 1948. (Mathematical technique mentioned in Chapter 17.)

21. Wilkes, M. V., *Automatic Digital Computers*, John Wiley and Sons, New York, 1956. (General introduction to logical design, with chapters on descriptions of computers, programming, and operation. Readable without knowledge of electrical engineering.)

22. Wilkes, M. V., D. J. Wheeler, and S. Gill, *The Preparation of Programs for an Electronic Digital Computer*, Addison-Wesley Press, Boston, 1951. (Describes programming for the EDSAC.)

23. ——, *The Fortran Automatic Coding System for the IBM 704*, International Business Machines Corporation, New York, 1956. (Technical description of the program mentioned in Chapter 18.)

24. ——, *The X-1 Assembly System*, Remington Rand Univac Division, Sperry Rand Corporation, New York, 1956. (Technical description of a program along the lines of those mentioned in Chapter 18.)

# INDEX

Abacus, 6
Absolute programming, 170
Absolute values, 18, 75
Access time, 27, 157, 227
Accumulator, 6, 7, 16, 18, 27, 68, 138
Accumulator left shift instruction, 26, 222
Accumulator plus jump instruction, 25, 26, 219
Accumulator right shift instruction, 222
Accumulator zero jump instruction, 76, 220
Accuracy of program, 162
Add absolute value instruction, 18, 75, 220
Add instruction, 16, 17, 220
Add to memory instruction, 80, 143, 221
Addition tables, 35
Address, 13, 25, 26, 27, 68, 115, 152
Address computation and modification, 67, 82, 105, 112, 113
Address of the address, 115, 116
Aiken, Howard, 8
Alphabetic information, 148, 151, 176
Alternators, 204
Analytical Differentiator, 216
Analytical Engine, 8, 231
Arabic number system, 31
Arithmetic unit, 1, 6, 7, 8
Assembly methods, 148, 172, 176, 213
Assertion box, 91
Asymptotic formulas, 163, 191
Attitude survey illustration, 93
Automatic coding, 211
Automatic light, 139

Automatic-manual switch, 139, 164
Automatic Sequence Controlled Calculator, 8
Auxiliary memory, 2, 3, 5, 7
Auxiliary tape equipment, 157
Averaging illustration, 107, 156

Babbage, Charles, 6, 8
Backus, John, 215
Base, of numbers, 31, 32
Base register, see Index register
B-box, see Index register
Bell computers, 49
B-lines, see Index register
Binary coded decimal, 47, 138.  See also Decimal digit codings
Binary numbers, 26, 30, 148
Binary search, 201
Bi-quinary numbers, 6, 47, 49
Bit, 30
Block transfer instruction, 223
Box, see Address
Break point jump instruction, 166, 220
Break point switch, 139, 166
Bucket, see Address
Burroughs E101, 234

Calling sequence, 114, 148, 179
Cambridge University, 9
Card Programmed Calculator, 233
Carriage return key, 140
Cell, see Address
Census Bureau, U. S., 8
Channel, 151
Check case, 159
Checkout, 11, 77, 135, 159, 211
Check sum, 154

Choice box, 89
Choices, elementary computer, 26, 98
Clear add instruction, 16, 220
Clear subtract instruction, 18, 220
Closed shop operation, 160
Code, 4
Coding, see Programming
Command, see Instruction
Compiling, 189, 213
Complement subtraction, 36
Complex arithmetic, 178, 181
Computing part of loop, 75, 77, 81
Conditional jumps, 25
Console, 138
Continued fractions, 207
Control, 1, 6, 7
Convergence, 206
Conversion, of fractions, 42
    of integers, 40
    of number bases, 30, 32, 39, 50
Counter, in loops, 76, 77, 146
Counting, 34
CPC, 233
Current instruction register, 6, 7, 138

Data reduction, 12, 107
DATATRON, 47, 216
Debugging, see Checkout
Decimal digit coding, bi-quinary, 49
    8-4-2-1, 47
    Excess-three, 47
    2-4-2*-1, 47, 48
    Two-out-of-five, 47, 48
Decimal point fixed in middle of the word, 53
Decimal point location, 17, 52
Decisions, elementary computer, 3, 26, 98
Decoding, of instructions, 3
Delay-line storage, 3, 9, 27, 227
Diagnostic programs, 163, 168
Difference Engine, 8
Display button, 140
Divide instruction, 22, 24, 55, 221
Divide stop, 23, 55, 63, 121
Divide stop light, 139
Double precision methods, 181, 191
Duotricenary numbers, 31
Dynamic diagnostic, 168

Eckert, J. P., 8
EDSAC, 9
EDVAC, 9
Effective address, 98, 99, 114, 219
ELECOM, 14, 48
Electrostatic storage, 3, 9, 27, 157
End-around-carry, 37
ENIAC, 8, 9, 37, 50, 231
Enter MQ key, 139
Equal index jump instruction, 101, 224
Errors in loop writing, 77, 106, 159
Excess-three coding of decimal digits, 47
Execute console instruction key, 139
Exponent, in floating point, 122
Exponential, 92, 185
Exponent-plus-fifty, 122, 147

Fast access loops, 227
Final address, 154, 168
Fixed connector, 90
Flaws, magnetic tape, 152
Flexowriter, 140
Floating add instruction, 128, 205, 225
Floating divide instruction, 128, 226
Floating multiply instruction, 128, 225
Floating point methods, 6, 53, 118, 121, 147, 181, 192, 204, 212
Floating subtract instruction, 128, 225
Flow charts, 87, 132, 161
FORTRAN, 215
Fractional part, in floating point, 122
Fractions, binary, 32
Function box, 88

Generators, 213, 214
Graphic method, 56

Halt and jump instruction, 82, 83, 115, 219
Halt box, 90
Harvard University, 8
Hexadecimal numbers, 31
Hollerith, Herman, 8
Hopper, Grace, 215
Horizontal record, 166

IBM card, 141, 142
IBM 650, 49, 165, 200, 216
IBM 701, 9

IBM 702, 122, 191
IBM 704, 9, 162, 168, 215
IBM 705, 9, 122, 191
Ice box, 233
Index control, 14, 78, 99, 177
Index register, 6, 7, 98, 138
Initial address, 144, 154, 168
Initializing part of loop, 75, 77, 81, 146, 166, 203, 232
In-out box, 90
Input, 1, 5, 7, 9, 15, 30, 118, 132
Input switches, 139
Instruction, 2, 4, 9, 14, 67, 68, 211
Instructional constant, 78
Integers, 33, 34
Intermediate storage, 155, 161
International Business Machines Corporation, 8
Interpolation, 81, 102
Interpreting, of instructions, 3
Interpretive programming methods, 178, 195, 212
Interrecord gap, 152
Iteration, 79, 135, 159

Jacquard loom, 8
JOHNIAC, 37
Jump table, 68, 182, 200
Jumps, 25, 66, 68, 98, 112

Kahramanian, Harry, 216
Key, magnetic tape, 153

Labeling connector, 91
Layout chart, 136, 137
Leibnitz, 6
Libraries, of subroutines, 118, 230
Linear interpolation, 81, 102
Linkages, 111, 179
Load card button, 139
Load index from accumulator instruction, 100, 223
Load index from memory instruction, 100, 223
Loading programs, 142
Load MQ instruction, 24, 223
Load typewriter button, 140
Location, see Address
Location counter, 6, 7, 16, 17, 138

"Loc" symbol, 69
Logical errors, 159
Long left shift instruction, 71, 203, 222
Long right shift instruction, 26, 203, 222
Loops, 25, 66, 74, 82, 233
Lower index instruction, 223

Maclaurin series, 206
Magnetic cores, 3, 9, 27, 30, 157
Magnetic drums, 3, 27, 150, 157, 227
Magnetic tape, 1, 5, 7, 9, 30, 141, 150
Mantissa, in floating point, 122
Mark I, 8, 231
Mark II, 47
Mark III, 48
Mark IV, 14
Massachusetts Institute of Technology, 9
Matrix algebra, 181, 191
Mauchley, J. W., 8
Memory, 1, 3, 5, 7, 8, 9
Memory dump, 166, 167, 168
Memory print, 166, 167, 168
Memory register, 19, 22, 138
Memory to index instruction, 100
Mercury storage, 3, 9, 227
MINIAC, 47
Minimum access programming, 228
Modifying part of loop, 75, 77, 81, 146
MONROBOT, 47, 53
Monte Carlo, 203
Moore School of Electrical Engineering, 8
MQ, 6, 7, 19, 27, 71, 138, 139
MQ sign jump instruction, 193, 220
Multiplication, by powers of two or ten, 26
Multiplication tables, 38
Multiplier-quotient, see MQ
Multiply instruction, 19, 54, 221
Multiply round instruction, 24, 221

National 102-D, 14, 47
Nesting, 105, 207
Newton-Raphson method, 79, 209
Nine's complements, 37
Normalize, 124, 205
Numerical analysis, 10

OARAC, 48
Octal numbers, 31, 32
Octonary numbers, 33
Off-line tape equipment, 157
On-line tape equipment, 157
Operation, 14
Optimizing designs, 12
Order, see Instruction
Origin, 172
Output, 1, 6, 7, 9, 30, 118, 132
Output planning chart, 136, 137
Overflow, 17, 54, 63
    in floating point, 123
Overflow jump instruction, 193, 219

Paper tape, 1, 8, 9, 74, 231
Parity bit, 151, 152, 155
Pascal, 6
Pigeonhole analogy, 13
Pin board, 234
Place value, 31, 32
Plugboards, 8, 9, 74, 231
Polynomial evaluation, 105
Post mortem, 168
Post office analogy, 13
Power series, 206
Power supply, 4
Preset, method in loops, 79
Prime numbers, 11
Program, 4
Programming, 10, 11, 27, 74, 80
Program stop light, 139
Pseudo instruction, 78, 180, 182
Pulse recording, 150, 152
Punch, on TYDAC, 141
Punched cards, 1, 8, 9, 30, 74, 231

Quaternary numbers, 33

Raise index instruction, 100, 223
Random access memory, 157
Rational approximation, 208
Reader, on TYDAC, 141
Reading, 1, 30
Read instruction, 141, 153, 224
Reasonable errors, 160
Reconversion, 37, 46
    number of binary places to give
        exact, 47
Records, magnetic tape, 152

Red tape operations, 98, 117, 168, 179
Reference marks, 91
Region, 171
Register, 3
Relative programming, 132, 133, 134,
    170, 213
Relays, 8
Relocation, 170, 171
Reset and clear button, 140
Reset button, 140
Reset, method in loops, 79
Rewind tape instruction, 154, 225
Roman number system, 31
Rounding, 22, 55, 124
Round instruction, 56, 222
Row, 152

Scale factor method, 59, 60, 80
Scientific representation, 121
Select instruction, 141, 153, 165, 224
Self-loading programs, 155, 156
Sequential control, 8
Set index and jump instruction, 101,
    113, 224
Shifting, 3, 26, 53, 55
Sign control, 18, 22, 25, 27, 75, 165,
    192
Significant figures, 52, 53, 121, 124, 130
Significant part, in floating point, 122
Simulation, 12
Sine, 185
Single stop key, 139, 164
Speeds, arithmetic, 27
Sperry Rand Corporation, 9
Square root, 79, 111, 118
Stop key, 140
Storage, see Memory
Store accumulator instruction, 16, 17,
    18, 76, 222
Store address instruction, 69, 75, 76,
    222
Store index in accumulator instruc-
    tion, 100, 223
Store index in memory instruction,
    100, 223
Store MQ instruction, 24, 223
Stored program computer, 4, 9, 52, 66,
    74, 231
Subroutines, 111, 118, 122, 128, 153,
    170, 214, 230

Substitution box, 90, 92
Subtract absolute value instruction,
    18, 221
Subtract instruction, 18, 221
Subtraction tables, 36
Suppression tests, 232
Switches, in flow charting, 92
Switch-jump instruction, 139, 220

Table look-up, 200, 206
Tape button, 140
Tape mark, 142, 152, 153
Tape stop, 151
Tape stop light, 138
Taylor series, 206
Temporary storage, 59, 146
Ten's complements, 36
Testing part of loop, 75, 77, 81
Three-address instructions, 76, 195
Tracing, 164, 167, 181
Track, on magnetic drum, 229
Transition card, 144, 146, 169
Triple precision, 192
TYDAC, 5, 13, 27
    block diagram, 7
    numerical operation codes, 218, 219

Typewriter, 140, 141, 144

Unconditional jump instruction, 25,
    219
Underflow, in floating point, 124
Univac, 37, 48, 152, 162, 215

Variable connector, 89
Vertical record, 166
Von Neumann, John, 9

Weight, in binary coding, 47
Whirlwind, 9
Word, 4, 13
Word count, 144
Write instruction, 141, 153, 225
Write tape mark instruction, 154,
    225
Writing, 4

X-punch, 141

Y-punch, 141

Zero index jump instruction, 101,
    224